Building Database-Driven
Flash Applications

NOEL JERKE AND DARIN BEARD

Building Database-Driven Flash Applications
Copyright ©2004 by Noel Jerke and Darin Beard

ISBN (pbk): 1-59059-110-0

Printed and bound in the United States of America 12345678910

Distributed to the book trade in the United States by Springer-Verlag New York, Inc., 175 Fifth Avenue, New York, NY 10010 and outside the United States by Springer-Verlag GmbH & Co. KG, Tiergartenstr. 17, 69112 Heidelberg, Germany.

In the United States: phone 1-800-SPRINGER, email orders@springer-ny.com, or visit http://www.springer-ny.com. Outside the United States: fax +49 6221 345229, email orders@springer.de, or visit http://www.springer.de.

For information on translations, please contact Apress directly at 2560 Ninth Street, Suite 219, Berkeley, CA 94710. Phone 510-549-5930, fax 510-549-5939, email info@apress.com, or visit http://www.apress.com.

The source code for this book is available to readers at http://www.apress.com in the Downloads section.

This book is dedicated to all of our newfound friends in Dallas—
Darin and his family included.
—Noel Jerke

For my wife, Becca, and our three children, Benjamin, Lydia, and Jack.
They are truly such an amazing blessing from God to me.
They have shown great patience in all my endeavors.
—Darin Beard

Contents at a Glance

Contents

About the Authors

Noel Jerke is currently an independent consultant with 12 years of experience in the information technology industry. He has a wide range of operational and hands-on technical experience. Clients have included Mary Kay, the American Diabetes Association, the Air Force, Jamba Juice, and Electronics Boutique.

Noel's background includes founding and successfully growing a software development consultancy. The company focuses on delivering Web and enterprise-level applications. His hands-on experience includes the full range of Microsoft technologies including ASP.NET, Visual Basic .NET, SQL Server, and the many different versions of Windows.

Noel has been married for more than 10 years and has three children. He resides in Dallas, Texas, and can be reached at noeljerke@att.net.

Darin Beard has been working with Web-based technology for almost a decade. As both a graphic designer and software developer, Darin has a unique perspective on the process of creating Web-based applications. He has experience in technology and software ranging from Adobe Photoshop and Illustrator to ASP, ASP.NET, HTML, PHP, JavaScript, and VBScript to Macromedia Flash to Microsoft SQL Server. His range of experience is extremely beneficial when working with Flash because he can approach a Flash project from both the graphical (design) and technical (code) directions.

Clients Darin has worked with include Hillwood, AMR, Cannon, American Airlines Center, Fellowship Church, RightNow.org, RenderAid.com, BlueFishTV, and others.

Darin currently lives in Dallas, Texas, with his wife of 12 years and his three children. He can be reached at darin.beard@sitetoolset.com.

About the
Technical Reviewer

 **John Morris** has been involved in the multimedia development community for more than 16 years. He has been a tutor/trainer of Macromedia and Adobe products and has developed Flash and Shockwave applications for Addison Wesley, Shockwave.com, and Macromedia. He has produced many popular titles on Shockwave.com and has acted as a Flash consultant for their Flash developer community. Recently, John has been leading the quality assurance effort for Macromedia's rich Internet application development showcased on its Web site (http://www.macromedia.com).

Acknowledgments

FIRST, I WOULD LIKE TO THANK Darin for developing the concept for the book. His background in programming and Flash made the book possible. Second, I would like to thank Apress for its support of this project. Also, a big thanks goes out to Martin Streicher, Kim Wimpsett, John Morris, and Sofia Marchant for helping us throughout the entire project. Finally, I would like to thank God for all of His many blessings, this book included.

—Noel Jerke

THANKS TO NOEL WHO GAVE me the opportunity to write this book and for the guidance he gave throughout the project (not to mention the patience he showed for the rookie). A big thank you to God for His grace and love in my life. Thank you to my family for their support and love always. Thank you Mom and Dad for the sacrifices you made for me along the way. Thank you Doug for sharing in my excitement and being my best critic. Thanks to Apress for believing in this book and being so good to us throughout the process. And a very special thank you to Mickey, who went out of his way to make sure I had the opportunity to go where I really wanted to go and who has been an inspiration to me.

—Darin Beard

Introduction

MACROMEDIA FLASH HAS emerged on the Web scene first as a fun and snazzy animation tool, and next as a deep and robust application development tool. There is still the stigma that Flash can only be good for animation. Although it can be great for animation, we have been using Flash as a database interface tool for several years and have seen fantastic results from it. The ability to take dynamic data from a database and display it in an attractive and useful manner is extremely valuable in the world of black Times New Roman in little squares on a white background. And to top it all off, it's not really very difficult to accomplish.

This book focuses on how to harness the power of database technology with Macromedia Flash. You can use the techniques demonstrated in this book with any server and database technologies. We chose in this book to utilize a range of Microsoft technologies including ASP and ASP.NET for the page programming and Access and SQL Server for the database programming. In addition, we demonstrate how to use Visual Studio, Visual Studio .NET, and Web Matrix for the integrated development environment.

We utilize these different technologies with the goal of providing example code that will be familiar to you, the reader. If you are using ASP and Access, you will find good examples to review and enable you to learn the techniques right out of the box. Of course, all of the chapters are valuable and show how the techniques are utilized. But, we wanted to ensure you had something you could set up and easily get running.

The first four chapters of the book provide an introduction to working with Flash and databases. We demonstrate basic concepts for working with external data and Flash. The last four chapters of the book provide complete examples that show how you can utilize Flash with complex database data.

Part One

Setting Up the Environment

CHAPTER 1
Introducing Flash MX

A COMMON MISCONCEPTION about Flash is that it is a program to make things move around the screen or to create a bandwidth-hogging Web site splash screen that turns into a glorified Skip Intro button for most people. It is true that you can use Flash for this purpose; however, it is a much more powerful tool than that.

You can use Flash as the interface for robust database-driven applications. Yes, that is right. A database and Flash can work together to create visually interesting and usable applications capable of extremely complex and valuable solutions. Used correctly, Flash can be an integral part of any database-driven application. You can use it to display data, manipulate and save data, create calculations based on the data, create charts and graphs, and organize and format data. The list is long and happy.

This book covers the basics of the tools needed to create applications such as an event calendar, online poll, trivia game, pie charts, line charts, and bar charts . . . all driven from data stored in a database. It takes you step by step through the creation process and shows you exactly how to do it.

If you have never used Flash as an authoring tool or have had little experience with it, you will learn a lot in this chapter. Specifically, this chapter covers where to get Flash MX, shows the system requirements to use it, goes through how to set up and use the Flash authoring interface, provides an overview of the drawing and manipulation tools, gives an ActionScripting primer, and shows how to create your first Flash movie.

This chapter is not meant to be a complete guide to using Flash MX. It gives you enough to be able to build the database-driven applications within this book. Obviously, the more experience you have with Flash MX, the easier it will be to build the applications—and the better your applications will be. If you require in-depth instructions, consider reading the Macromedia documentation and working through the tutorials that come with Flash MX.

 NOTE *This book refers to Flash applications or designs as* movies. *That term has been used to describe Flash output for years—mostly because the "movies" have a timeline, frames, a stage (the place where the action takes place), and actors (objects on the Flash Stage). It sounds like a movie to us!*

Where to Get Flash MX

The first thing you will want to do is get a copy of Flash MX. You can download a trial version of Flash MX from http://www.macromedia.com. The trial version is a complete version of the software with no limitations except that it allows you to use it for only 30 days at which time it disables itself and you must purchase a copy to continue using it. You can also purchase Flash MX from http://www.macromedia.com.

Understanding the System Requirements

What does it take to run Flash? The following requirements come from the *Using Flash* documentation that is bundled with Flash MX.

Authoring Requirements

Authoring is simply the process of creating Flash movies using the Flash MX authoring software. The following are the system requirements necessary to run Flash MX.

For Microsoft Windows:

- An Intel Pentium 200MHz or equivalent processor running Windows 98 SE, Windows ME, Windows NT 4, Windows 2000, or Windows XP

- 64MB of RAM (128MB recommended)

- 85MB of available disk space

- A 16-bit color monitor capable of 1024×768 resolution

- A CD-ROM drive

For the Macintosh:

- A Power Macintosh running Mac OS 9.1 (or later) or Mac OS X version 10.1 (or later)

- 64MB RAM of free application memory (128MB recommended)

- 85MB of available disk space

- A color monitor capable of displaying 16-bit (thousands of colors) at 1024×768 resolution

- A CD-ROM drive

Playback Requirements

Playback requirements refer to the system and browser you need to play Flash movies.

The following operating systems can play Flash movies:

- Microsoft Windows 95, Windows 98, Windows ME, Windows NT 4, Windows 2000, and Windows XP (or later)

- Macintosh PowerPC with system 8.6 or later (including Mac OS X version 10.1 or later)

The following browsers support Flash movies:

- A Netscape plug-in that works with Netscape 4 (or later) in Windows or works with Netscape 4.5 (or later) or Internet Explorer 5 (or later) on Mac OS. You can find the plug-in as a free download at http://www.macromedia.com.

- To run ActiveX controls, you need Microsoft Internet Explorer 4 or later (Windows 95, Windows 98, Windows ME, Windows NT 4, Windows 2000, Windows XP, or a later version).

- AOL 7 on Windows and AOL 5 on Mac OS

- Opera 6 on Windows and Opera 5 on Mac OS

Understanding Panels

Now that you have Flash MX installed and are ready for action, you will set up the authoring environment. The first things you need to set up are your panels.

What Are Panels?

Panels are windows or palettes that Flash uses to modify settings or properties or to store elements such as objects, sounds, MovieClips, and so on. Each panel has its own set of information that it conveys or sets. You will use some panels more often than others.

One of the most-used panels is the Properties Panel. This panel's content changes based on which tool or object you have selected within the Flash authoring environment. It allows you to set properties of a tool you are using or an object on the Stage.

You can see a complete list of the panels available in Flash MX and turn them on and off (visibility) by using the Window menu.

Arranging and Saving Panels

One of the nice features of Flash MX is the ability to arrange your panels in a way that fits your needs and then save that arrangement. You could, conceivably, have several different panel arrangements saved, each for a different type of work or focus.

Selecting Window ➤ Panel Sets in the menu bar shows a list of preset panel arrangements for different needs (see Figure 1-1). These are based on screen resolution and the focus of your work, either designer (more graphically oriented) or developer (more code oriented). These presets are a good starting place when arranging your panels.

You can move these panels around by grabbing the upper-left corner of their title bars and dragging. They anchor themselves to where you drag and release them.

You can also collapse them when you are not using them to make space for other work on the screen. Clicking the title bar of the panel opens (expands) and closes (collapses) that panel.

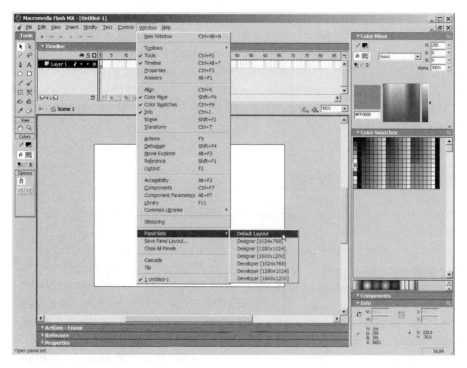

Figure 1-1. The panel sets

Once you have your panels set up the way that works best for you, select Window ➤ Save Panel Layout. Flash MX will prompt you for a name. Give the panel set a descriptive name that tells you what this particular layout is for and click OK. Now your new panel set will show up in the Window ➤ Panel Sets menu.

The Bare Basics of the Authoring Environment

The following sections quickly run through the Flash MX authoring environment. The sections discuss the organization of your movie using scenes, layers, and the important Timeline. If you want to review the authoring environment in more detail, the Flash documentation and examples provide additional details.

Understanding Scenes

Scenes in Flash are just like scenes in a movie or show. When one scene plays out, the next starts. You can create different scenes within the same Flash movie.

You can use scenes to organize a movie thematically. For example, you could use separate scenes for an introduction, a preliminary message, and the interface.

When you publish a Flash movie that contains more than one scene, the scenes in the movie play in the order they fall within the Flash document. Alternatively, you can tell Flash to go from one scene to another based on an evaluation of circumstances. Scenes are not required and are rarely used in the applications you will create in this book.

Understanding Layers

Layers are the tools you use to separate the different objects and clips in your Flash movie.

Macromedia describes layers as being "like transparent sheets of acetate stacked on top of each other." Layers are a way of organizing your objects and artwork on the Flash Stage. You can place an object in a layer that will appear on top of every other layer below it. It allows you to "stack" objects in the order you want them. Furthermore, it allows you to work on an object in one layer without affecting the objects in the other layers.

Layers become important in your Flash design and layout. To animate an object in your Flash movie, you must include the object on the Timeline in its own layer (you will learn more about the Timeline in the next section, "Using the Timeline").

There are some easy controls to create, manipulate, and organize the layers in your movie. Specifically, Figure 1-2 shows three icons across the top of the screen: an eye, a padlock, and a square. Each icon is a column heading that controls the visibility of the layers on your screen. Clicking the eye column *next to a layer* will toggle the visibility of that layer on and off. If you need to hide a layer to work on something underneath it, you use this button.

Figure 1-2. Controlling layers

You use the padlock column to toggle the layer locked or unlocked. While locked, you cannot select, edit, or modify anything in that layer.

The square button toggles the layer between Preview mode and Outline mode. Preview mode displays how the movie will look while playing, and Outline mode provides a quick view of objects and items on the Stage.

TIP *If you click the icons at the top of the columns, you can toggle these options for all layers simultaneously.*

You will also see a few icons at the bottom of Figure 1-2. On the far left is one that looks like a document with a little plus sign (+) on it. This is the Insert Layer button, which inserts a new layer directly above the currently selected layer.

The button to the right of the Insert Layer button is the Add Motion Guide button. It looks like a little ball bouncing, and it also has a plus sign (+). Clicking this button adds a *motion guide* layer. Motion guides define a path that an object can be forced to follow during its movement and are principally used by animators (in this book, you will not utilize motion guides).

The third button, the Insert Layer Folder button, looks like a folder with a plus sign (+). Clicking this button adds a layer folder. You can use layer folders to hold several layers. Folders are great for organizing your layers. For instance, if you have a logo that animates on the screen and the pieces are in five different layers, you could put all five of those layers into a layer folder so you could collapse it while you are not working on it. Also, if you use the visibility buttons discussed previously on the folder, you affect every layer in the folder simultaneously.

The last button on the far right, the Delete Layer button, looks like a trash can. Clicking this button deletes whichever layer, or layers, is selected.

TIP *You can select multiple layers by pressing either the Control key or the Shift key while clicking different layers.*

One last note about layers: Double-clicking the layer name highlights it so you can rename it to something more descriptive than *Layer 1* or *Layer 2*. This helps when you have 30 layers all doing different things and you want to find a particular layer to edit.

Using the Timeline

The Timeline is one of the most important instruments in the Flash MX authoring environment (see Figure 1-3). It is where you tell Flash what to do and when to do it. This section gives you an overview of how the Timeline works and how to manipulate it.

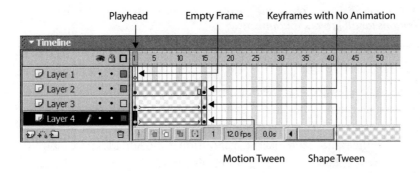

Figure 1-3. The Timeline

If you look at Figure 1-3, you will notice to the right of Layer 1 is a series of squares (or rectangles). Each of those squares represents one frame holder on the Timeline. On the top of the Timeline are numbers that represent where in the Timeline those frames fall. On the bottom of the Timeline are some numbers that help you know where you are. The first box on the left shows the frame you currently have selected. Next is the frames per second (fps), the speed at which the movie is set to run. With a little math, the third frame tells you the "time" that the selected frame represents in your Timeline.

In the top area where the frame numbers are is a pinkish red square with a red line drawn down through all the layers in the movie. This is the *playhead*. It shows what frame is currently being displayed on your screen. While you are previewing the movie in Authoring mode, the playhead moves across the Timeline in real time. You can also grab and drag the playhead to a new location or just click a frame number or marker somewhere on the Timeline, and Flash will jump to that frame immediately.

To place elements in your Flash movie on the Timeline, you need to create frames and keyframes (described next).

NOTE *Flash uses two types of animation:* keyframe, *where objects move to a new location in each frame, and* tween, *where you specify a beginning and ending position so Flash calculates the movement in the frames between the two points.*

Frames are simply places where you can place objects and shapes within the Timeline. *Keyframes* are frames that have objects or shapes in them and are used as beginning and ending phases of animations and actions. In other words, keyframes are how you define animation. In frame-by-frame animation, every frame will be a keyframe. In tween animations, only the places where a phase in the animation happens are marked with keyframes; Flash fills in the frames between the keyframes.

An empty frame on the Timeline displays as a white rectangle with a hollow circle in it. This shape indicates a frame with no objects or shapes. After putting something in that frame, the circle in the frame will turn solid. This is a keyframe. Tweened frames display as either light blue (*motion tweens*) or light green (*shape tweens*).

When a frame is selected, it displays as black, and anything inside the frame (hollow circle, solid circle, animation arrows) reverses and displays as white.

By highlighting a frame on your Timeline and pressing the F5 key (or selecting Insert ➤ Insert Frame), you can create a blank frame on the Timeline. By default all frames except the first one are empty frame holders in a new movie. An empty frame holder is not an actual frame, just a space where a frame could be created. Pressing F6 (or Insert ➤ Keyframe) creates a keyframe on the Timeline. Pressing Shift+F6 deletes a selected keyframe, and pressing Shift+F5 deletes a selected frame, making that frame holder empty again.

Flash MX automatically does some of these things for you as you work. For instance, if you drag and drop an item from the object library (discussed later) onto your Stage, Flash automatically creates a keyframe at the frame that was selected.

TIP *You can also select a keyframe and drag it to a new location on the Timeline.*

Using Flash MX's Tools

When we say *tools*, we are describing the set of drawing and painting tools Flash incorporates into the authoring environment. These tools are what you use to create and edit drawings, shapes, and objects within your movies.

The following sections quickly run through the authoring toolset. The toolbar is, by default, located on the left side of the Flash authoring environment (see Figure 1-4). You should familiarize yourself with the different symbols for each tool.

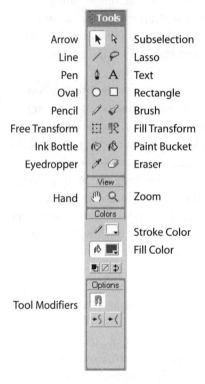

Figure 1-4. Flash drawing and painting toolset

Using the Arrow Tool

The Arrow, or Selection, tool is the most-used tool in the toolset. You use it to select any object, line, MovieClip, and so on. You can also use it to click and drag items around the Stage. If you click and hold a blank area of the Stage and drag your mouse, you will see a selection square moving from where you clicked originally until you let go of the button. This selects everything within this square as you release the mouse button.

Using the Subselection Tool

You use the Subselection tool in conjunction with the Pen tool to select and adjust curves. See "Using the Pen Tool" later in this chapter.

Using the Line Tool

You use the Line tool to draw lines. It sounds basic because it is. Choose the Line tool and set the line's thickness and color in the Properties Panel. After you set your line properties, click and drag on the Stage to draw the line.

TIP *Holding Shift while drawing a line constrains that line to increments of 0, 45, 90 (and so on) degrees.*

After drawing the line, you can use the Selection tool to select the line and change its properties such as thickness or color.

TIP *If you deselect the line and then use the Selection tool to click, hold, and drag the middle of the line, it will drag the line into a curved shape. You can also grab the endpoints of a deselected line and drag to change where the line starts or ends.*

Using the Lasso Tool

You use the Lasso tool to create a custom-shaped selection other than a square, circle, and so on. For instance, if you had a large red rectangle and wanted to select an organically shaped section from the center of it, you could use the Lasso tool and draw a selection shape (see Figure 1-5).

Figure 1-5. Lasso selection

The Lasso tool can also be useful if you have a number of small items close to each other on the Stage. You can zoom in and use the Lasso tool to encompass only what you need selected, much like "lassoing" them.

Using the Pen Tool

You use the Pen tool to draw precise paths as straight lines or smooth, flowing curves (Bezier). To draw straight lines, you click at points and the line fills in between them. To draw curves, click and drag each point to create "handles" for each point. You can then use the Subselection tool to modify and edit each point's handles, and thus you edit the curve.

The Pen tool is one of the more complex tools in the toolset; we recommend reading the help documentation that comes with Flash MX if you are interested in more complex options for using the Pen tool.

Using the Text Tool

You use the Text tool to create vectored text on your Stage. You can use the Properties Panel to set the font, size, color, alignment, spacing, and so on.

There are three types of textboxes in Flash MX: static, dynamic, and input. You will use all three in your database-backed applications. In the Properties Panel of the Text tool, you can choose which type you want using the drop-down list (see Figure 1-6).

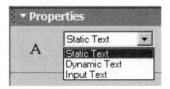

Figure 1-6. Text properties

Static textboxes are textboxes that you type text in when authoring the movie, and the text does not change.

Dynamic textboxes are objects used to display variables in text form. In the Properties Panel you can set the instance name (the name of the object to call programmatically using ActionScript) and the variable name (the actual variable that the textbox represents). Dynamic textboxes will be an integral part of your application design and function.

Input textboxes are similar to dynamic textboxes in that they have an instance name and variable name that can be assigned to them and they are dynamic in nature. The main difference is that input textboxes are specifically for receiving user text input such as in a form.

Using the Oval Tool

You use the Oval tool to draw round shapes. When drawing with the Oval tool, the foreground color will be the Fill Color, and the outline color will be the Stroke Color. You can use the Properties Panel to set the thickness and style of the outline as well as the Fill Color and Stroke Color.

Using the Rectangle Tool

You use the Rectangle tool to draw square/rectangle shapes. The Rectangle tool has the same options available as the Oval tool.

Using the Pencil Tool

The Pencil tool lets you draw lines "free hand" (using the Stroke Color or color set in the Properties Panel).

Using the Brush Tool

The Brush tool works like the Pencil tool except it uses the Fill Color and does not create "stroke" or "outline" graphics. In other words, instead of drawing lines, it draws shapes, which is the other type of graphic that Flash MX uses. Each has their own properties as well as their own ways of modification and editing.

Using the Free Transform Tool

The Free Transform, or Scale, tool allows you to select an object and scale, rotate, stretch, skew, or otherwise manipulate it on the Stage. When this tool is selected and you click any object or shape on the Stage, it highlights the object and produces little square "handles" on the corners and sides. Clicking and dragging one of these handles modifies the shape or scale of the object.

If you hold your cursor next to one of the corner handles, your cursor will change into a round line with an arrow at one end. This is the *rotate cursor*. When this cursor is visible, you click and drag to rotate the object or shape. It is the same with putting your cursor next to one of the side handles. It will change to a line with two arrows pointing in opposite directions. This is the *skew cursor*. Click and drag to skew the shape of the object or shape.

Using the Fill Transform Tool

The Fill Transform tool works much like the Free Transform tool, but it transforms the gradient color fills of objects.

There are two main kinds of color fills: solid and gradient. *Gradient* is when two or more colors are applied to the object and they gradually change from one to the other in some fashion. Sometimes it is a radial gradient, sometimes linear. You can set the type of gradient used in the Color Mixer Panel (see Figure 1-7).

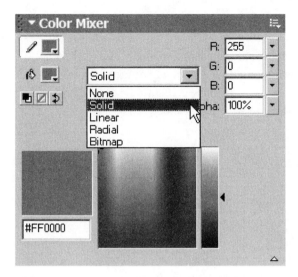

Figure 1-7. Color Mixer Panel fill selector

Choosing the Fill Transform tool and then clicking the object with the gradient fill displays an outline representing the fill's modification shape. If the fill is a gradient, the shape will be round and have three handles on it: one for scale, one for rotation, and one for width. Linear fills only have two handles: rotate and width.

Just grab the handle and drag to modify the fill. The best way to learn this tool is to play with it. It is all in the feel.

Using the Ink Bottle Tool

The Ink Bottle tool is a fill tool for lines and strokes. Set the Stroke Color and click any line with this tool, and the line will be filled with the Stroke Color. If you select several lines or an entire outline of a shape and click them with the Ink Bottle tool, all the lines will be filled with that color.

Using the Paint Bucket Tool

Just like the Ink Bottle tool, the Paint Bucket tool is a fill tool, but it works for shapes and not lines. It works exactly like the Ink Bottle tool.

Using the Eyedropper Tool

You use the Eyedropper tool to select colors from shapes on the Stage already. Click either the Fill Color icon or the Stroke Color icon in your toolbar, select the Eyedropper tool, and click the color you want. The color will be either the Fill Color or the Stroke Color, depending on which you selected.

Using the Eraser Tool

The Eraser tool works like the Brush tool except that it erases whatever you "draw" on.

NOTE *The Eraser tool only works on shapes and lines and will not erase objects or clips. You can edit shapes and lines inside of objects and clips using the Eraser tool if you open the object or clip in edit mode first.*

Using the Hand Tool

The Hand tool is very, uh, handy (sorry, we could not resist!). It is especially helpful when you are zoomed in close and need to move the Stage around to find something currently off the screen. Select the Hand tool and then click and drag on the Stage in the direction you want to move the Stage. It does not move any objects, just your view. It works just like grabbing the Stage with your hand and sliding it around.

Using the Zoom Options

Zoom in and out on your Stage to adjust fine details or alignment. When selected, the Options section of the toolbar shows the Zoom In and Zoom Out options. Choose which you want and click the Stage where you want to zoom.

Setting the Stroke Color

The Stroke Color is the color for lines, outlines, and strokes either as they are drawn or after they are drawn.

Clicking the color chip icon on this tool will pop up a color palette, and your cursor will turn into an eyedropper (see Figure 1-8). You can click any color in the palette to choose that color or click anywhere on your screen to grab that color with the eyedropper. In the upper-right corner of the pop-up palette is a small color wheel icon. Clicking that opens a standard color chooser. You can also enter the hexadecimal (*#nnnnnn*) color value if working with Hypertext Markup Language (HTML).

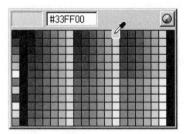

Figure 1-8. Pop-up color palette

Using the Fill Color Tool

The Fill Color is the color for shapes either as they are drawn or after they are drawn. It has the same pop-up color palette that the Stroke Color has.

NOTE *That was the "sonic-boom" tour of the Flash MX authoring toolset. For more in-depth information on the toolset, consider reading all of the documentation and working through the tutorials that Macromedia provides with Flash MX to get more familiar with the authoring environment.*

Getting an ActionScript Primer

Drawing ovals, lines, and curves is all very cool indeed, but the real deal is ActionScripting. ActionScript is the scripting language that Flash MX uses to control what you want the application to do. ActionScript is similar to JavaScript in syntax and style.

Flash MX comes with an ActionScript dictionary in the documentation. It is a complete reference to all objects, functions, methods, and so on.

TIP *You can access the ActionScript dictionary at any time within the Flash authoring environment by pressing F1, which opens the Flash help. Just choose the ActionScript Dictionary option in the left-side navigation.*

The following sections give you a quick rundown of the important Action-Script elements that will be necessary in the applications you will build later in this book.

Some of the following topics are not pure ActionScripting topics but use ActionScripting as you will use it in your applications.

 NOTE *The ActionScript constructors in the following sections come from the Macromedia Flash MX ActionScript dictionary.*

A *constructor* is the logical order and syntax of how a function, command, element, or method is constructed.

Using Buttons

Buttons are objects within Flash MX and function exactly as what they are: buttons. They are not, by definition, ActionScripting elements; however, you use Action-Script to define what buttons will do. They have four built-in states: Up, Over, Down, and Hit.

Up is the button state when nothing is interacting with it. Over is the state when the cursor is over the button. Down is how the button reacts when being clicked and held down. Hit is the area of the button that is live or active—basically, the area that can be rolled over or pressed.

Let's create a button. In the menu bar, select File ➤ New.

Flash MX comes with a library of common objects to use, including buttons, sounds, and others. So let's use one of these common buttons. Select Window ➤ Common Libraries ➤ Buttons. This opens a window with several sets of buttons (see Figure 1-9). Double-click the Circle Buttons folder. Find Circle Button–Next and drag it to your Stage. You should see a circle with a triangle in it.

Figure 1-9. Common buttons library

If you double-click the button on the Stage with the Arrow tool, you will open that button in edit mode. Notice that the button consists of four frames, one for each of the states mentioned previously. Click each state and see how the button changes for each one. Note that the Hit state is a solid circle. You do not see the Hit state in the button. It is only used to tell Flash what part of that button is active. If you used just the outline and triangle for the Hit state, the white space around the triangle would *not* be clickable, making the button difficult to click. This is especially important if the button is made up of text.

Now, at the top of your Stage, in the header/title bar, click the word *Scene 1*. This should take you out of edit mode and into the main Timeline. Pressing Control+E will do the same thing.

Next, choose Control ➤ Test Movie (or press Control+Enter) to open your movie in Preview mode. You should see your button on the screen. Roll over the button and click it to see how it reacts.

Switch back to the authoring window by pressing Control+Tab or choosing Window ➤ Untitled1 (or whatever your movie is called—without the .swf extension).

Next, you will learn how to apply actions to the button's events.

TIP *Throughout this book we refer to using the Control key in "shortcut" key combinations. Obviously, this is a key found on PCs. In most cases, the same shortcut key combinations work on Macs by substituting the Command key for the Control key.*

Using Button Events

Button events are how you tell Flash what to do with a button when a user clicks it.

Let's continue with the next button. Using the Selection/Arrow tool, select the button by clicking it. Now open the Actions Panel.

There are two modes in which the Actions Panel functions: Normal and Expert. In Normal mode you can add, delete, or change the order of statements in the Script pane; you can also enter parameters for actions in textboxes above the Script pane. In Expert mode, you can still choose from the same list, but there are no parameter boxes. You enter the code directly.

Which method you use is a matter of taste. We choose Expert mode usually because it is faster for us. As beginners, we used Normal mode to learn the syntax of ActionScript.

You can change the mode by clicking on the upper-right corner of the panel and choosing the option you desire.

TIP *If you are programming using Expert mode and want to check the syntax of your code, you can temporarily switch to Normal mode. If you have syntax errors in your code, however, Flash will not let you switch to Normal mode. If it switches to Normal mode without incident, you know that your syntax is correct.*

In the title bar of the Actions Panel, it will say *Actions–Frame* or *Actions–Button* or whatever you have selected. To edit the actions of the button, use the Arrow tool and click the button. Now the Actions Panel title bar should say *Actions–Button*.

Buttons have several events built into them. You can find them in the Actions Toolbox under Objects ➤ Movie ➤ Button ➤ Events. If you hold your cursor over each event for a couple of seconds, a tool tip pops up that describes what each is. Also, clicking when selecting the event displays the description in the panel.

The syntax for using a button event is as follows:

```
on(release) {
    //do something
}
```

This code simply tells the button when it is released to fire whatever the `//do something` tells it to do (everything following `//` is considered a comment in ActionScript, so this button would not actually do anything).

So, you can use any of the button events using the same syntax as previously to fire events for that button. As you learn more commands and functions, you will create buttons that actually do something.

Using Variables

The following sections show how to use variables.

Usage

The following shows the syntax for using variables:

```
var variableName1 [= value1] [...,variableNameN [=valueN]]
```

Parameters

The following are the parameters for variables:

- variableName: An identifier

- value: The value assigned to the variable

Variables in Flash can be declared locally or globally. If a variable is declared within a function, it is local and will expire at the end of the function. The same applies to a variable declared within a code block, {}.

You can declare a global variable using the following:

```
_global.variableName1 [= value1] [...,variableNameN [=valueN]]
```

You can also set a variable in a specific location within your movie and *target* that variable when you call it. You will learn about targeting a little later in the "Using Targeting" section; it is an important part of ActionScripting.

Example

The following examples use the var or _global action to declare and assign variables:

```
var x;
var z = 2;
var a = 5, v = 7;
var q, r, s = t;
_global.x = 11;
```

Using Loops

What would scripting be without loops to process through a DataSet or group of items? Flash employs three types of loops: do while, while, and for. Each considers a condition and executes statements while the condition evaluates as requested.

In the applications in this book, you will use different loops to move through a DataSet or group of items and disperse the data to variables and locations within the application.

do while

The following sections show how to use the do while loop.

Usage

The following shows the syntax for using do while:

```
do {
    statement(s)
} while (condition)
```

Parameters

The following are the parameters for do while:

- condition: The condition to evaluate

- statement(s): The statement(s) to execute as long as the condition parameter evaluates to true

Example

This example starts counting from 1 and keeps counting until it reaches 10; the condition will no longer be less than 10, so it will evaluate to false, and the loop will stop:

```
var intCount;
intCount = 1;
do {
    intCount++;
} while (intCount < 10)
```

while

The following sections show how to use the while loop.

Usage

The following shows the syntax for while:

```
while(condition) {
    statement(s);
}
```

Parameters

The following are the parameters for `while`:

- `condition`: The expression that is reevaluated each time the `while` action executes. If the statement evaluates to `true`, the statement runs.

- `statement(s)`: The code to execute if the condition evaluates to `true`.

Example

The following example duplicates five MovieClips on the Stage, each with a randomly generated x and y position, `xscale` and `yscale`, and an `_alpha` property to achieve a scattered effect. The variable `foo` is initialized with the value zero. The `condition` parameter is set so that the `while` loop will run five times or as long as the value of the variable `foo` is less than five. Inside the `while` loop, a MovieClip is duplicated, and `setProperty` is used to adjust the various properties of the duplicated MovieClip. The last statement of the loop increments `foo` so that when the value reaches five, the `condition` parameter evaluates to `false`, and the loop will not execute:

```
on(release) {
    foo = 0;
    while(foo < 5) {
        duplicateMovieClip("_root.flower", "mc" + foo, foo);
        setProperty("mc" + foo, _x, random(275));
        setProperty("mc" + foo, _y, random(275));
        setProperty("mc" + foo, _alpha, random(275));
        setProperty("mc" + foo, _xscale, random(200));
        setProperty("mc" + foo, _yscale, random(200));
        foo++;
    }
}
```

for

The following sections show how to use the `for` loop.

Usage

The following shows the syntax of `for`:

```
for(init; condition; next) {
    statement(s);
}
```

Parameters

The following are the parameters you can use with `for`:

- `init`: An expression to evaluate before beginning the looping sequence, typically an assignment expression. A `var` statement is also permitted for this parameter.

- `condition`: An expression that evaluates to `true` or `false`. The condition is evaluated before each loop iteration; the loop exits when the condition evaluates to `false`.

- `next`: An expression to evaluate after each loop iteration, usually an assignment expression using the ++ (increment) or -- (decrement) operator.

- `statement(s)`: An instruction or instructions to execute within the body of the loop.

Example

The following is an example of using `for` to perform the same action repeatedly. In the following code, the `for` loop adds the numbers from 1 to 100:

```
var sum = 0;
for (var i=1; i<=100; i++) {
    sum = sum + i;
}
```

Using Arrays

Arrays are objects whose values are indicated by a number that represents its place within the array. These representative numbers are the *index*. Flash arrays are zero based, meaning that the first index will always be [0].

Arrays are a good way to store ordered data because you can apply methods to that array to move through it easily forward and backward, sort its items, delete items, modify items, and so on.

Usage

The following shows the syntax of an array:

```
new Array()
new Array(length)
new Array(element0, element1, element2,...elementN)
```

Parameters

The following are the parameters of an array:

- length: An integer specifying the number of elements in the array. In the case of noncontiguous elements, the length parameter specifies the index number of the last element in the array plus one.

- element0...elementN: A list of two or more arbitrary values. The values can be numbers, strings, objects, or other arrays. The first element in an array always has an index or position of zero.

Methods

The following are the methods of an array:

- Array.cat: Concatenates the parameters and returns them as a new array

- Array.join: Joins all elements of an array into a string

- Array.pop: Removes the last element of an array and returns its value

- `Array.push`: Adds one or more elements to the end of an array and returns the array's new length

- `Array.reverse`: Reverses the direction of an array

- `Array.shift`: Removes the first element from an array and returns its value

- `Array.slice`: Extracts a section of an array and returns it as a new array

- `Array.sort`: Sorts an array in place

- `Array.sortOn`: Sorts an array based on a field in the array

- `Array.splice`: Adds and/or removes elements from an array

- `Array.toString`: Returns a string value representing the elements in the Array object

- `Array.unshift`: Adds one or more elements to the beginning of an array and returns the array's new length

Properties

The following is the property of an array:

- Array.length: Returns the length of the array

Example

The following example creates a new Array object with an initial length of zero:

```
myArray = new Array();
```

The following example creates the new Array object go_gos, with an initial length of five:

```
go_gos = new Array("Belinda", "Gina", "Kathy", "Charlotte", "Jane");
trace(go_gos.join(" + "));
```

The initial elements of the go_gos array are as follows:

```
go_gos[0] = "Belinda";
go_gos[1] = "Gina";
go_gos[2] = "Kathy";
go_gos[3] = "Charlotte";
go_gos[4] = "Jane";
```

The following code adds a sixth element to the go_gos array and changes the second element:

```
go_gos[5] = "Donna";
go_gos[1] = "Nina"
trace(go_gos.join(" + "));
```

Using the Date/Time Object

You use the Date object to retrieve date and time values either from the client machine or from universal date/time (formerly Greenwich Mean Time, or GMT). Many times we will pass a date from the server to our application and use the Date object to process that date into whatever format we need. This way we have control over whether that date and time are correct because they are based on what the server says instead of relying on the client machine having the correct date and time.

Usage

The following shows the syntax for the Date object:

```
new Date()
new Date(year, month [, date [, hour [, minute [, second [, millisecond ]]]]])
```

Parameters

The following shows the parameters for the Date object:

- year: A value of 0 to 99 indicates 1900 though 1999; otherwise, all four digits of the year must be specified.

- month: An integer from 0 (January) to 11 (December).

- date: An integer from 1 to 31. This parameter is optional.

- hour: An integer from 0 (midnight) to 23 (11 P.M.).

- minute: An integer from 0 to 59. This parameter is optional.

- second: An integer from 0 to 59. This parameter is optional.

- millisecond: An integer from 0 to 999. This parameter is optional.

Methods

The following shows the methods for the Date object:

- Date.getDate: Returns the day of the month according to local time

- Date.getDay: Returns the day of the week according to local time

- Date.getFullYear: Returns the four-digit year according to local time

- Date.getHours: Returns the hour according to local time

- Date.getMilliseconds: Returns the milliseconds according to local time

- Date.getMinutes: Returns the minutes according to local time

- Date.getMonth: Returns the month according to local time

- Date.getSeconds: Returns the seconds according to local time

- Date.getTime: Returns the number of milliseconds since midnight January 1, 1970, universal time

- Date.getTimezoneOffset: Returns the difference, in minutes, between the computer's local time and the universal time

- Date.getUTCDate: Returns the day (date) of the month according to universal time

- `Date.getUTCDay`: Returns the day of the week according to universal time

- `Date.getUTCFullYear`: Returns the four-digit year according to universal time

- `Date.getUTCHours`: Returns the hour according to universal time

- `Date.getUTCMilliseconds`: Returns the milliseconds according to universal time

- `Date.getUTCMinutes`: Returns the minutes according to universal time

- `Date.getUTCMonth`: Returns the month according to universal time

- `Date.getUTCSeconds`: Returns the seconds according to universal time

- `Date.getYear`: Returns the year according to local time

- `Date.setDate`: Sets the day of the month according to local time and returns the new time in milliseconds

- `Date.setFullYear`: Sets the full year according to local time and returns the new time in milliseconds

- `Date.setHours`: Sets the hour according to local time and returns the new time in milliseconds

- `Date.setMilliseconds`: Sets the milliseconds according to local time and returns the new time in milliseconds

- `Date.setMinutes`: Sets the minutes according to local time and returns the new time in milliseconds

- `Date.setMonth`: Sets the month according to local time and returns the new time in milliseconds

- `Date.setSeconds`: Sets the seconds according to local time and returns the new time in milliseconds

- `Date.setTime`: Sets the date in milliseconds and returns the new time in milliseconds

- `Date.setUTCDate`: Sets the date according to universal time and returns the new time in milliseconds

- `Date.setUTCFullYear`: Sets the year according to universal time and returns the new time in milliseconds

- `Date.setUTCHours`: Sets the hour according to universal time and returns the new time in milliseconds

- `Date.setUTCMilliseconds`: Sets the milliseconds according to universal time and returns the new time in milliseconds

- `Date.setUTCMinutes`: Sets the minutes according to universal time and returns the new time in milliseconds

- `Date.setUTCMonth`: Sets the month according to universal time and returns the new time in milliseconds

- `Date.setUTCSeconds`: Sets the seconds according to universal time and returns the new time in milliseconds

- `Date.setYear`: Sets the year according to local time

- `Date.toString`: Returns a string value representing the date and time stored in the specified Date object

- `Date.UTC`: Returns the number of milliseconds between midnight on January 1, 1970, universal time, and the specified time

Example

The following example retrieves the current date and time:

```
now = new Date();
```

The following example creates a new Date object for Gary's birthday, which is August 7, 1974:

```
gary_birthday = new Date (74, 7, 7);
```

The following example creates a new Date object, concatenates the returned values of the Date object methods `getMonth`, `getDate`, and `getFullYear`, and displays them in the text field specified by the variable `dateTextField`:

```
myDate = new Date();
dateTextField = ((myDate.getMonth() + 1) + "/" + myDate.getDate() +
"/" + myDate.getFullYear());
```

Using the Math Object

The Math object is a top-level object that can be called without using a constructor. You use the methods and properties to access and manipulate mathematical constants and functions. The Math object must always be called using `Math.method(parameter)` or `Math.constant`.

Methods

The following are the methods for the Math object:

- `Math.abs`: Computes an absolute value

- `Math.acos`: Computes an arc cosine

- `Math.asin`: Computes an arc sine

- `Math.atan`: Computes an arc tangent

- `Math.atan2`: Computes an angle from the x-axis to the point

- `Math.ceil`: Rounds a number up to the nearest integer

- `Math.cos`: Computes a cosine

- `Math.exp`: Computes an exponential value

- `Math.floor`: Rounds a number down to the nearest integer

- `Math.log`: Computes a natural logarithm

- `Math.max`: Returns the larger of the two integers

- `Math.min`: Returns the smaller of the two integers

- `Math.pow`: Computes x raised to the power of y

- `Math.random`: Returns a pseudorandom number between 0.0 and 1.0

- `Math.round`: Rounds to the nearest integer

- `Math.sin`: Computes a sine

- `Math.sqrt`: Computes a square root

- `Math.tan`: Computes a tangent

Properties

The following are the properties for the Math object:

- `Math.E`: Euler's constant and the base of natural logarithms (approximately 2.718)

- `Math.LN2`: The natural logarithm of 2 (approximately 0.693)

- `Math.LOG2E`: The base 2 logarithm of e (approximately 1.442)

- `Math.LN10`: The natural logarithm of 10 (approximately 2.302)

- `Math.LOG10E`: The base 10 logarithm of e (approximately 0.434)

- `Math.PI`: The ratio of the circumference of a circle to its diameter (approximately 3.14159)

- `Math.SQRT1_2`: The reciprocal of the square root of 1/2 (approximately 0.707)

- `Math.SQRT2`: The square root of 2 (approximately 1.414)

Using MovieClips

MovieClips are the meat and potatoes of what you are going to do with Flash MX. MovieClips are objects that have an instance name so they can be *targeted*, and they have their own independent Timeline. The main Timeline is considered the root or parent MovieClip. Each additional MovieClip you place in your movie is a child clip of the root clip.

MovieClips have 26 methods, 8 drawing methods (to use a MovieClip to draw with), 30 properties, and 18 event handlers or events. You can use all of these methods, properties, and events to dynamically manipulate your Flash movie to fit your needs. This book will not cover all of the possible methods, properties, and events, but you can find good information on all of them in the ActionScript dictionary included with Flash MX.

TIP *If you are in Flash MX, pressing F1 at any time will open the Flash help that includes the entire ActionScript dictionary for easy reference.*

You can attach actions, or ActionScripting, to a MovieClip using the onClipEvent triggers (see the "Using Movie Events" section later in this chapter).

Using MovieClip Methods

You do not need to use a constructor when calling MovieClip methods; instead, you use the MovieClip's instance name (for example, myMovieClip.play();).

Methods

The following are the MovieClip methods:

- MovieClip.attachMovie: Attaches a movie in the library

- MovieClip.createEmptyMovieClip: Creates an empty MovieClip

- MovieClip.createTextField: Creates an empty text field

- MovieClip.duplicateMovieClip: Duplicates the specified MovieClip

- `MovieClip.getBounds`: Returns the minimum and maximum x and y coordinates of a movie in a specified coordinate space

- `MovieClip.getBytesLoaded`: Returns the number of bytes loaded for the specified MovieClip

- `MovieClip.getBytesTotal`: Returns the size of the MovieClip in bytes

- `MovieClip.getDepth`: Returns the depth of a MovieClip

- `MovieClip.getURL`: Retrieves a document from a Uniform Resource Locator (URL)

- `MovieClip.globalToLocal`: Converts the Point object from Stage coordinates to the local coordinates of the specified MovieClip

- `MovieClip.gotoAndPlay`: Sends the playhead to a specific frame in the MovieClip and plays the movie

- `MovieClip.gotoAndStop`: Sends the playhead to a specific frame in the MovieClip and stops the movie

- `MovieClip.hitTest`: Returns true if the bounding box of the specified MovieClip intersects the bounding box of the target MovieClip

- `MovieClip.loadMovie`: Loads the specified movie into the MovieClip

- `MovieClip.loadVariables`: Loads variables from a URL or other location into the MovieClip

- `MovieClip.localToGlobal`: Converts a Point object from the local coordinates of the MovieClip to the global Stage coordinates

- `MovieClip.nextFrame`: Sends the playhead to the next frame of the MovieClip

- `MovieClip.play`: Plays the specified MovieClip

- `MovieClip.prevFrame`: Sends the playhead to the previous frame of the MovieClip

- MovieClip.removeMovieClip: Removes the MovieClip from the Timeline if it was created with a duplicateMovieClip action or method or the attachMovie method

- MovieClip.setMask: Specifies a MovieClip as a mask for another MovieClip

- MovieClip.startDrag: Specifies a MovieClip as draggable and begins dragging the MovieClip

- MovieClip.stop: Stops the currently playing movie

- MovieClip.stopDrag: Stops the dragging of any MovieClip that is being dragged

- MovieClip.swapDepths: Swaps the depth level of two movies

- MovieClip.unloadMovie: Removes a movie that was loaded with the loadMovie action

Using MovieClip Properties

The following section does not cover all 30 MovieClip properties, but it does list the most important properties for your application development. You retrieve each of these properties using the instance name of the MovieClip; for instance, myMovieClip._width would return the width of the MovieClip named myMovieClip.

Properties

The following are the MovieClip properties:

- MovieClip._alpha: The transparency value of a MovieClip instance

- MovieClip._currentframe: The frame number in which the playhead is currently located

- MovieClip._height: The height of a MovieClip instance in pixels

- MovieClip._name: The instance name of a MovieClip instance

- MovieClip._parent: A reference to the MovieClip that encloses the MovieClip

- `MovieClip._rotation`: The degree of rotation of a MovieClip instance

- `MovieClip._target`: The target path of a MovieClip instance

- `MovieClip._visible`: A Boolean value that determines whether a MovieClip instance is hidden or visible

- `MovieClip._width`: The width of a MovieClip instance in pixels

- `MovieClip._x`: The x coordinate of a MovieClip instance

- `MovieClip._xmouse`: The x coordinate of the cursor within a MovieClip instance

- `MovieClip._xscale`: The value specifying the percentage for horizontally scaling a MovieClip

- `MovieClip._y`: The y coordinate of a MovieClip instance

- `MovieClip._ymouse`: The y coordinate of the cursor within a MovieClip instance

- `MovieClip._yscale`: The value specifying the percentage for vertically scaling a MovieClip

Using Movie Events

You use movie events to attach ActionScripts to a MovieClip intended to fire at a certain time. You will use `onClipEvent` events extensively in your applications.

To attach code to a clip using the `onClipEvent` event, you select the MovieClip to which you want to add an event handler and put the `onClipEvent(event)` trigger in the Actions Panel as shown in the next section.

Usage

The following shows the syntax for `onClipEvent`:

```
onClipEvent(movieEvent){
    statement(s);
}
```

Events

The following are the events for `onClipEvent`:

- `load`: The action is initiated as soon as the MovieClip is instantiated and appears in the Timeline.

- `unload`: The action is initiated in the first frame after the MovieClip is removed from the Timeline. The actions associated with the `Unload` MovieClip event are processed before any actions are attached to the affected frame.

- `enterFrame`: The action is triggered continually at the frame rate of the movie. The actions associated with the `enterFrame` clip event are processed before any frame actions are attached to the affected frames.

- `mouseMove`: The action is initiated every time the mouse is moved. Use the `_xmouse` and `_ymouse` properties to determine the current mouse position.

- `mouseDown`: The action is initiated when the left mouse button is pressed.

- `mouseUp`: The action is initiated when the left mouse button is released.

- `keyDown`: The action is initiated when a key is pressed. Use the `Key.getCode` method to retrieve information about the last key pressed.

- `keyUp`: The action is initiated when a key is released. Use the `Key.getCode` method to retrieve information about the last key pressed.

- `data`: The action is initiated when data is received in a `loadVariables` or `loadMovie` action. When specified with a `loadVariables` action, the data event occurs only once, when the last variable is loaded. When specified with a `loadMovie` action, the data event occurs repeatedly, as each section of data is retrieved.

- `statement(s)`: The instructions to execute when the `mouseEvent` event takes place.

Example

The following statement includes the script from an external file when the movie is exported; the actions in the included script run when the MovieClip they are attached to loads:

```
onClipEvent(load) {
    #include "myScript.as"
}
```

The following example uses onClipEvent with the keyDown movie event. The keyDown movie event is usually used in conjunction with one or more methods and properties of the Key object. The following script uses the Key.getCode method to find out which key the user has pressed; if the pressed key matches the Key.RIGHT property, the movie is sent to the next frame; if the pressed key matches the Key.LEFT property, the movie is sent to the previous frame:

```
onClipEvent(keyDown) {
    if (Key.getCode() == Key.RIGHT) {
        _parent.nextFrame();
    } else if (Key.getCode() == Key.LEFT){
        _parent.prevFrame();
    }
}
```

The following example uses onClipEvent with the mouseMove movie event. The _xmouse and _ymouse properties track the position of the mouse each time the mouse moves:

```
onClipEvent(mouseMove) {
    stageX=_root.xmouse;
    stageY=_root.ymouse;
}
```

Using Targeting

Targeting is the way you tell Flash where objects are within the code. This is the *path*, if you will. It is how you target objects within the movie. Targeting is one of the more complex issues with which you will deal. Beginning Flash designers typically have some trouble with this subject, but this book will try to make it as simple as possible.

For example, Figure 1-10 shows a hierarchy of three MovieClips and one variable. The top-level MovieClip is the main Timeline and is referred to as _root. Inside of the _root clip is a clip named clipOne. Inside of clipOne is another clip named clipTwo. Inside of clipTwo is a variable named variableOne. The figure shows the full path (or target) for each level.

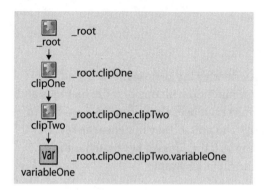

Figure 1-10. Targeting hierarchy example

Now, what if you were writing code inside the clipTwo clip and wanted to target the root clip to get the value of a variable stored there? You would simply use _root to call the root. If you wanted to call the clipOne clip from within the clipTwo clip, you could either start from the root and work back up, _root.clipOne, or you could use _parent, which targets the parent clip of the clip where the code is being executed. So, the _parent of clipTwo would be clipOne. If you used _parent._parent from the clipTwo clip, it would be the same thing as calling _root in this case. You are calling the _parent of the _parent, moving two levels up, which is the root. *Ugh.*

Why in the world would you want to do something like that? That just makes it more complicated, right? Well, yes, it does, but there are times when it will be necessary. Flash has the ability to load external movies (SWF files) into movies. Let's say, for example, that you loaded a movie (let's call it movieTwo) into your root movie, and you are writing code inside the movieTwo movie. You are two levels (clips) deep within the movieTwo movie and want to call the root of the movieTwo movie. If you were to use _root, it would call the root of the main movie and not the movieTwo movie. Using _root will always call the root of the main Timeline; if there are multiple movies involved, the main Timeline is the first movie that opens. Because of this, you would have to use _parent however many times necessary to back out to the root of the movieTwo movie.

Another reason to use _parent is if you are using dynamic clip names and you need to create a sort of generic path from the code. You will not always know what the name of the clip will be if it was dynamically generated, so you cannot necessarily call it by name. Instead of calling the full path, you can just back up as needed to get to the level you desire.

To take the targeting one step further, let's look at the variable `variableOne` in the `clipTwo` clip. Now let's say you are writing some code on the root Timeline and want to poll that variable and get the value of it. What would the path look like? It would be `_root.clipOne.clipTwo.variableOne`.

You can also use the array access operators to target the same variable as `_root.clipOne.clipTwo["variableOne"]`.

We hope this is clear enough to understand. It is not really that difficult once you get your mind wrapped around it. It just takes a little bit to get all the nuances of Flash targeting digested.

Duplicating MovieClips

In the application design in this book, it will be necessary to create a MovieClip that formats and holds data, such as a day on a calendar, and then duplicate that MovieClip and move it to a new location, such as the next day on the calendar. To do this, you use the `duplicateMovieClip` method.

Usage

The following shows the syntax for `duplicateMovieClip`:

```
duplicateMovieClip(target, newname, depth)
```

Parameters

The following are the parameters:

- `target`: The target path of the MovieClip to duplicate.

- `newname`: A unique identifier for the duplicated MovieClip.

- `depth`: A unique depth level for the duplicated MovieClip. The depth level is a stacking order for duplicated MovieClips. This stacking order is much like the stacking order of layers in the Timeline; MovieClips with a lower depth level are hidden under clips with a higher stacking order. You must assign each duplicated MovieClip a unique depth level to prevent it from replacing MovieClips on occupied depths.

Example

The following is an example:

```
DuplicateMovieClip("_root.Windows", "Windows2",2);
```

The depth will become extremely important as you start dynamically generating large numbers of MovieClips in your applications. If the depths are not set correctly, clips could cover other clips as they get out of order or even replace a clip if the same depth is accidentally reused.

Drawing Shapes Using MovieClips

You can use MovieClips to dynamically draw shapes in your movie.

Methods

You utilize the following methods to create charts and graphs dynamically from data collected from a database in some of your applications:

- MovieClip.beginFill: Begins drawing a fill on the Stage

- MovieClip.beginGradientFill: Begins drawing a gradient fill on the Stage

- MovieClip.clear: Removes all the drawing commands associated with a MovieClip instance

- MovieClip.curveTo: Draws a curve using the latest line style

- MovieClip.endFill: Ends the fill specified by beginFill or beginGradientFill

- MovieClip.lineStyle: Defines the stroke of lines created with the lineTo and curveTo methods

- MovieClip.lineTo: Draws a line using the current line style

- MovieClip.moveTo: Moves the current drawing position to specified coordinates

Example

The following example creates an empty MovieClip, named `triangle`. It then turns on the clip's `Fill` method, sets an outline style, and moves the `triangle` clip to the starting position. The `triangle` clip then moves to three points in a triangle shape, and as it moves, it draws and fills a triangle on the Stage. Finally, the clip's `Fill` method is turned off:

```
_root.createEmptyMovieClip ("triangle", 1);
    with (_root.triangle){
        beginFill (0x0000FF, 50);
        lineStyle (5, 0xFF00FF, 100);
        moveTo (200, 200);
        lineTo (300, 300);
        lineTo (100, 300);
        lineTo (200, 200);
        endFill();
}
```

Building Dynamic Flash Objects

You have moved through the tools and bare basics of the Flash MX authoring toolset and ActionScripting. It is now time to learn some of the advanced techniques that will be key in creating Flash MX database-driven applications.

Retrieving data from a database will always be dynamic in some ways. Most likely you will not know exactly how many records are being returned or what the exact values will be, and that is the point. You want your application to be able to dynamically change in response to changes in the data. To do this, you must dynamically generate elements within your Flash environment based on what you retrieve from the database.

Creating Dynamic Variable Names

Creating new variables with dynamic names (var1, var2, var3...) is a process that will be necessary as you build your applications. For this you will use the set() function.

Usage

The following shows the syntax of set():

```
set(varname, value)
```

Example

The following example:

```
for (i=0;i<10;i++) {
    set (["v" + i],i);
}
```

generates this list of variables:

```
v0 = 0
v1 = 1
v2 = 2
v3 = 3
v4 = 4
v5 = 5
v6 = 6
v7 = 7
v8 = 8
v9 = 9
```

There are a couple of things happening within this example. First, [ ] are being used to create the dynamic clip name. Flash is linking everything between the brackets together into one name programmatically. Next, a plus sign (+) is being used to concatenate (combine) strings into one string. Finally, set() is being used to set a variable to a value. You must use the set() function here because using dynamically named variables in the traditional varname=value format will not work. The same thing applies when setting MovieClip properties using dynamic names. You will have to use setProperty() or getProperty() with dynamically named MovieClips.

Using Dynamic Targeting

Sometimes, such as in a calendar, you will have to dynamically target clips and variables. You will use the eval() function for this; eval() takes a dynamic name and then evaluates and returns the value for it.

Usage

The following shows the syntax of eval():

```
eval(expression);
```

Parameters

The following is the parameter:

- expression: A string containing the name of a variable, property, object, or MovieClip to retrieve

Example

This example targets a variable named var inside a clip named clip12 where x=12:

```
eval(["_root.clip" + x].var);
```

Creating Dynamic MovieClips

Creating MovieClips dynamically is almost always necessary when dealing with database data. Usually you will use a loop to move through the data and create MovieClips with incrementing numbers attached to their instance names.

Example

The following example takes a MovieClip in the root named clip and duplicates it 10 times, incrementing the new name each time. It also sets a new dynamic depth with each duplication to avoid clips overlapping or accidentally replacing each other:

```
for(i=0;i<10;i++) {
    duplicateMovieClip("_root.clip",["clip" + i], i+10);
}
```

NOTE *A MovieClip's depth is the stacking order of objects in the movie. A MovieClip at a depth of five will be "underneath" or be covered by a MovieClip at a depth of six should the two clips overlap at anytime.*

The previous code generates the following clips:

```
clip0 depth of 10
clip1 depth of 11
clip2 depth of 12
clip3 depth of 13
clip4 depth of 14
clip5 depth of 15
clip6 depth of 16
clip7 depth of 17
clip8 depth of 18
clip9 depth of 19
```

Creating a Simple Movie

Now that you have tackled the basics, it is time to try out what you have learned. In this section, you will build a simple movie that incorporates some of the topics covered so far.

Open Flash MX and select File ➤ New (or Control+N).

NOTE *If you just opened Flash, by default there is a blank (new) movie already created for you. In that case, there is no need to create a new movie.*

In your toolbar, choose the Rectangle tool. In the Fill Color, click the color chip and select a bright blue. For the Stroke Color, select red. Now move your cursor to the Stage and then click and drag a rectangle, releasing when you get it to a good button size in the middle of your Stage (see Figure 1-11).

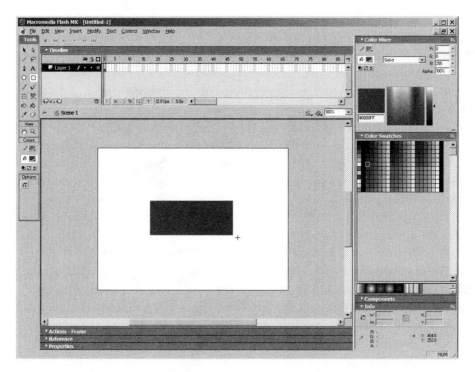

Figure 1-11. Drawing a rectangle

Now, on the toolbar, choose the Arrow tool. Double-click the center of your rectangle. That should select both the fill and the outline of your new shape. Press F8 (or select Insert ➤ Convert to Symbol). A dialog box will ask for the name of your symbol and what type of symbol it is. In the Name box, type *btnBlue* and select the Button radio button (see Figure 1-12). Click OK. Your rectangle is now a button.

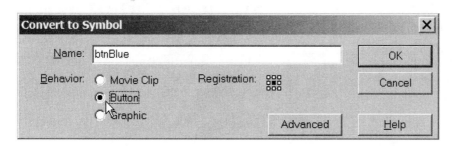

Figure 1-12. Converting a rectangle to a symbol

Double-click the button. This takes you into edit mode. Your rectangle is now editable. You will give the button a different look for each of its four states. The first thing to do is look for the Timeline with the four states at the top of your screen. Click the black dot under the Up state. Press F6 three times (or select Insert ➤ Keyframe three times). This creates a keyframe of your button for each of the four states.

Next, click the black dot under the Over state. Double-click in the middle of your button, selecting both the fill and outline of the shape. On the toolbar, select the Stroke Color chip and move your cursor around the Stage. It should look like an eyedropper, and the color chip on the Stroke Color tool should change to whatever your cursor moves over. Move over the blue color of the button's Fill Color and click. The outline's color should now be blue. Now change the color of the button's Fill Color to something else.

Now click the black dot under the Down state. Change the Fill Color and Stroke Color for this state to something you have not used yet. Now, with both the fill and outline of the object selected in the Down state, press Control+Alt+S (or select Modify ➤ Transform ➤ Scale and Rotate). You will see a dialog box with two options, one for a scale percentage and one for degrees of rotation. You will just enter a scale. Enter *90* for the scale, make sure the rotation is zero, and choose OK.

Press Control+E (or select Edit ➤ Edit Document), which should take you back to the main Timeline and Stage. Now let's see how the button looks. Press Control+Enter (or select Control ➤ Test Movie). This compiles the movie and opens it in a test window. The movie is playing just like it will when published. Roll over the button and click it to see how it works. It is not the most beautiful thing in the world, but it is still pretty cool.

Now let's make that button actually do something. Press Control+Tab or select Window ➤ Untitled1 (or whatever your movie is named, but make sure to select the name without the .swf extension).

You will place a textbox on the Stage and use the button to add text to it. Add a layer to your movie using the Insert Layer button, the button at the bottom of the layers list that looks like a document with a plus sign (+) on it. On your toolbar, choose the Text tool. Open the Properties Panel, and for text type, choose Dynamic Text. On the Stage, wherever you have room, click and drag sideways about the same length of your button and release. In the Properties Panel there are now more options (see Figure 1-13). Directly under the text type drop-down list is a box that has <*Instance Name*> in it. Type *textbox* into that box. This instance name is one way you can access your dynamic textbox using ActionScripting. On the right of the Properties Panel is a Var box. In that box, type *output*, which becomes the name of the variable that fills this textbox.

Figure 1-13. The text's Properties Panel

Using your Arrow tool, click your blue button again. Open the Actions Panel. Make sure the title bar of your Actions Panel says *Actions–Button*. Now you are going to add some ActionScript to this button in the form of button events.

NOTE *You will have to use Expert mode to type this code in directly. You can switch to Expert mode by clicking the Options icon in the upper-right corner of the Actions Panel title bar.*

Enter the following into the Actions Panel:

```
on(rollOver) {
    //sets the variable output in the root to "ROLLOVER"
    _root.output = "ROLLOVER";
}
on(rollOut, dragOut) {
    //sets the variable output in the root to nothing
    _root.output = "";
}
on(release){
    //sets the text property of the textbox object to "CLICK"
    _root.textbox.text = "CLICK";
}
```

You used two different methods of setting the text in the textbox. In rollOver previously, you simply set the variable in the root movie (output) to be equal to the text string you wanted to show in the textbox. You used the same method for the second event; however, you set the variable to be an empty string. In the previous release event, you set the .text property of the textbox object to the string you wanted to display. The first method is for outputting the text based on the value held in a variable. The latter method is for changing text in a textbox programmatically whether or not there is a variable involved.

Now press Control+Enter and test out your button. Your textbox should say *ROLLOVER* when you roll over the button and then clear the text again when you roll out. It should also say *CLICK* if you click and release the button. Notice that if you click and hold down the button, drag your mouse outside of the button, and then release, it does not say *CLICK*. That is because you set the release event to display *CLICK*, and by releasing outside the button's Hit state, you have instead caused the dragOut and releaseOutside events to fire. You have the dragOut event set to clear the text in the textbox so that is what your button does in this case.

Figure 1-14 shows the button in its Up state, Over state, and right after the release event has fired.

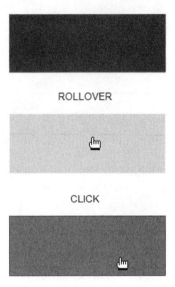

ROLLOVER

CLICK

Figure 1-14. Movie output

How cool is that? You have created your first movie with a button, textbox, and some nifty ActionScript to boot.

Summary

That was a "hair-on-fire" run-through of Flash MX requirements, bare basics, tools, and ActionScript basics. You also got a little bit of hands-on experience by building a simple button event–driven movie. You should have a general idea of the Flash tools and methods you are going to use to develop database-driven applications. Up next, you will look at how to set up the Web server and database environment.

CHAPTER 2

Setting Up the Web Server and Database Environment

THE DATABASE-DRIVEN Flash application equation has two halfs. Chapter 1, "Introducing Flash MX," covered the basics of working with Flash, and now you need to think about what type of database and Web environment you want for the other half. The good news is there are many different ways to place a database behind your Flash front ends. The bad news is some are simple to set up and some are not so simple (despite what the Microsoft marketing literature might say).

This chapter explores all Web server and database environments and then examines the basics with Microsoft's Web and database technology. Later chapters use variations of the different technologies to demonstrate each and provide samples that will work in your chosen environment, but for the basics of database access, this chapter concentrates on a single vendor.

Picking the Right Technologies

There are essentially four different types of technology to consider when setting up a database and Web server environment:

- The base server (operating system) technology

- The Web server that will be utilized

- The database technology

- Any development tools required to work in that environment

For each of those options there are different vendors that you can mix and match together. You can choose to go with an all-Microsoft solution, go with a solution based on Linux, or mix and match vendors. More than likely your choices will be driven by your existing environment, your budget, and your skills and familiarity with a technology.

Exploring Microsoft-Based Solutions

Microsoft provides a wide range of options for implementing Web server technology and Web-based development. Table 2-1 shows the different technology options for the four different technology categories.

Table 2-1. Microsoft Technology Options

TECHNOLOGY	SOFTWARE	DESCRIPTION
Server	Windows 2000	Provides the basic operating system for running the Web server.
Server	Windows XP	Next-generation version of Microsoft operating system technology.
Web server	Internet Information Services (IIS) 5.0	Microsoft's basic Web server that runs on Windows 2000 and Windows XP.
Web server	IIS 6.0/.NET	The next generation of Microsoft's Web server that takes advantage of the .NET technologies and focuses on running secure and scalable .NET Web applications.
Database	Microsoft Access	Microsoft's entry-level database. You can utilize it for building stand-alone applications or as the database behind a Web server. It is great for low-cost database requirements.
Database	Microsoft SQL Server 2000	Microsoft's enterprise-level data base solution, utilized for running large databases that require a high level of transactions.
Development tools	Visual Studio 6.0	With the Visual Interdev component, this is Microsoft's non-.NET development environment. For Web development, it is the primary tool utilized for building Active Server Pages (ASP) with VBScript.

Table 2-1. Microsoft Technology Options (continued)

TECHNOLOGY	SOFTWARE	DESCRIPTION
Development tools	Visual Studio .NET	Microsoft's latest development toolset that supports developing ASP.NET Web applications using a variety of programming languages, including Visual Basic .NET and C#.
Development tools	Web Matrix	Microsoft supports a free development tool called Web Matrix, which makes it easy to develop simple ASP.NET Web applications. This is a perfect tool for basic development and provides the ability to connect to databases. Note that Web Matrix also comes with its own simple Web server for testing pages built into the tool.

NOTE *Microsoft Access and Microsoft SQL Server 2000 come with development and administration tools. For Microsoft Access, the Access application environment provides tools for creating databases, queries, reports, forms, and so on. Microsoft SQL Server comes with enterprise management tools, which provide the ability to define and maintain databases.*

There are two key choices to make when considering Microsoft-based solutions. The first is whether to go with .NET as the development environment. The plus is that it is a robust next-generation technology and is the future of Microsoft's development platform. The minus is that it requires a more advanced approach to development (even with Web Matrix). ASP is still one of the most popular Web development environments and does not require .NET. ASP pages are simple to program and require only knowledge of VBScript (a light version of Visual Basic) and Hypertext Markup Language (HTML).

NOTE *Traditional ASP pages can run in the .NET environment and be developed with Visual Studio .NET.*

The second key choice is the database technology. Microsoft Access provides basic database needs where transaction scalability is not a key requirement. Depending on the type of database transactions, the number of simultaneous users of the database can scale to hundreds and thousands. Access is also much easier to administrate and more intuitive for users who are unfamiliar with advanced database techniques. SQL Server, on the other hand, is designed to run high-volume databases where transactions reach into the millions per second. Administration is also more complicated for SQL Server primarily because it is a true server technology vs. a stand-alone application.

To help determine the best approach to setting up a Web site with significant coding and database requirements, Table 2-2 provides some guidance based on different requirements scenarios.

Table 2-2. Recommended Configurations

TECHNOLOGIES	TARGET USE
Windows 2000/XP, IIS 5.0, Visual Studio 6.0, Microsoft Access	If you need to develop in ASP (which likely means you are doing it already) with light database requirements, then this is the best configuration.
Windows 2000/XP, IIS 5.0, Visual Studio 6.0, SQL Server 2000	If you need to develop in ASP and have advanced database requirements, this is the best configuration.
Windows 2000/XP, IIS 6.0, Web Matrix, Microsoft Access	If you are ready to do basic ASP.NET development and have basic database requirements, this will be the simplest environment to set up (and the most cost effective).
Windows 2000/XP, IIS 6.0, Visual Studio .NET, Microsoft SQL Server 2000	If you need more advanced development and database capabilities, the full power of Microsoft's enterprise development environment will be appropriate.

Through the examples in this book, you will explore each technology combination. This will allow you to review how Web development in the different environments works and test the appropriate code.

Exploring Microsoft Alternatives

There are a wide range of alternative options to Microsoft technology. For each of the major components (operating system, Web server, database, and development tools), you have a large number of options to choose from or to mix and match together. As mentioned, your choice of technologies may be driven by available technical skills and cost.

The most fundamental decision is what operating system to select. You can have a Microsoft-based operating system or go for a free (or low-cost) operating system such as Linux (http://www.kernel.org). Your choice of operating system does not necessarily lock you into a specific vendor for the rest of your application. Each option has its plusses and minuses; this book will not delve into that discussion (or argument) here. Depending on the operating system you select, you can use different combinations of technology. One of the most popular Web servers for both the Linux and Microsoft operating environments is the open-source Apache Web server (http://www.apache.org).

There are many different database vendors in the marketplace. Two prominent alternatives to Microsoft SQL Server include Oracle (http://www.oracle.com) and MySQL (http://www.mysql.com). Oracle is the powerhouse database that is now branching into a full application development platform. Oracle is available on multiple operating system platforms. It can also be expensive. MySQL is an open-source database technology also available on multiple platforms, including Windows and, naturally, Linux. MySQL is free in some cases and has low licensing fees for others.

There are also a wide range of options for programming tools and languages. Perl (http://www.perl.org), for example, is one of the original Web programming languages and is still an option available on many platforms. Java has been highly touted, and there are numerous Web development tools that provide a development environment for Java, including BEA WebLogic and IBM WebSphere. For Linux in particular, PHP (http://www.php.org) has become a popular server-side scripting language.

....

Using LAMP, or Linux/Apache/MySQL/(Perl/Python/PHP)

LAMP is quickly becoming a popular open-source solution for Web development. It combines the most popular and best-of-breed tools for Web development. Sun has a specific initiative called *SunLAMP* that focuses on providing this solution with Sun hardware. IBM and Hewlett-Packard also have similar offerings. LAMP is emerging as a strong and low-cost competitor to Microsoft development solutions.

....

The good news is that there are plenty of options for setting up Web application platforms that range from low cost and simple to extremely complex and robust. The key is to find the right set of solutions to fit with your requirements.

Setting Up the System

As mentioned, this book focuses on building examples based on different configurations of Microsoft technology. The following sections of the chapter cover the basics of getting connected to a database from a Web server page. You will use the fundamental techniques demonstrated throughout the rest of the book.

The three examples you will explore in this chapter focus on the two primary development environments, ASP and ASP.NET, and the two primary databases, Access and SQL Server. The examples in this book mix and match these environments, but the techniques for accessing data are the same.

Preparing the Web Server Environment

Before going through the examples of how to connect to a database, you need to set up your Web server environment. You need either Windows 2000 or Windows XP (Professional or Server edition). To add the Microsoft Web server, IIS, go to the Control Panel. Select Add or Remove Programs and then select Add/Remove Windows Components. Now select Internet Information Services (IIS) and follow the instructions. The version of IIS you are installing depends on the operating system you are utilizing.

If you plan to do .NET programming, you need to add the .NET Framework. If you intend on using Visual Studio .NET, then the framework will come with the installation. If you intend on using Web Matrix, you can download and install .NET from Microsoft at `http://msdn.microsoft.com/netframework/default.asp`.

 NOTE *The examples outlined in the following sections assume you are setting up the development projects on the same server as your Web server.*

Preparing the Database

For the examples used in this book, you need either Microsoft Access or Microsoft SQL Server. You can purchase Microsoft Access from any major computer software retailer. Microsoft has an interesting option for SQL Server. You can download the Microsoft SQL Server Desktop Engine (MSDE) at `http://www.asp.net/msde/default.aspx`. It is a fully functioning version of SQL Server but is limited on the extent it can be utilized. For additional information, check out the Microsoft Knowledge Base article at http://support.microsoft.com/default.aspx?scid=kb;en-us;Q324998 and the FAQ on MSDE at http://www.microsoft.com/sql/howtobuy/msdeuse.asp?LN=en-us&gssnb=1. Or, if you are using Visual Studio .NET enterprise, you can optionally install MSDE. This provides a development environment for creating SQL Server–driven Web sites.

When installing SQL Server, select the appropriate security option. SQL Server defaults to integrated Windows security, which requires your login to have the appropriate access to SQL Server. Or, you can select to use SQL Server security and create specific login accounts in SQL Server.

NOTE *This book uses the Standard Query Language (SQL) for working with data. Basic familiarity with SQL will be required. To make the example simpler, the book will* not *be using stored procedures to work with the data. If you are comfortable working with stored procedures, you can certainly move any of this SQL code into stored procedures.*

Understanding Microsoft's Universal Data Access

Before building the data access examples, it is important to have some basic understanding of Microsoft's approach to data access. Universal Data Access is a strategy for providing wide access to data from multiple sources. Universal Data Access provides high-performance access to a variety of information sources, including relational and nonrelational data, and an easy-to-use programming interface available from a variety of tools. These technologies enable developers to integrate diverse data sources into their applications.

A key component of Universal Data Access is Microsoft Data Access Components (MDAC) that provide easy-to-use, high-performance access to all types of data. Developers creating traditional client/server and Web-based data-driven applications use these components to easily integrate information from a variety of sources. MDAC consists of a version of ActiveX Data Objects (ADO), OLE DB, and Open Database Connectivity (ODBC). For more information, see http://www.microsoft.com/data/default.htm.

The book's examples will specifically use Microsoft's ADO technology. For ASP-based applications, the examples utilize standard ADO. For .NET applications, the example utilizes ADO.NET. There are entire books written on ADO technology. This book focuses on showing techniques for making basic database connections and reading and writing data.

NOTE *If you would like further information on ADO, check out the multiple books Apress offers on the subject (*http://www.apress.com/*).*

Seeing ASP and Microsoft Access Data Access in Action

The first data access example is going to utilize ASP pages (not ASP.NET) and Microsoft Access. You will create a simple database of contact data. You will then display that data in a formatted table in the Web page. You will also use Visual Studio to create the ASP page that connects to the database.

The database has the basic contact data in a single table. The following steps guide you through creating the database:

1. Open Microsoft Access and create a blank database.

2. Save the database as *Contacts.mdb* in a folder called *DataAccessExample1* in the wwwroot folder on your machine. Typically, the wwwroot folder is located on your hard drive at c:\inetpub. Note that you need to create the DataAccessExample1 folder first. You should now have a screen that looks like Figure 2-1.

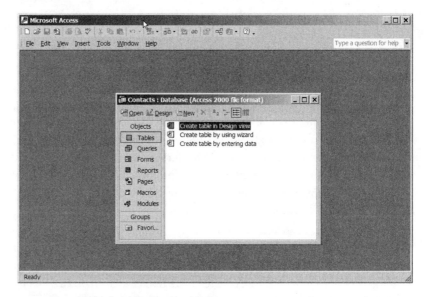

Figure 2-1. New Access database setup

3. Double-click the Create Table in Design View option. This will allow you to define your contact data table.

4. Set up the fields for the table as shown in Table 2-3.

Table 2-3. Table Field Definitions

FIELD NAME	DATA TYPE	DESCRIPTION
idContact	Autonumber/primary key	Primary key (unique identifier) of the table. Note: Make sure you indicate this is the primary key of the table by selecting the field and clicking the key icon on the toolbar.
chrFirstName	Text (field size 20)	First name of the contact.
chrLastName	Text (field size 20)	Last name of the contact.
chrAddress	Text (field size 50)	Street address of the contact.
chrCity	Text (field size 50)	City for the contact.
chrState	Text (field size 20)	State for the contact.
chrZip	Text (field size 10)	ZIP code of the contact.
chrPhone	Text (field size 15)	Phone number of the contact.
chrEmail	Text (field size 50)	Email address of the contact.

5. Now save the table as *ContactData*. Figure 2-2 shows the table.

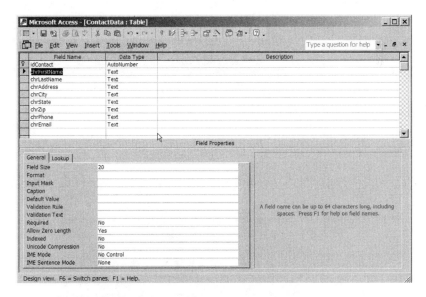

Figure 2-2. The ContactData table

NOTE *You need to enter test data into the database for the following code examples. In Access, open the table by double-clicking it. It opens in the Datasheet view. Then enter the sample data.*

That is all it takes to define your contact database. Now you are ready to begin the code development with Visual Studio 6.0.

 NOTE *You can also do ASP development with Visual Studio .NET.*

The following steps guide you through setting up the project and creating your data-driven page:

1. Start Visual Interdev 6.0.

2. Set up the project as *DataAccessExample1* and save it in the DataAccessExample1 folder you created earlier. Figure 2-3 shows the project's setup screen.

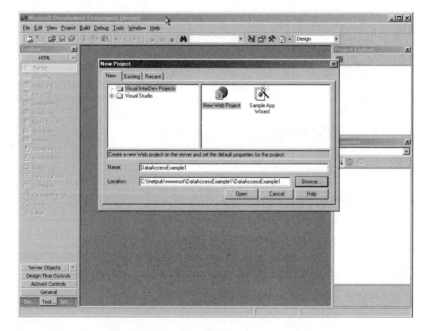

Figure 2-3. Visual Interdev project setup

3. Next, you will be prompted by a series of screens to set up the project. For the first step, indicate the Web server where the project will run (typically localhost because it is created on the same server).

4. On the second step, create a new Web application called *DataAccessExample1*.

5. On step 3, do not apply a layout.

6. On step 4, do not apply a theme and then click Finish.

7. From the File menu, create a new ASP file called *DataAccess.asp*. Add the code in Listing 2-1 to the page.

Listing 2-1. DataAccess.asp

```
<%@ Language=VBScript%>
<%
Option Explicit
%>
<html>
<head>
</head>
<title>Data Access Example 1</title>
<body>

<%

dim sSQL
dim sConn
dim ObjConn
dim oRec

' Use the view we created in the Access database to retrieve the contacts
sSQL = "select * from ContactData"

' The connection string to the database
' NOTE:  Change the path to your MDB as appropriate
sConn = "PROVIDER=MSDASQL;DRIVER={Microsoft Access Driver (*.mdb)};" & _
        "DBQ=c:\inetpub\wwwroot\dataaccessexample1\contacts.mdb;"
```

```
'  Create an ADO connection
set ObjConn = Server.CreateObject("AdoDb.Connection")

'  Open the connection
ObjConn.open sConn

'  Execute the query and store the
'  returned data in a record set
Set oRec = objConn.Execute(sSQL)

%>


<!--  Build the table header -->
<table cellspacing="2" cellpadding="2" rules="all" border="1" id="dgContacts"
        style="border-style:Groove;Z-INDEX: 101; LEFT: 15px;
        POSITION: absolute; TOP: 61px">
        <tr>
                <th>idContact</th>
                <th>chrFirstName</th>
                <th>chrLastName</th>
                <th>chrAddress</th>
                <th>chrCity</th>
                <th>chrState</th>
                <th>chrZip</th>
                <th>chrPhone</th>
                <th>chrEmail</th>
        </tr>
<%

        '  Loop through each contact
        do until oRec.eof
%>
        <!--  Display the data for each field -->
        <tr>
                <td><%=oRec("idContact")%></td>
                <td><%=oRec("chrFirstName")%></td>
                <td><%=oRec("chrLastName")%></td>
                <td><%=oRec("chrAddress")%></td>
                <td><%=oRec("chrCity")%></td>
                <td><%=oRec("chrState")%></td>
                <td><%=oRec("chrZip")%></td>
                <td><%=oRec("chrPhone")%></td>
                <td>
                  <a href="<%=oRec("chrEmail")%>"><%=oRec("chrEmail")%></a>
                </td>
        </tr>
<%
```

```
'  Move to the next record
oRec.movenext

'  Loop back
Loop
%>
```

```
</table>
```

```
</body>
</html>
```

The page has two primary components. The first section sets up the database connection. The first step creates a SQL statement string to retrieve all of the records from the ContactData table. Next, it creates a string that contains a connection definition to tell the ADO engine where the Access database is located and that you want a connection to it. The driver is Microsoft Access and the DBQ setting tells where the Access .mdb is located on the file system.

Next, you create an ADO Connection object using the CreateObject method of the ASP Server object. Using the Connection object, the Execute method is used to execute the SQL statement, and the data results are returned in a record set.

Once you have your data, you loop through the contacts and build a table using mixed VBScript and HTML. This is the primary coding technique for showing database data using ASP pages. As you will see in the next examples, with .NET there are several new options for working with data. To see the page in action, open a browser and browse to http://localhost/DataAccessExample1/DataAccess.asp. Figure 2-4 shows the displayed data based on the code in Listing 2-1.

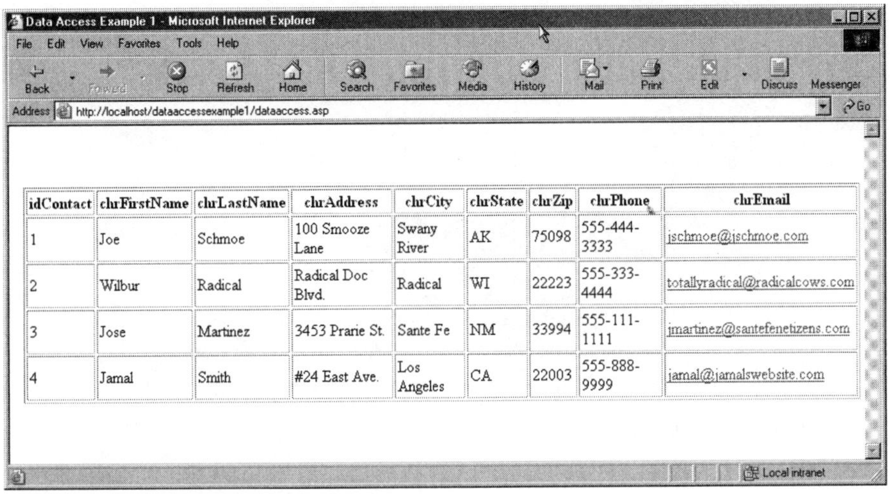

Figure 2-4. Displayed contact data

ASP is one of the most popular Web development environments and still has a significant base of existing pages and development. It certainly works fine for interacting with Flash from a database perspective.

Seeing ASP.NET, Web Matrix, and SQL Server Data Access in Action

The next example utilizes the free ASP.NET Web development tool, Web Matrix. In addition, it moves from Access to SQL Server for the database.

To create the Contacts database using the Web Matrix interface, follow these steps:

1. Start Web Matrix.

2. Click the Data tab on the right workspace window.

3. On the top portion of the Data window, click the New Connection icon. Your screen should look like Figure 2-5.

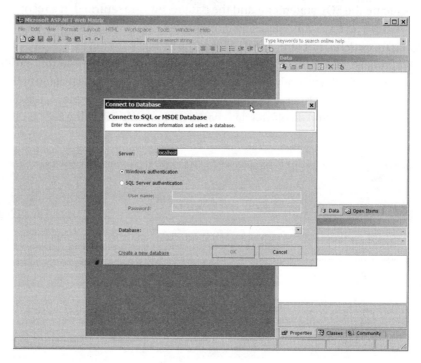

Figure 2-5. Database connection setup

4. Click the Create a New Database link.

5. When prompted for the database name, enter *Contacts*.

6. Your screen should now look like Figure 2-6.

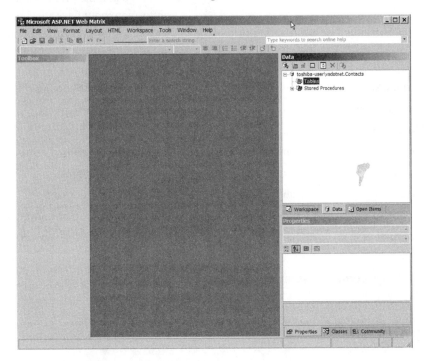

Figure 2-6. New Contacts database

7. Now click the Tables item and click the New Item icon on the top of the Data window.

8. Enter the table name as *ContactData* in the Create New Table window.

9. Now create the columns (fields) of the table by clicking the New button. Set up the column properties as shown in Table 2-4.

Table 2-4. Column Properties

COLUMN NAME	DATA TYPE	DESCRIPTION
idContact	int	Primary key (unique identifier) of the table. Make sure the field is required and the primary key and auto-increment flags are checked. With each new record inserted, an incremented value is created for the ID.
chrFirstName	varchar (field size 20)	First name of the contact.
chrLastName	varchar (field size 20)	Last name of the contact.
chrAddress	varchar (field size 50)	Street address of the contact.
chrCity	varchar (field size 50)	City for the contact.
chrState	varchar (field size 20)	State for the contact.
chrZip	varchar (field size 10)	ZIP code of the contact.
chrPhone	varchar (field size 15)	Phone number of the contact.
chrEmail	varchar (field size 50)	Email address of the contact.

When complete, your screen should look like Figure 2-7.

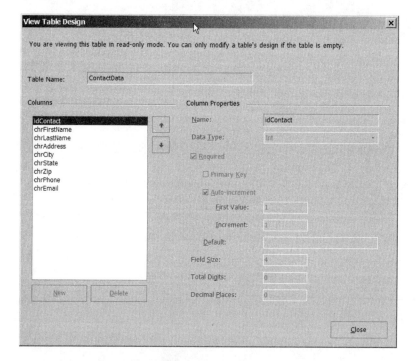

Figure 2-7. The ContactData table

NOTE *You need to enter test data into the database for the following code examples. Select the newly created table and click the Edit button on the Data window to enter data.*

Now you are ready to build the code for the page. Web Matrix has a great data presentation capability where a table from a database can be dragged onto a Web page. Follow these steps to automatically display the contact data in the Web browser:

1. Create a new ASP.NET page by selecting File ➤ New.

2. Save it as *DataAccess.aspx*.

3. Click the ContactData table you just created.

4. Drag and drop it on the DataAccess.aspx page.

5. You will see a data table created automatically, as shown in Figure 2-8.

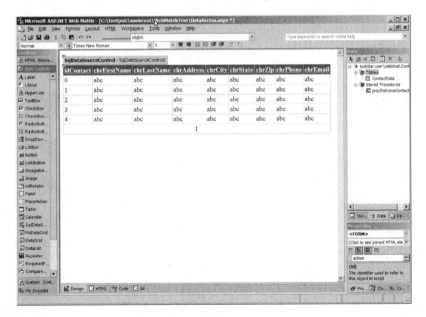

Figure 2-8. ContactData table's HTML design

6. On the View menu, select Start to display the page, as shown in Figure 2-9.

NOTE *Web Matrix will prompt you to use its built-in Web server or IIS. You can choose to use either.*

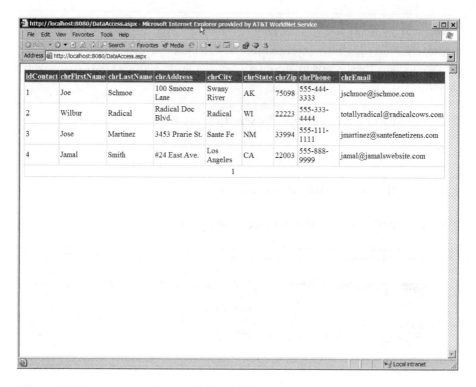

Figure 2-9. Contact data displayed in a Web page

Listing 2-2 shows the generated code (click the HTML tab at the bottom of the file window to see the code generated).

Listing 2-2. ContactData's HTML Display Code

```
<html>
<head>
</head>
<body>
    <form runat="server">
        <p>
            <wmx:SqlDataSourceControl id="SqlDataSourceControl1"
                runat="server"
```

```
                UpdateCommand=""
                SelectCommand="select * from contactdata"
                AutoGenerateUpdateCommand="False"
                ConnectionString="server='mysqlserver';
                trusted_connection=true; Database='Contacts'"
                DeleteCommand=""></wmx:SqlDataSourceControl>
    </p>
    <p>
        <wmx:MxDataGrid id="MxDataGrid1" runat="server"
            DataSource="<%# SqlDataSourceControl1 %>"></wmx:MxDataGrid>
    </p>
    </form>
</body>
</html>
```

This code creates a server-side SQLDataSource object with the appropriate connection data and query to retrieve the data. Then it ties a server-side DataGrid
control to the data source. When the page runs on the server, the data source
retrieves the data and the DataGrid builds the HTML to display the data. That all
happens pretty transparently, but it does not allow you to work directly with the
data, which you need to do to interface with Flash.

To see how to work with the data directly, you will build an HTML table on the
fly to display the data. This works differently than the process in the previous ASP
example. In this case, you will use the .NET Framework programming environment for the code development.

On the DataAccess.aspx page, make sure you are in the Design view. Follow
these steps to add new controls to the page:

1. Choose HTML Elements in the Toolbox and drag a horizontal rule onto
    the page below the DataGrid.

2. Next, from the Web Controls tab of the Toolbox, drag a button onto the
    page below the horizontal rule. In the Properties window, name the con-
    trol *btnContact* in the (ID) field and set the text property to *Create Contact
    Table*. At the end of the table, click and hit Return to go to the next line.

3. Finally, drag a Table control from the Web Controls tab to the bottom of
    your page. Figure 2-10 shows the page after completion. Use the Proper-
    ties window to name the control *tblContact* in the (ID) field.

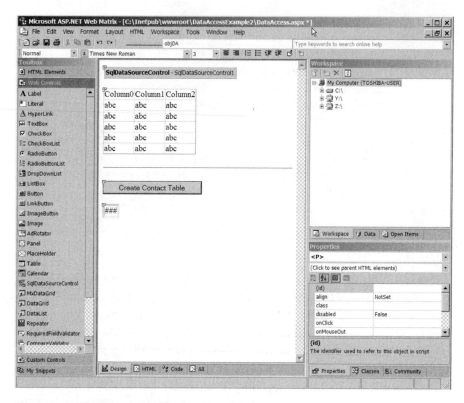

Figure 2-10. Added page elements

Next, you will add code to the click event of the button control. When the user clicks the button, rows and columns are added to the Table object to display the contact data. Listing 2-3 shows the code for the click event of the button along with the rest of the page code. To automatically create the click event in the server-side code, double-click the button in the design interface. Once you have entered the Code view, then enter the code in Listing 2-3 to the btnContact_Click subroutine (sub).

Listing 2-3. DataAccess.aspx Page Code

```
<%@ Page Language="VB" %>
<%@ Register TagPrefix="wmx" Namespace="Microsoft.Saturn.Framework.Web.UI"
Assembly="Microsoft.Saturn.Framework, Version=0.5.464.0, Culture=neutral,
PublicKeyToken=6f763c9966660626" %>
<script runat="server">

    Sub btnContact_Click(sender As Object, e As EventArgs)
        Dim intCounter As Integer
```

```
Dim tRowHeader As New TableRow()
Dim strConn As String
Dim sqlConnection As System.Data.SqlClient.SqlConnection
Dim strSQL As String
Dim sqlCommand As System.Data.SqlClient.SqlCommand
Dim dataAdapter As System.Data.SqlClient.SqlDataAdapter
Dim objDS As System.Data.DataSet = New System.Data.DataSet

' Build the data connection
strConn = "data source=mysqlserver;initial" & _
        "catalog=Contacts;integrated security=SSPI;" & _
        "workstation id=myserver;packet size=4096"

' Create a connection to the database
sqlConnection = New System.Data.SqlClient.SqlConnection(strConn)

' Build the call to the stored procedure
strSQL = "select * from ContactData"

' Build the SQL command
sqlCommand = New _
      System.Data.SqlClient.SqlCommand(strSQL, sqlConnection)

' Open the SQL adapter with the connection and the SQL statement
' to be executed
dataAdapter = New System.Data.SqlClient.SqlDataAdapter(sqlCommand)

' Fill the DataSet object
dataAdapter.Fill(objDS)

' Build the header rows with the appropriate column data
' Create a table cell object
Dim tHeaderCell1 As New TableHeaderCell()

' Set the text for the cell
tHeaderCell1.Text = "Contact ID"

' Add new TableCell object to row
tRowHeader.Cells.Add(tHeaderCell1)

Dim tHeaderCell2 As New TableHeaderCell()
tHeaderCell2.Text = "Name"
tRowHeader.Cells.Add(tHeaderCell2)
```

```vb
Dim tHeaderCell3 As New TableHeaderCell()
tHeaderCell3.Text = "Address"
tRowHeader.Cells.Add(tHeaderCell3)

Dim tHeaderCell4 As New TableHeaderCell()
tHeaderCell4.Text = "Phone"
tRowHeader.Cells.Add(tHeaderCell4)

Dim tHeaderCell5 As New TableHeaderCell()
tHeaderCell5.Text = "Email"
tRowHeader.Cells.Add(tHeaderCell5)

' Add a new row to table
tblContact.Rows.Add(tRowHeader)

'  Loop through the contact data and build row
'  for each contact
For intCounter = 0 To objDS.Tables(0).Rows.Count - 1

    ' Create a new table row object
    Dim tRow As New TableRow()

    ' Create a new table cell
    Dim tCell1 As New TableCell()
    ' Set the table cell to the contact data
    ' Note the data is referenced by calling the
    ' appropriate data row and the appropriate item in the
    ' data row
    tCell1.Text = objDS.Tables(0).Rows(intCounter).Item("idContact") _
                    & vbCrLf

    ' Add new TableCell object to the row
    tRow.Cells.Add(tCell1)

    Dim tCell2 As New TableCell()
    tCell2.Text = _
    objDS.Tables(0).Rows(intCounter).Item("chrLastName") & _
    ", " & objDS.Tables(0).Rows(intCounter).Item("chrFirstName") & _
    vbCrLf

    tRow.Cells.Add(tCell2)

    Dim tCell3 As New TableCell()
```

```
            tCell3.Text = objDS.Tables(0).Rows(intCounter).Item("chrCity") _
                & ", " & _
                objDS.Tables(0).Rows(intCounter).Item("chrState") & " " & _
                objDS.Tables(0).Rows(intCounter).Item("chrZip") & vbCrLf
            tRow.Cells.Add(tCell3)

            Dim tCell4 As New TableCell()
            tCell4.Text = objDS.Tables(0).Rows(intCounter).Item("chrPhone")
            tRow.Cells.Add(tCell4)

            Dim tCell5 As New TableCell()
            tCell5.Text = "<a href=""" & _
                objDS.Tables(0).Rows(intCounter).Item("chrEmail") & """>" & _
                objDS.Tables(0).Rows(intCounter).Item("chrEmail") & "</a>" & _
                vbCrLf
            tRow.Cells.Add(tCell5)


        ' Add the contact row to table
         tblContact.Rows.Add(tRow)


         Next
    End Sub


</script>
<html>
<head>
</head>
<body>
    <form runat="server">
        <p>
            <wmx:SqlDataSourceControl id="SqlDataSourceControl1" runat="server"
            UpdateCommand="" SelectCommand="execute procRetrieveContacts"
            AutoGenerateUpdateCommand="False"
            ConnectionString="server='mysqlserver';
            trusted_connection=true; Database='Contacts'"
            DeleteCommand=""></wmx:SqlDataSourceControl>
        </p>
        <p>
            <wmx:MxDataGrid id="MxDataGrid1" runat="server"
            DataSource="<%# SqlDataSourceControl1 %>"></wmx:MxDataGrid>
        </p>
        <hr />
        <p>
```

```
            <asp:Button id="btnContact" onclick="btnContact_Click" runat="server"
            Text="Create Contact Table"></asp:Button>
        </p>
        <p>
            <asp:Table id="tblContact" runat="server" GridLines="Both"
            BorderStyle="Groove"></asp:Table>
        </p>
        <!-- Insert content here -->
    </form>
</body>
</html>
```

The first part of the code creates variables and objects for working with the database and table. Classes within the .NET Framework provide functionality that can be instantiated and utilized. In this case, the code creates several SQL data objects for working with the database. To learn more about .NET classes, use the Object Browser provided with Web Matrix and review the online support for Web Matrix at http://www.asp.net.

The code focuses on retrieving data from the database. Note that the connection created to the database utilizes integrated Windows security for access permission to the database. You can change this to use SQL Server permissions as appropriate. Set the initial "catalog" or database to your Contacts database.

Next, create the query to return all of the contact data using an SQL select statement. To execute the SQL statement, a SQL command statement is created. The command to execute the connection is passed to the SQL Command object.

The data is returned to a DataAdapter object. The DataAdapter serves as a bridge for retrieving and saving data between a DataSet and SQL Server. In this case, the DataAdapter is used to fill your DataSet, objDS. A DataSet stores retrieved data from the database in a memory cache. You will use the DataSet to display data on the page.

The first step in drawing the display table is creating the header cells. You use the methods of the Table control placed on the page to dynamically add rows and columns to the table. To get started, create a header row object with the TableRow() method and new cells with the TableHeaderCell() method. You can then set the text value of each cell and add the call to the newly created row using the cell.add method of the table row object. You do this to display the combined contact name, contact address, phone, and email. Once the header row is complete, you place the Rows method of the table on the page to display the row.

Once the header row is created, the rest of the contact data is looped through the functions and a new row is built to display each contact data for each cell set to the appropriate database values.

To retrieve the data from the database, the data has to be referenced appropriately. Because a DataSet can contain multiple result sets of data, the ContactData of the collection of tables has to be referenced. In this case, the DataSet only contains data from the single ContactData table. Thus, the reference into the tables collection is zero to indicate the first table. The rows collection of the table collection contains the actual contact data. Each item of the row relates to a specific field. With each row of data, the data fields are referenced by name to retrieve the data and set the cell text. When the row is complete and all of the cells have been added, the Rows method of the table placed on the page is utilized to add the row to the display.

Figure 2-11 shows the result after clicking the button.

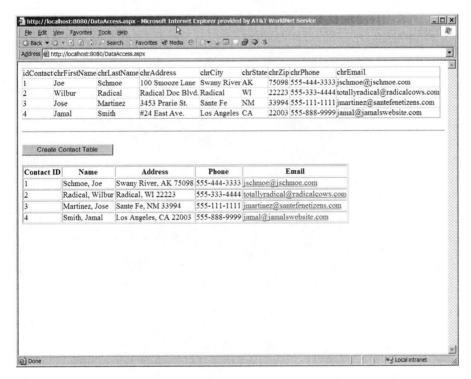

Figure 2-11. Dynamic contact data display

Note the differences between the dynamically generated grid display on the top of the page and the display at the bottom of the page. By accessing the data directly, you have more control over how you work with the data.

Web Matrix provides a quick and easy way to do .NET development. The interface is fairly intuitive. The primary disadvantages of the tool are the inability to harness the full power of Visual Basic and reduced support for navigating the .NET class structure. But, for simple projects, Web Matrix provides an easy-to-use and cost-effective solution for driving data to your Flash front ends.

Seeing Visual Studio .NET, ASP.NET, and Microsoft SQL Server Data Access in Action

The final example in this chapter uses the full Visual Studio .NET environment and SQL Server. In this case, you can use the full Visual Basic development environment to build the ASP.NET pages. Some of the power of the Visual Studio environment will not be apparent in the code examples in the book and will seem similar to Web Matrix, but Visual Studio is truly a more sophisticated and robust development environment.

The first task is to create a new project. The following steps outline the process:

1. Start Visual Studio .NET, as shown in Figure 2-12.

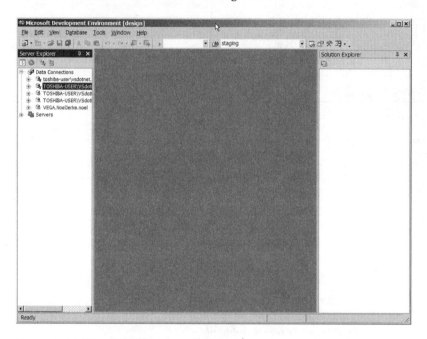

Figure 2-12. Visual Studio startup page

2. Select File ➤ New Project. Select the option to create a new ASP.NET Web Application project.

3. Provide a project name of *DataAccessExample* and save it in a folder called *DataAccessExample3* in the wwwroot directory of your inetpub folder.

4. Once the project is created, rename the WebForm1.aspx file to *DataAccess.aspx.*

5. On the View menu, select Server Explorer to show the Server Explorer window.

6. Expand the list until you have the option SQL Servers.

7. Right-click SQL Server and register the instance of your server by entering the address/name and security settings as appropriate.

8. Now right-click your SQL server and select New Database. At this stage, your screen should look like Figure 2-13.

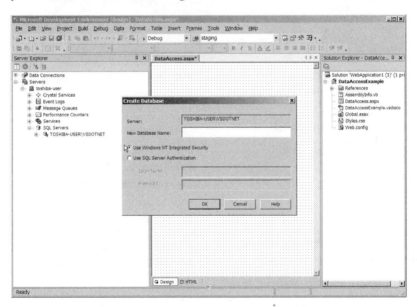

Figure 2-13. The Create Database screen

9. Enter the name of the database *Contacts* and click OK. The database will be created for you.

10. Now, you can create a new table by selecting Database ➤ New Table. A field design screen comes up for defining the data, as shown in Figure 2-14.

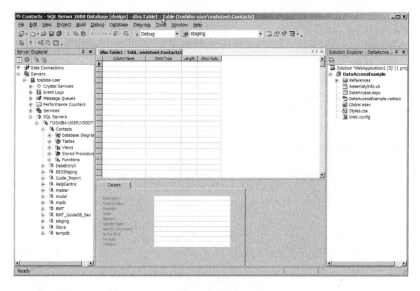

Figure 2-14. Creating a new table

11. Next, you can set up the table. Use the field definitions outlined in Table 2-5 to create the table.

Table 2-5. Field Definitions

FIELD NAME	DATA TYPE	DESCRIPTION
idContact	int	Primary key (unique identifier) of the table. Make sure the Identity flag is set to true so that the value will be automatically incremented.
chrFirstName	varchar (field size 20)	First name of the contact.
chrLastName	varchar (field size 20)	Last name of the contact.
chrAddress	varchar (field size 50)	Street address of the contact.
chrCity	varchar (field size 50)	City for the contact.
chrState	varchar (field size 20)	State for the contact.
chrZip	varchar (field size 10)	ZIP code of the contact.
chrPhone	varchar (field size 15)	Phone number of the contact.
chrEmail	varchar (field size 50)	Email address of the contact.

If you want, you can also use the SQL script shown in Listing 2-4 to create the table by using SQL Server management tools or building a stored procedure and executing it.

Listing 2-4. Table SQL Server Creation Script

```
if exists (select * from dbo.sysobjects where id= object_id(N'[dbo].[ContactData]')
and OBJECTPROPERTY(id, N'IsUserTable') = 1)
drop table [dbo].[ContactData]
GO
if not exists
(select * from dbo.sysobjects where id = object_id(N'[dbo].[ContactData]')
and OBJECTPROPERTY(id, N'IsUserTable') = 1)
 BEGIN
CREATE TABLE [dbo].[ContactData] (
     [idContact] [int] IDENTITY (1, 1) NOT NULL ,
     [chrFirstName] [varchar] (20) COLLATE SQL_Latin1_General_CP1_CI_AS NULL ,
     [chrLastName] [varchar] (20) COLLATE SQL_Latin1_General_CP1_CI_AS NULL ,
     [chrAddress] [varchar] (50) COLLATE SQL_Latin1_General_CP1_CI_AS NULL ,
     [chrCity] [varchar] (50) COLLATE SQL_Latin1_General_CP1_CI_AS NULL ,
     [chrState] [varchar] (20) COLLATE SQL_Latin1_General_CP1_CI_AS NULL ,
     [chrZip] [varchar] (10) COLLATE SQL_Latin1_General_CP1_CI_AS NULL ,
     [chrPhone] [varchar] (15) COLLATE SQL_Latin1_General_CP1_CI_AS NULL ,
     [chrEmail] [varchar] (50) COLLATE SQL_Latin1_General_CP1_CI_AS NULL
) ON [PRIMARY]
END

GO
```

12. Save the table as *ContactData*.

13. Enter some sample data. You can do this by right-clicking the Contact-Data table and selecting Retrieve Data from Table. A grid-based screen opens for data entry.

TIP *You do not need to enter a value for idContact. Because it is an identity field, a sequential number will be automatically generated.*

Now you have completed the project setup. Your new project should look similar to Figure 2-15.

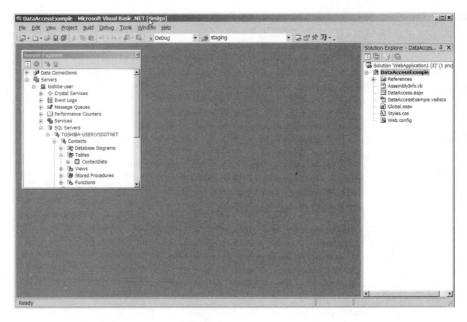

Figure 2-15. Completed project setup

Now that you have set up the database, you can write code to retrieve and display its data. We will demonstrate two approaches, the first with the Web form DataGrid control and the second with a table built on the fly.

To design the Web interface, follow these steps:

1. Open the DataAccess.aspx page for editing. Ensure that the page is in Design vs. HTML mode.

2. Select View ➤ Toolbox to display the Toolbox.

3. On the Toolbox, click the Web Forms tab.

4. From the list of tools, click the DataGrid control and drag it onto to the DataAccess.aspx page. Your form should now look like Figure 2-16.

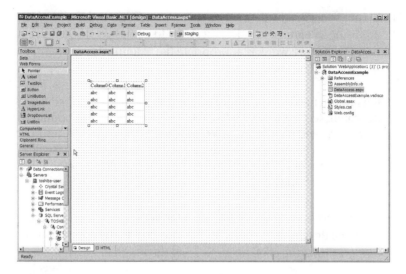

Figure 2-16. Adding a DataGrid

5. Right-click the DataGrid and select Properties to bring up the Properties window. Name the control *dgContacts*.

6. Next, go to the HTML tab on the Toolbox.

7. Select the Horizontal Rule control and drag it below the DataGrid.

8. A button will be placed on the form that, when clicked, will build a table on the fly to display the contact data. Click the Web Forms tab of the Toolbox and drag a Button control below the horizontal rule. In the Properties window for the control, set the ID (name) to *btnContact*.

9. On the Web Forms tab of the Toolbox, drag a Table control below the button. In the Properties window for the control, set the name to *tblContact*.

10. Next, you need to build a connection to the database. Click the Data tab on the Toolbox. Drag a SQLConnection control onto the page. A new window opens on the page with the SQLConnection control. On the Properties window for the control, change the connection name to *ContactsConnection*. Set the `connectionstring` property to the following:

```
data source=mysqlserver;initial catalog=Contacts;
integrated security=SSPI;persist security info=False;
workstation id=myserver;packet size=4096
```

11. In the string, set the data source to be your SQL database server. If you are not using integrated Windows security to access your SQL Server, set the user ID and password as appropriate (an example is commented out in the page code).

12. Finally, you need a SQLCommand control to execute commands against the database. On the Data tab of the Toolbox, drag a SQLCommand control to the page and name it *RetrieveContacts*. Set the commandtext property to *select * from contactdata* to return all of the contact data. It also needs a SQLConnection object to execute the command against. For the Connection property, select the ContactsConnection connection from the drop-down box.

Figure 2-17 shows the final result. The interface for the page is completed, but no code has been developed to hook up the interface to the data—that is your next step. Listing 2-5 shows the code for generating the interface.

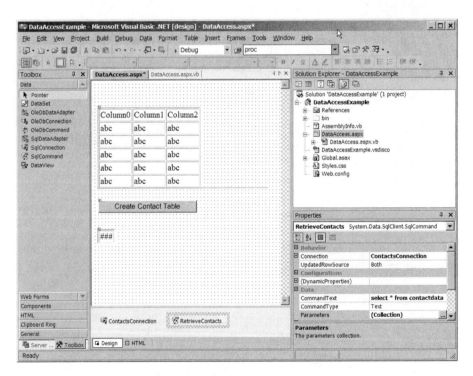

Figure 2-17. Completed Web form design

Listing 2-5. DataAccess HTML Code

```
<%@ Page Language="vb" AutoEventWireup="false" Codebehind="DataAccess.aspx.vb"
    Inherits="DataAccessExample.WebForm1"%>
<!DOCTYPE HTML PUBLIC "-//W3C//DTD HTML 4.0 Transitional//EN">
<HTML>
    <HEAD>
            <title>WebForm1</title>
            <meta content="Microsoft Visual Studio.NET 7.0" name="GENERATOR">
            <meta content="Visual Basic 7.0" name="CODE_LANGUAGE">
            <meta content="JavaScript" name="vs_defaultClientScript">
            <meta content="http://schemas.microsoft.com/intellisense/ie5"
                name="vs_targetSchema">
    </HEAD>
      <body MS_POSITIONING="GridLayout">
            <form id="Form1" method="post" runat="server">
              <asp:DataGrid id="dgContacts" style="Z-INDEX: 101;
                    LEFT: 15px; POSITION: absolute; TOP: 61px" runat="server"
                    BorderStyle="Groove" CellPadding="2" CellSpacing="2">
               </asp:DataGrid>
              <HR style="Z-INDEX: 102; LEFT: 13px; WIDTH: 94.5%;
                    POSITION: absolute; TOP: 243px; HEIGHT: 1px"
                    width="94.5%" SIZE="1">
              <asp:Table id="tblContact" style="Z-INDEX: 103; LEFT: 14px;
                    POSITION: absolute; TOP: 337px" runat="server"
                    BorderStyle="Groove" BorderColor="Transparent"
                    GridLines="Both"   CellPadding="2" CellSpacing="2">
             </asp:Table>
              <asp:Button id="btnContact" style="Z-INDEX: 104; LEFT: 16px;
                    POSITION: absolute; TOP: 272px" runat="server"
                    Text="Create Contact Table"></asp:Button></form>
    </body>
</HTML>
```

Fortunately, the HTML code is automatically generated for the display interface. The designer interface in Visual Studio generates the appropriate HTML code to tell the Web server and the .NET Framework that you want to utilize the DataGrid, Button, and Table server-side controls.

You place the code to interface with the database in a *code-behind* file. Visual Studio creates a separate file from the .aspx page with an .aspx.vb extension. This signifies that you can utilize Visual Basic for interacting with the Web form that was just created. This file is automatically created with all of the appropriate connections to the Web form. To see the DataAccess.aspx.vb file created in the project, click the Show All Files button on the Server Explorer window. When that happens, a plus sign (+) shows up by the DataAccess.aspx file. Click that plus sign (+) to see the .vb file.

Double-click the .vb file to see the page as it is set up. Even though you have not written a line of code yet, the page has quite a bit of code that interfaces to the appropriate .NET classes to ensure the DataGrid will appear, SQL connections can be opened, and all of the other critical items are in place to allow coding of the Web form. In fact, there is a section of the page called *Web Form Designer Generated Code* that is hidden and can be viewed by clicking the plus sign (+). This code defines all of the routines required to create the controls you just placed on the page.

To implement the functionality of the page, you will add code to two specific events. The first is the Page_Load event. This subroutine is fired off when the page is first loaded in the browser. Here the DataGrid will be bound to the contact data and displayed.

The second event is the click event of the button that was added to the page. When the button is clicked, the code will be executed to build a table on the fly to display the contact data. Listing 2-6 shows the code for the page, including the Web Form Designer–generated code.

Listing 2-6. DataAccess.aspx.vb

```
 Public Class WebForm1
Inherits System.Web.UI.Page
Protected WithEvents tblContact As System.Web.UI.WebControls.Table
Protected WithEvents btnContact As System.Web.UI.WebControls.Button
Protected WithEvents ContactsConnection As System.Data.SqlClient.SqlConnection
Protected WithEvents RetrieveContacts As System.Data.SqlClient.SqlCommand
Protected WithEvents dgContacts As System.Web.UI.WebControls.DataGrid


#Region " Web Form Designer Generated Code "

'This call is required by the Web Form Designer.
<System.Diagnostics.DebuggerStepThrough()> Private Sub InitializeComponent()
    Me.ContactsConnection = New System.Data.SqlClient.SqlConnection()
    Me.RetrieveContacts = New System.Data.SqlClient.SqlCommand()
    '
    'ContactsConnection
    '
    Me.ContactsConnection.ConnectionString = _
        "data source=mysqlserver;"initial catalog=Contacts;" & _
        "integrated security=SSPI;persist security info=False;" & _
        "workstation id=myserver;packet size=4096"
    '
```

```vbnet
    'RetrieveContacts
    '
    Me.RetrieveContacts.CommandText = "select * from contactdata"
    Me.RetrieveContacts.Connection = Me.ContactsConnection

End Sub

Private Sub Page_Init(ByVal sender As System.Object, _
        ByVal e As System.EventArgs) Handles MyBase.Init
    'CODEGEN: This method call is required by the Web Form Designer
    'Do not modify it using the code editor.
    InitializeComponent()
End Sub

#End Region

Private Sub Page_Load(ByVal sender As System.Object, _
        ByVal e As System.EventArgs) Handles MyBase.Load

    ' Create a new SQL DataReader
    Dim dr As SqlClient.SqlDataReader

    ' Open the connection
    ContactsConnection.Open()

    ' Retrieve the contacts by executing the SQL Command object
    ' which executes the select command
    dr = RetrieveContacts.ExecuteReader()

    ' Assigning the data to the DataGrid
    dgContacts.DataSource = dr

    ' Bind the data
    dgContacts.DataBind()

End Sub

Private Sub btnContact_Click(ByVal sender As Object, _
        ByVal e As System.EventArgs) Handles btnContact.Click

    Dim intCounter As Integer
    Dim strConn As String
    Dim objDA As SqlClient.SqlDataAdapter
    Dim objDS As New Data.DataSet()
```

```vb
Dim strSQL As String
Dim tRowHeader As New TableRow()

'  Build the connection string
'  Replace the source and catalog (DB) with
'  the appropriate name
strConn = "data source=mysqlserver;" & _
          "initial catalog=Contacts;integrated security=SSPI;" & _
          "workstation id=myserver;packet size=4096"

'  Note this is an alternative connection string for accessing
'  the database with a specific login
'  Change the User ID and password as appropriate
'strConn = "data source=mysqlserver;" & _
          "initial catalog=contacts;user id=sqluserid;" & _
          "password=sqluserpassword;packet size=4096"

'  Build a SQL select command to return
'  the contacts data
strSQL = "select * from contactdata"

'  Open the SQL adapter with the connection and the SQL statement
'  to be executed
objDA = New SqlClient.SqlDataAdapter(strSQL, strConn)

'  Fill the DataSet object
objDA.Fill(objDS)

'  Build the header rows with the appropriate column data
'  Create a table cell object
Dim tHeaderCell1 As New TableHeaderCell()

'  Set the text for the cell
tHeaderCell1.Text = "Contact ID"

' Add new TableCell object to row
tRowHeader.Cells.Add(tHeaderCell1)

Dim tHeaderCell2 As New TableHeaderCell()
tHeaderCell2.Text = "Name"
tRowHeader.Cells.Add(tHeaderCell2)

Dim tHeaderCell3 As New TableHeaderCell()
tHeaderCell3.Text = "Address"
tRowHeader.Cells.Add(tHeaderCell3)
```

```vbnet
Dim tHeaderCell4 As New TableHeaderCell()
tHeaderCell4.Text = "Phone"
tRowHeader.Cells.Add(tHeaderCell4)

Dim tHeaderCell5 As New TableHeaderCell()
tHeaderCell5.Text = "Email"
tRowHeader.Cells.Add(tHeaderCell5)

' Add a new row to table
tblContact.Rows.Add(tRowHeader)

'  Loop through the contact data and build row
'  for each contact
For intCounter = 0 To objDS.Tables(0).Rows.Count - 1

    '  Create a new table row object
    Dim tRow As New TableRow()

    '  Create a new table cell
    Dim tCell1 As New TableCell()

    '  Set the table cell to the contact data
    '  Note the data is referenced by calling the
    '  appropriate data row and the appropriate item in the
    '  data row
    tCell1.Text = objDS.Tables(0).Rows(intCounter).Item("idContact") & _
        vbCrLf

    ' Add new TableCell object to the row
    tRow.Cells.Add(tCell1)

    Dim tCell2 As New TableCell()
    tCell2.Text = objDS.Tables(0).Rows(intCounter).Item("chrLastName") _
        & ", " & _
        objDS.Tables(0).Rows(intCounter).Item("chrFirstName") & vbCrLf
    tRow.Cells.Add(tCell2)

    Dim tCell3 As New TableCell()
    tCell3.Text = objDS.Tables(0).Rows(intCounter).Item("chrCity") & _
        ", " & _
        objDS.Tables(0).Rows(intCounter).Item("chrState") & " " & _
        objDS.Tables(0).Rows(intCounter).Item("chrZip") & vbCrLf
    tRow.Cells.Add(tCell3)
```

```
            Dim tCell4 As New TableCell()
            tCell4.Text = objDS.Tables(0).Rows(intCounter).Item("chrPhone")
            tRow.Cells.Add(tCell4)

            Dim tCell5 As New TableCell()
            tCell5.Text = "<a href=""" & _
                objDS.Tables(0).Rows(intCounter).Item("chrEmail") & """>" & _
                objDS.Tables(0).Rows(intCounter).Item("chrEmail") & "</a>" & vbCrLf
            tRow.Cells.Add(tCell5)

            ' Add the contact row to table
            tblContact.Rows.Add(tRow)
        Next
    End Sub
End Class
```

The first subroutine, page_load, utilizes the SQLConnection and SQLCommand objects added in the page designer. To retrieve the contact data, you must open a connection to the database. The Open method of the SQLConnection object is called to open the connection to the database.

A DataReader object is created to read data from a database. DataReader objects are useful for reading data from a database and moving forward through the data (which is all you need to do for display). The Execute method of the SQL command is invoked, and it takes the text in the commandtext property (select * from contactdata) and executes it against the connection established to the Contacts database.

The data is returned and stored in the DataReader objects. The datasource property of the DataGrid control is set to the DataReader objects that has the contact data, and then the DataBind method of the DataGrid is invoked to display the data on the page. The results of a page run should look like Figure 2-18.

You must include a final set of code for the click event of the Button control. The first section of the click event includes variables and objects created for working with the database and table. For the data objects, appropriate .NET classes are referenced.

When the button is clicked, the Table control will be populated with the contact data. The first step in creating the display table is creating the header cells. A Table control was placed on the page and its methods can be used to add rows and columns to the table. A header row object is dynamically created using the TableRow() method, and new cells are created with the TableHeaderCell() method. The text value of each cell can then be set, and then the cell is added to the newly created row using the `cell.add` method of the table row object. You do this to display the combined contact name, address, phone, and email. Once the header row is complete, the `Rows` method of the table placed on the page is used to display the row.

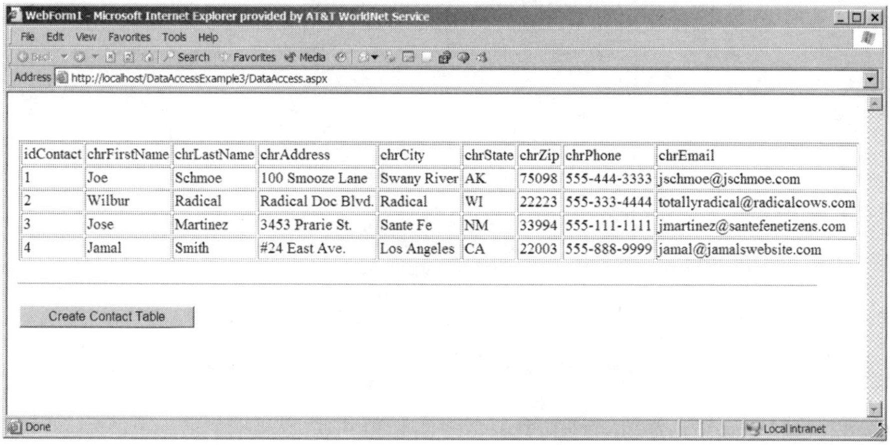

Figure 2-18. Populated DataGrid

Once you have created the header row, you can create rows to display the contact data. You will use the same method as creating the header row but instead use standard cells vs. header cells. The data for each cell is set to the appropriate database values.

To retrieve the data from the database, appropriate referencing of the `DataSet` is key. Because a `DataSet` can contain multiple result sets of data, the ContactData table in the collection of tables has to be referenced. In this case, the `DataSet` only contains data from the ContactData table. Thus, the reference into the tables collection is zero to indicate the first table. The rows collection of the table collection contains the actual contact data. Each item of the row relates to a specific field. As each data row is referenced, each field is referenced by name to retrieve the data and set it to the cell. When the row is complete and all of the cells have been added, the `Rows` method of the table placed on the page is utilized to add the row to the display.

You can see the result shown in Figure 2-19 by clicking the button.

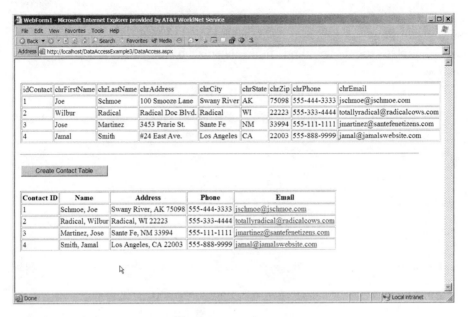

Figure 2-19. Dynamic contact data display

Once again, note the differences between the dynamically generated grid display on the top of the page and the display on the bottom of the page. Accessing the data directly gives you more control over how you work with the data.

Visual Studio .NET provides a powerful environment for building complex Web applications. If your requirements focus on building robust applications with a Flash front end, Visual Studio, ASP.NET, and SQL Server make up the likely appropriate development environment.

Summary

This chapter touched on the topic of server setup and data access. This introduction provides enough information and detail to be able to work with the examples in the book. As demonstrated, you have many different options for working with Web servers and data. If you need more in-depth information or are working in a more complex environment, look for additional resources to learn more about Web servers and databases. Those resources may be provided by your vendor, books, or other sources of information. In the next chapter, you will build your first Flash application that works with simple data.

CHAPTER 3

Creating Your First Flash Application

NOW THAT YOU HAVE LEARNED the basics of the Flash MX authoring tools and of ActionScripting, you are going to build something you can actually use. Every Web site has some sort of navigation to let the user move throughout the site. There are many ways to build navigation for a Web site, but you are going to build some Flash navigation.

Using Flash navigation can be really cool because you can create nice mouseovers and interactive buttons that react more than standard Hypertext Markup Language (HTML) and JavaScript buttons and that do it more easily. You can create this Flash navigation using less code than the HTML and JavaScript versions, as well. However, there are some drawbacks to using Flash for navigation. If the visitor to the site does not have the Flash plug-in installed or they are behind a firewall that blocks Flash movie files for some reason (we have heard of companies blocking Flash content for their employees although this is rare), then that user will *not* be able to see and use the Flash navigation. Therefore, that user will not be able to navigate through the site. One way to solve this problem is to have two versions of the navigation, one Flash and one HTML, and use a "sniffer" to determine if the user has the Flash plug-in installed.

This is not meant to scare anyone off from using Flash. Macromedia.com claims that more than 97.8 percent of all Web users have the Macromedia Flash Player. From our experience, this is pretty accurate. We recently captured some statistics from traffic on a particular Flash site; over a three month period, 96.8 percent of the visitors had the Flash 6 plug-in installed, 2.8 percent had the Flash 5 plug-in installed, and 0.4 percent had no Flash plug-in installed. That is not bad at all.

Another negative to using Flash for navigation is what we call the "update factor." This is simply the process of changing or updating the navigation should something on the site change. Someone would have to go back to the authoring environment, create new buttons or change the text and Uniform Resource Locators (URLs) of existing buttons, regenerate the movie, and upload it. Then return visitors would have to redownload the movie, even if it was cached, because it had changed. With larger movies, that can be annoying if changes happen frequently.

The good news is that there is a perfect solution for this problem...dynamic Flash movies. You can build your navigation using Flash and make it dynamic so you can change the navigation anytime you want without having to edit the Flash at all. You can change the text on the buttons, change the number of buttons, and even make the Flash navigation display submenu items based on where you are in the site. Does that mean that the navigation has to be boring, ugly, and static with no real animation or movement? Nope. In this chapter, you will build dynamic, smart navigation with interactive buttons, subnavigation buttons, and the ability to animate onto the screen as the page loads.

When you are finished, you will have a useable, working, dynamic Flash navigation bar to use on any site. This chapter focuses on planning and creating the Flash navigation; in the next chapter, you will write the code to make it work. So, at the end of this chapter you should have a good feel for how to create objects and manipulate their properties within the Flash authoring environment.

Planning the Navigation Project

One of the most important and time-saving techniques is to plan what you are going to do before you actually start building anything. This will save you from having to rework something because you come across an issue that you had not thought of originally. This is not to say that will not happen anyway sometimes…it certainly does. But the likelihood of it happening is far less if you think through and plan before you start.

What Should the Flash Application Do?

The primary item to consider before even opening the Flash authoring toolset is what you want/need the Flash application to do. It sounds goofy, but get down to the root of it and draw diagrams of the logic to define the capabilities of the Flash application (see Figure 3-1).

Figure 3-1 is a basic logic diagram of what you want the Flash navigation bar to do. As you can see, you want to input some data to the application that tells it what the navigation options are, what the suboptions are, and what the URLs are to all the options. It should also probably contain some flag so the application knows which page it currently is on in the site. The application then should duplicate enough buttons (each with three button states built into it) to match the options in the input data. Finally, the application will animate all the duplicated buttons into their places and await a surfer's click—at which time the application will send the surfer to the chosen URL and the process will reload at the new location with a new set of data.

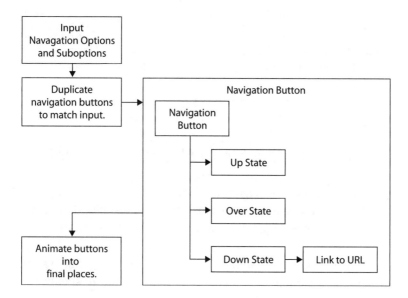

Figure 3-1. Basic logic diagram

This sounds pretty simple…and actually it is. You will be surprised to see how much easier this is to do than you might have imagined.

What Should the Application Look Like?

So, you know what the application is supposed to do, now you need to consider what you need it to look like. There are many issues that fall into this area: color schemes of the site, button styles, fonts, background graphics, location of the navigation on the page, space that the navigation must fit within, and so on. Because you are creating navigation that will be generic enough to plug into a site rather easily, you are going to stick with left-side navigation with some standard, slightly beveled buttons. The great thing about a dynamic Flash application is that the design is relatively easy to modify later because most of the items in the application are duplicated from one or just a few items in the application itself. You can change one or a few items, and it changes them all.

NOTE *When planning the application's look, usually we do mock-ups using Adobe Photoshop or Adobe Illustrator until we get the look we like and either output graphics to import into Flash or re-create the graphics within Flash itself.*

How Will the Flash Application Fit into the Page?

Where the Flash will be located on the page will affect how you lay out the movie. A top navigation will most likely be more of a horizontal format with options next to each other. A side navigation will be more of a vertical format with options stacked on top of each other.

Because you are creating side navigation in this chapter, you are going to stack your buttons one on top of the other and indent the suboption buttons slightly to set them apart from the top-level navigation buttons.

Understanding the Size Needs and Limitations

It is important to know how much space you will have to fit your Flash application onto the page. Although your Flash navigation is dynamic in data, the size cannot change. So you need to make sure you allow enough space to add all the navigation options you need without using too much space that causes big, fat, empty spaces.

Know exactly what the dimensions of the Flash application need to be *before* you start on it. This is extremely difficult to change after you have already started building a dynamic Flash application.

Understanding File Size and Raster Graphics vs. Vector Graphics

There has always been, and probably always will be, debates over *raster* (or bitmapped) graphics and *vector* graphics. Raster/bitmap images consist of rows of pixels, square or rectangular in shape usually. As you zoom into a bitmap graphic you will see the "jaggies" or stair-step pattern from the pixels. This is known as *aliasing*. Vector graphics are images that are mathematically defined by lines and shapes in a given two-dimensional or three-dimensional space. Because vector graphics are not confined to pixels in their raw state but instead are converted to pixels for display on the fly, they can easily scale without displaying the "jaggy" or aliased patterns of bitmapped images.

Figure 3-2 shows two gray circles with black outlines that look similar. Figure 3-3 has zoomed in to the same two circles, and you can clearly see which is a bitmap graphic (left) and which is vector based (right).

Figure 3-2. Bitmap and vector images

Figure 3-3. Bitmap (left) and vector (right) images

There are benefits to using bitmap graphics. You can create subtle and interesting effects that are far more difficult to achieve using vector graphics. A good example of this is soft drop shadows. They are almost impossible to achieve using vector graphics, but they are simple to do using bitmap graphics.

The biggest issue concerning the two types of graphics within Flash is that bitmap graphics are more expensive to the file size of the final movie. The bigger the file size of the final movie, the longer the user will have to sit and wait for it to download. Vector graphics are usually smaller in file size and, therefore, load much more quickly than bitmap images.

NOTE *Our opinion on the matter is somewhere in between. We use a good mixture of bitmap and vector graphics. Many of the movies we have produced in the past were heavily bitmap laden and thus an expensive download for the user. We now use vector graphics for as much as we can to keep file size down, but we use bitmaps for the "fancy" graphics needed to make our movies/applications look the way we want them to look.*

In the dynamic navigation application in this chapter, you will use vector graphics and some techniques to make those graphics look like they have a little more depth than just a block of color. This will keep the file size down and still look nice.

Choosing Fonts

Another file/download size issue arises with fonts used in your movies. Flash can embed fonts into the movie as you output it for Web consumption. If the fonts were not embedded and the user views the movie without the fonts installed, they would not see the text created in the movie where it was placed. Instead, they would see a default system font instead. This could possibly destroy all the careful spacing and placing you might have done.

The more fonts you put into the movie, the larger the file size is going to be. Some fonts are larger in file size than others. Just looking in our Fonts directory, our fonts range from 3KB to more than 20MB in size. So, wisely choosing fonts to avoid a huge download is a good plan. We tend to pick one, two, or maybe three fonts and try to consistently stick to them within a Flash movie.

In dynamic textboxes you can actually set how much of the font to embed into the movie. For instance, if you know that a particular textbox is only going to display numeric characters, you can set the textbox properties to embed only numeric characters. This can greatly reduce the amount of needless file size. You certainly do not want to make users download something that is not even being used. You will learn more about how to do this later.

There is one good thing about font embedding: If you embed part or all of a font in one textbox, it is embedded into the movie for any other textboxes with that font. A font is only embedded into a Flash movie one time no matter how many times it is used within the movie.

In this chapter's navigation application, you are going to use one font throughout the movie.

Using Preloaders

A *preloader* is a bit of graphics and code that display how much of the movie is loaded as the user waits and watches as it downloads. Usually this is used for larger movies that take a little longer to download.

With the evolution of ActionScripting, preloaders are more powerful than they were in the past. They now know the file size of a movie and can calculate download speed and time remaining.

Preloaders have another function that is more subtle; they hold the movie at a prelocation while the rest of the parts load. If the movie were allowed to just go where it could as it loaded, things would appear and work sporadically as it finished loading. With a preloader, you can tell the movie to stop and hold until everything is loaded and then continue.

If the movie is longer and larger, you can preload just enough to allow the movie to play while the rest of it loads during the playback. As long as the playback does not catch up to what is not loaded yet, users will never know that the movie is still loading while they are watching it. This is called *streaming*.

NOTE *To stream a movie, it is necessary to determine the slowest connection speed for which to preload the movie. So, if you expect quite a bit of 56Kbps traffic, you could set the movie to preload enough of the movie that a 56Kbps user would need so that the movie could start while the rest loads in the background without the user ever catching up to what is not loaded. Flash can tell how much this would be in relation to the number of frames in the preview window. You will learn more about this later.*

In a movie that will be as small in size as this navigation bar, you will put a small and simple preloader on it just to show that the navigation is loading, even though most people will not have a chance to really see much of the preloader because of the speed with which it will load.

CAUTION *Streaming Flash movies is generally reserved for animation type movies. Streaming a Flash application is not going to be beneficial or even possible 99 percent of the time. We, nearly always, preload the entire application before starting the interface for use.*

Building Your Project

You have moved through the planning stage and know what your movie is supposed to do and what you want it to look like. Now you can start building it.

So let's jump right in. Open Flash MX and get a fresh, new movie on the screen.

Setting Movie Properties

The first thing to do is make your Stage the size you want it, change the background color to what you want, and set the frame rate (if needed). The Properties Panel displays some settings that are the basic movie properties (see Figure 3-4).

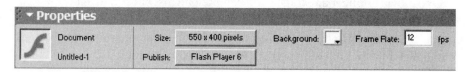

Figure 3-4. Movie properties

In the Properties Panel, click the Size button (Figure 3-4 shows it saying 550×400) to open the Document Properties dialog box. You can set several things from here. For the dynamic navigation movie, enter *150* for the width and enter *30* for the height, as shown in Figure 3-5.

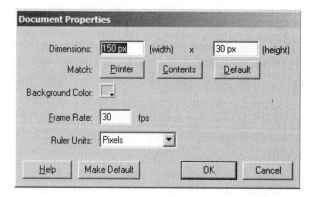

Figure 3-5. The Document Properties dialog box

Click the little color chip icon to open a color chooser box. You can choose a background color by clicking one of the "paint chips" or entering a hexadecimal color value in the textbox provided. Just enter *CCCCCC* in the textbox and press Enter. The color chip should change to light gray.

The frame rate is how many frames per second (fps) the Flash movie will attempt to play back when viewed. We say *attempt* because if the processor of the computer cannot process the frames fast enough to play back at the specified rate, the movie will not play back properly. It will just play the movie as fast as it can. So, setting the frame rate to some ridiculous number is unnecessary. Standard video-tape plays at about 30fps, and we do not recommend setting the movie's frame rate any higher than this for normal operation. That being said, this navigation does not rely on the frame rate for much of anything because there is little animation involved. But let's set it to 30 anyway.

After those settings are all in, click OK.

Creating the Buttons

Now you are going to create the button that will be duplicated for each dynamic navigation option that is sent to your Flash movie.

From the Toolbox, choose the Rectangle tool. In the Properties Panel, you can set the properties of the rectangle before drawing the rectangle (see Figure 3-6).

Figure 3-6. Rectangle properties

You are going to change the Fill Color of the rectangle (the bottom paint chip with the pouring paint bucket next to it in the Properties Panel). Click the Fill Color paint chip and enter *666666* in the textbox. This should be a dark gray color. Leave the Stroke Color black.

Now click and hold the left mouse button anywhere on the movie's Stage, drag it down and to the right, and then release. The size does not matter at this point because you are going to set the size using the Properties Panel later. Just make it big enough to be able to see and select it.

Now choose the Arrow tool from the Toolbox and then select the entire rectangle and outlines by double-clicking in the center of the rectangle. In the Properties Panel, you will see options for setting the values of the shape. You are going to set the size of your rectangle to the size you want your button to be. Enter *148* for the width (W) and *20* for the height (H).

With the shape still selected, press F8 (or select Insert ▶ Convert to Symbol) to open the Convert to Symbol dialog box. In the Name field, enter *button*. For the behavior, be sure to select Button (see Figure 3-7). Then click OK.

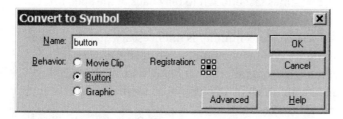

Figure 3-7. The Convert to Symbol dialog box

Now the rectangle is officially a button. Make sure it is selected, and in the Properties Panel, set the x position (X) to *1* and the y position (Y) to *-20*. This will place the button just above the top of the Stage. We did this because this button will only be used to duplicate other buttons, and the starting point will be just above the navigation top (see Figure 3-8 for what the property settings should look like).

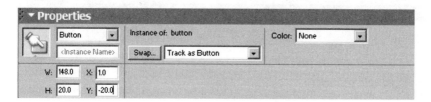

Figure 3-8. The button's Properties Panel

You will give your button a little bit of a three-dimensional look and modify the states for it. Double-click the button on the Stage to select it and choose Edit ▶ Edit Symbol (or select it and press Control+E). You should see something like Figure 3-9.

Using the Arrow tool, click anywhere on the Stage where there is not an object to deselect the button. Click on the outline located on the top edge of the button. This should select it.

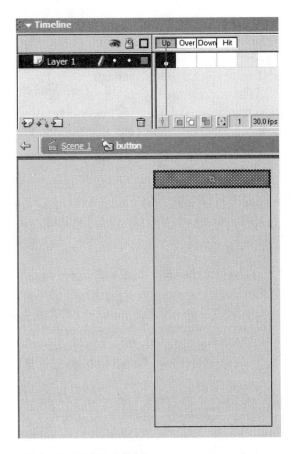

Figure 3-9. Editing the button

TIP *Selecting an outline can be challenging at first. A good thing to know is when your pointer (the Arrow tool) is in position over an outline, the cursor will change slightly to either an arrow with a partially curved line underneath it or an arrow with two lines forming a corner underneath it. The latter is if your cursor is over where two lines meet.*

Now hold down the Shift key and select the outline on the left edge of the button. That should add the left outline to the selection. Now, in the Properties Panel, click the Stroke Color paint chip and choose white for the new color. Click anywhere on the Stage that is not part of the button to deselect the outlines. Now the button looks a little more three-dimensional.

Let's create the different states for the button. Click the black dot (keyframe) under the Up state to select it. When the keyframe is selected, the dot is white and the box is black. Press F6 (or choose Insert ➤ Keyframe) three times. There should now be an identical keyframe for each state. Select the Over state by clicking its keyframe. Deselect any part of the shape that is selected (by clicking anywhere on the Stage that is off the button). Click in the center of the button, just selecting the gray part of it. Use the Properties Panel and change the gray color to *0000FF* (full blue). Select the Down state by clicking its keyframe. Again, deselect the button parts. Now you want to just select the top and left (white) outlines. Change these to black. Next, select the right and bottom outlines and change these to white. When you are done, find where it says *Scene 1* just under the states and their keyframes and then click Scene 1. Clicking Scene 1 should exit symbol-editing mode and take you back to the main Timeline (or press Control+E to do the same thing).

Press Control+Enter (or select Control ➤ Test Movie) and play with the button. Roll over it and click it. How easy was that?

So, you have a button but you need some text on that button to tell users what it is. Go back to the movie by closing the preview window. Click the button and press F8 (or select Insert ➤ Convert to Symbol). Enter *buttonClip* for the name, choose Movie Clip for the behavior, and click OK. You just created a MovieClip with your button in it.

Select and edit the buttonClip (double-click it and press Control+E, or select it and choose Edit ➤ Edit Symbol). Now the MovieClip's Timeline is displayed with a single keyframe in the first frame. That keyframe contains the button. You want to add a layer using the Insert Layer button. Make sure this new layer is above (on top of) the button's layer.

Choose the Text tool from the Toolbox. In the Properties Panel, set the textbox to Dynamic Text, the font to Verdana, and the size to 11. Make sure the Fill Color is set to black and the text orientation is set to be center justified. Also, to the right of the Single Line drop-down selector is the Ab button. That option toggles whether the text within the textbox is selectable by the user. You do not want your button text to be selectable, so make sure that button is toggled off.

With all the properties set, click near the upper-left corner of the button, drag to the right edge of the button, and release. This draws a textbox on the button. Most likely, the textbox is not exactly centered on the button, so let's use the Align Panel to get the alignment perfect. Choose the Arrow tool from the Toolbox and make sure the new textbox is selected by clicking it. Open the Align Panel by pressing Control+K (or selecting Window ➤ Align). Make sure the To Stage button is toggled down. In the top row of buttons are two sets of three buttons. The first three buttons are to align objects horizontally. Click the center button of the first set to center the textbox horizontally. The second set of three buttons are for aligning vertically. Click the center button of the second set to center the textbox. Now the textbox should be smack-dab in the center of the button.

With the Arrow tool, make sure the textbox is selected and look at the Properties Panel. Set the instance name (see Figure 3-10) to *option* and the variable name (see Figure 3-11) to *strOption*.

Figure 3-10. Setting the instance name

Figure 3-11. Setting the variable name

These are the names you will use in the scripting to set the values for the text on the buttons. You will do that in the next chapter.

Okay, you are almost there. Using the Arrow tool, click the keyframe that contains the textbox to select it and press Control+Alt+C (or select Edit ➤ Copy Frames). Create another new layer above the textbox layer. Select the first frame in the newest layer and press Control+Alt+V (or select Edit ➤ Paste Frames). This makes a new layer with an exact copy of the textbox in it. Deselect everything (click anywhere on the Stage off of the button and textboxes using the Arrow tool). With the Arrow tool, click the textbox on top. Using the Properties Panel, change its color to white. Press Control+1 or select View ➤ Magnification ➤ 100%. While the top white textbox is still selected, use the arrow keys on the keyboard and press the up and left arrow keys one time each. This should nudge the textbox up and to the left slightly.

You just created two textboxes, one white and one black, that will show the same text, but the black will look like a shadow of the white text because of the slight offset of the two. Pretty clever, huh? It will make the text easier to read and a little snazzier to look at, too.

Save the movie as *dynamicNav.fla*.

NOTE *You can compare your version of dynamicNav.fla to dynamicNav-PreScript.fla, which is available in the Downloads section of the Apress Web site (*http://www.apress.com*).*

You have completed all the objects you need for your dynamic navigation. Yes, really! That is all there is to it—one button with a couple of textboxes. Figure 3-12 is what it should look like so far. (It is not much to look at yet.) If you were to test the movie, it would just be a gray background with nothing else on it at this point. But after you add the scripting, it will be your dynamic Flash navigation.

Figure 3-12. Navigation objects completed

Summary

In this chapter, you built the graphic flash foundation for the dynamic navigation bar and set up the foundation for making it dynamic. In the next chapter, you will add ActionScript code to the page to make the navigation bar dynamic. In addition, you will review how to pass variable data into the movie to define what navigation menu options should be displayed. The next chapter will even touch a little bit on using Extensible Markup Language (XML) data to drive the navigation menu.

CHAPTER 4

Adding ActionScript to Your Flash Application

IN CHAPTER 3, "Creating Your First Flash Application," you built the foundation for a dynamic Web navigation bar using Flash. Without some ActionScript to make it work, however, it will do absolutely nothing. This chapter takes you through the process of adding the scripting to the navigation. These are the basic ActionScript techniques that you will use in all of the database-driven Flash applications in this book.

Doing More Planning

In the previous chapter, you planned what you wanted the navigation to do and look like. Now you must plan how the data part of your application will work.

Understanding Data Vehicles

There are several methods of passing data to and from Flash. First, the data can be stored in a database and accessed through Active Server Pages (ASP) or some other scripting language. Second, Macromedia has a product called Flash Remoting MX, which Macromedia.com describes as follows:

> *Macromedia Flash Remoting MX provides the connection between Macromedia Flash and your Web application server, making it fast and easy to create Rich Internet Applications that blend content, applications, and communications. Easily integrate rich Macromedia Flash content with applications built using Macromedia ColdFusion, Microsoft .NET, Java, and SOAP-based Web services using the powerful—yet simple—programming model provided with Flash Remoting MX.*

See http://www.macromedia.com/software/flashremoting/ for more information on Flash Remoting MX.

In addition, the data can also be stored in a plain-text file and read directly into Flash.

Finally, another data vehicle is Extensible Markup Language (XML). Flash has native XML tools built into the ActionScript language for reading and parsing XML. Because of the need to store a navigation structure, including subnavigation options and Uniform Resource Locators (URLs) for each option, you are going to utilize the XML abilities of Flash in this chapter.

XML is a simple text format with origins in Standard Generalized Markup Language (SGML). XML is a markup language for documents containing structured information, which is information that contains content with some indication of what role that content plays. Almost all documents have some structure. A markup language is a method to identify structures in a document. The XML specification defines a standard way to add markup to documents.

 NOTE *You can find more information about XML at* http://www.w3.org/XML/.

You will use the XML format to create a navigation structure and assign values to each navigation option so that Flash can display and link each option and to track which suboptions should be visible.

Determining the Data Structure

You must determine your navigation structure and what information each option will have for Flash to work. Listing 4-1 shows what the navigation data structure needs to contain. Figure 4-1 shows a graphical representation of the same structure.

Listing 4-1. Data Structure

```
numopts - the number of main navigation options
opt - nav option (id as attribute)
optText - the text to display
url - the link for this option
numsubopts - the number of suboptions found under this main option
subopt - sub nav option (id of main option for this suboption as attribute
         and sid as attribute)
optText - text to display for this suboption
url - link for this suboption
```

```
numopts
 └─ opt (id as attribute)
    ├ optText
    ├ url
    ├ numsubopts
    └ subopt (id and sid as attributes)
       ├optText
       └url
```

Figure 4-1. The data structure

This may look and sound a little confusing, but Listing 4-2 shows the sample XML file you will use as your navigation in this chapter. It also shows how the structure in Listing 4-1 is formatted when in XML format. Simply open a text editor (Notepad.exe on the PC, for example), enter the text from Listing 4-2, and save it as *nav.xml*. Place this file in the same directory as the Flash navigation movie (the .swf file).

Listing 4-2. Sample XML Navigation

```
<nav numopts="4">
    <opt id="1">
        <optText>Home</optText>
        <url>index.html</url>
        <numsubopts>0</numsubopts>
    </opt>
    <opt id="2">
     <optText>About Us</optText>
        <url>about.html</url>
        <numsubopts>0</numsubopts>
    </opt>
    <opt id="3">
        <optText>Services</optText>
        <url>services.html</url>
        <numsubopts>3</numsubopts>
        <subopt sid="1" id="3">
            <optText>Web Design</optText>
            <url>web.html</url>
        </subopt>
        <subopt sid="2" id="3">
            <optText>Code</optText>
```

```
                <url>code.html</url>
        </subopt>
        <subopt sid="3" id="3">
            <optText>Database</optText>
            <url>db.html</url>
        </subopt>
    </opt>
    <opt id="4">
        <optText>Contact Us</optText>
        <url>contact.html</url>
        <numsubopts>0</numsubopts>
    </opt>
</nav>
```

Applying the Plan and Techniques

With the XML created, you can move on to building the Flash XML parser to read
that data and do what you need with it.

Setting Up the Data Parsing

To be able to load the XML navigation into Flash, you have to set up some Action-
Script that utilizes Flash MX's native XML object.

Open Flash MX and load the navigation Flash movie, dynamicNav.fla, that you
created in Chapter 3. Click Layer 1 and insert a new layer above it. You can do this
by clicking the Insert Layer button or by choosing Insert ➤ Layer from the menu.
Double-click the name of the new layer to highlight it and rename it to *Control*.
Go ahead and rename the other layer to *Nav*.

Click Frame 1 of the Control layer. Open your Actions Panel. It should say
Actions–Frame in the title bar of the Actions Panel. If it does not, click the frame
again to make it active. You need to insert the functions in Listing 4-3 into this
frame.

 NOTE *You need to be running your Actions Panel in Expert mode to be able to
directly type commands into it (or to cut and paste into it). By default, the
Actions Panel is set to Normal mode, which does not allow you to type commands directly into it. To change the mode, click the upper-right corner of the
Actions Panel and choose the Expert Mode option from the drop-down menu.*

Listing 4-3. XML Parsing Functions

```
stop(); // to stop the movie in Frame 1 while the XML loads
//function to facilitate insertion of new array record
function NavOption(id, txt, link, numsubopts) {
 this.id = id;
 this.txt = txt;
 this.link = link;
 this.numsupopts = numsubopts;
}


//function to facilitate insertion of new array record
function NavSubOption(id, sid, txt, link) {
 this.id = id;
 this.sid = sid;
 this.txt = txt;
 this.link = link;
}


//parse the XML file and insert each option into arrays
function makeArray(success) {
 var i, j, k, mainTag, txt, link, numsubopts, subtxt, sublink;
 if (success) {
  for (i=0; i<=navXML.childNodes.length; i++) {
   if (this.childNodes[i].nodeValue == null
   && this.childNodes[i].nodeName == "nav") {
    mainTag = this.childNodes[i];
    _root.numOpts = mainTag.attributes["numopts"];
   }
  }

  for (i=0; i<=mainTag.childNodes.length; i++) {
   if (mainTag.childNodes[i].nodeName == "opt") {
    id = mainTag.childNodes[i].attributes["id"];
    for (j=0; j<mainTag.childNodes[i].childNodes.length; j++) {
     if (mainTag.childNodes[i].childNodes[j].nodeName != null) {
      if (mainTag.childNodes[i].childNodes[j].nodeName == "optText") {
       txt = mainTag.childNodes[i].childNodes[j].firstChild.nodeValue;
      } else if (mainTag.childNodes[i].childNodes[j].nodeName == "url") {
       link = mainTag.childNodes[i].childNodes[j].firstChild.nodeValue;
      } else if (mainTag.childNodes[i].childNodes[j].nodeName == "numsubopts") {
       numsubopts = mainTag.childNodes[i].childNodes[j].firstChild.nodeValue;
      } else if (mainTag.childNodes[i].childNodes[j].nodeName == "subopt") {
```

```
          subid = mainTag.childNodes[i].childNodes[j].attributes["sid"];
          mainid = mainTag.childNodes[i].childNodes[j].attributes["id"];
          for(k=0; k<mainTag.childNodes[i].childNodes[j].childNodes.length; k++) {
           if (mainTag.childNodes[i].childNodes[j].childNodes[k].nodeName ==↵
"optText") {
             subtxt = mainTag.childNodes[i].childNodes[j].childNodes[k].↵
firstChild.nodeValue;
           } else if (mainTag.childNodes[i].childNodes[j].childNodes[k].↵
nodeName == "url") {
             sublink = mainTag.childNodes[i].childNodes[j].childNodes[k]↵
.firstChild.nodeValue;
           }
          }
          thisSubOption = new NavSubOption(mainid, subid, subtxt, sublink);
          navSubOptions.push(thisSubOption);
          delete thisSubOption;
         }
        }
       }
     thisOption = new NavOption(id, txt, link, numsubopts);
     navOptions.push(thisOption);
     delete thisOption;
    }
   }
   _root.gotoAndStop("buildNav");
  }
}


//array for nav options
var navOptions = [];
//array for nav suboptions
var navSubOptions = [];

//create XML object
navXML = new XML();
//ignore white space in XML file (keeps from generating uneccessary tags)
navXML.ignoreWhite = true;
//after XML is loaded, fire the makeArray function
navXML.onLoad = makeArray;
//load the XML
navXML.load("nav.xml");
```

CAUTION *Modifying the structure of the XML sample provided within this chapter will result in the XML parser shown in Listing 4-3 not working properly. This parser was written specifically for this particular XML structure. You can modify the data in the XML file, but the structure must remain consistent.*

This section will not go into great detail about what is happening in the XML parser shown in Listing 4-3, but the basic overview is that it takes the XML file, moves through each tag, determines what that tag is and what its options and data are, and then inserts the data into one of two arrays. It does this by traversing the XML tree and reading the data values. It looks ugly but is fairly basic. If you want to dig into it in detail, run subsegments of the code to see what is read from the XML file.

One array is the main navigation options, and the other is for displaying the active suboptions. Once the XML data is parsed into the appropriate arrays, you send the Flash movie to a frame that will contain the code to duplicate and create the menu buttons.

 NOTE *If you want more information about Flash's native XML object and the methods it contains, see the documentation that comes with Flash MX.*

Next, click Frame 1 of the Nav layer and release. Now click and drag Frame 1 over to Frame 5 in the Nav layer. This should move the keyframe that was in Frame 1 to Frame 5 and leave a blank keyframe in Frame 1.

Next, click Frame 5 of the Control layer and press F7 (or choose Insert ➤ Blank Keyframe). In the Properties Panel, with Frame 5 of the Control layer selected, type *buildNav* in the Frame Label box. Click the MovieClip on the Stage (in the Nav layer), and enter *buttonClip* for the Instance Name.

Finally, click Frame 5 of the Control layer. Enter the code in Listing 4-4 using the Actions Panel.

Listing 4-4. Build Navigation ActionScript

```
stop();
buttonClip._visible=false;
var blnSubPast = false;
var i = 0;
var x = 0;
```

```
var so = 0;
//loop through navOptions array and create menu items
for (i=0; i<navOptions.length; i++) {
 duplicateMovieClip(buttonClip,["buttonClip"+i],i+100);
 if (blnSubPast) {
  setProperty(["buttonClip"+i],_y,buttonClip._y+(23*(i+1+so)));
  set(["buttonClip"+i+".endY"],buttonClip._y+(23*(i+1+so)));
 }else{
  setProperty(["buttonClip"+i],_y,buttonClip._y+(23*(i+1)));
  set(["buttonClip"+i+".endY"],buttonClip._y+(23*(i+1)));
 }
 set(["buttonClip"+i+".strOption"],navOptions[i].txt);
 set(["buttonClip"+i+".strURL"],navOptions[i].link);
 set(["buttonClip"+i+".intNum"],i);
 //if this option is the active option,
 //and this option has suboptions
 //then parse the suboptions
 if (_root.activeOpt == navOptions[i].id and navOptions[i].numsubopts > 0) {
  blnSubPast = true; //to tell Flash that suboptions have been processed
  //loop through navSubOptions and only display the suboptions of the active option
  for (j=0; j<navSubOptions.length; j++) {
   if (navSubOptions[j].id == navOptions[i].id) {
    so++;
    duplicateMovieClip(buttonClip,["buttonClipS"+j],j+1000);
    setProperty(["buttonClipS"+j],_y,buttonClip._y+(23*(j+i+1)));
    set(["buttonClipS"+j+".endY"],buttonClip._y+(23*(j+i+1)));
    set(["buttonClipS"+j+".strOption"],"::" + navSubOptions[j].txt);
    set(["buttonClipS"+j+".strURL"], navSubOptions[j].link);
    set(["buttonClipS"+j+".intNum"],j);
   }
  }
 }
}
```

Listing 4-4 shows the code that takes the data Flash received from the XML, duplicates the button clips, and moves them to their proper position on the navigation.

Double-click the buttonClip to move into edit mode. Hide the top two layers (using the Hide Layer toggle next to the layer name (see Chapter 1, "Introducing Flash MX," for more information about the Hide Layer toggle). Only the layer with the actual menu button in it should be visible now. Click the button and add the code in Listing 4-5 to the Actions Panel for that button.

Listing 4-5. Menu Button Scripting

```
on (release) {
 getURL(strURL);
}
```

This simply tells your Flash navigation button to send the browser to whatever URL was set in this button's strURL variable. That variable was set in the navigation build of this application.

Be sure the nav.xml file is located in the same directory that this Flash file is saved in and press Control+Enter (or choose Control ➤ Test Movie). There should be a gray menu with four menu options on it. Clicking any of them will cause your application to error because those links do not actually exist. However, you can easily customize the XML file by adding your own menu text and links. Just change the current options and URLs in the nav.xml file to what you want them to be and add as many new options and suboptions as you need for your navigation. Finally, save the file. The Flash navigation will parse your options and display the navigation you need, as shown in Figure 4-2.

NOTE *You must keep the same structure in the XML file that is there now. Options and suboptions must be formatted exactly like described. If there is any deviation from this format, the XML will not be parsed correctly by the parser that was written for the navigation movie.*

Figure 4-2. The navigation in default state

One Final Note

The Flash navigation you have just built is looking for a particular variable value so that it knows which page it is on so that in turn it knows which subnavigation options to display and where to display them. That variable is named activeOpt. If no value is set for this variable, then the Flash navigation only displays the main navigation options and no suboptions.

The trick to telling the application the value for each page is to use the QueryString of the Flash calls in the page code. Listing 4-6 shows a sample of what the Flash call would look like in your page.

Listing 4-6. Flash Call

```
<OBJECT classid="clsid:D27CDB6E-AE6D-11cf-96B8-444553540000"
    codebase=
    "http://download.macromedia.com/pub/shockwave/cabs/flash/swflash⤶
.cab#version=6,0,0,0"
  WIDTH="150"
  HEIGHT="300"
  id="dynamicNav "
  ALIGN="">
  <PARAM NAME=movie VALUE="dynamicNav-.swf">
  <PARAM NAME=loop VALUE=false>
  <PARAM NAME=menu VALUE=false>
  <PARAM NAME=quality VALUE=high>
  <PARAM NAME=bgcolor VALUE=#CCCCCC>
  <EMBED
    src="dynamicNav-.swf"
    loop=false
    menu=false
    quality=high
    bgcolor=#CCCCCC
    WIDTH="150"
    HEIGHT="300"
    NAME="dynamicNav- "
    ALIGN=""
    TYPE="application/x-shockwave-flash"
    PLUGINSPAGE="http://www.macromedia.com/go/getflashplayer">
  </EMBED>
</OBJECT>
```

Notice that there are two separate places where the filename of the movie is used. One is within the OBJECT tag in a parameter named movie, and the other is within the EMBED tag as src. This is because Microsoft Internet Explorer and Netscape use different methods when adding the Flash objects to a page. Internet Explorer uses the OBJECT tags, and Netscape uses the EMBED tags. So to add anything to the QueryString that calls your Flash movie, it will be necessary to add it to *both* places where the file is called. If you add the QueryString values only to the OBJECT tag, for example, then only people using Internet Explorer will be able to use that data.

 NOTE *The* QueryString *of a URL is a string of name values found on the end of a URL. An example URL could be* http://www.somesite.com/ flashMovie.swf?variable1=value1. *The QueryString of this URL is everything after the question mark (?), which is* variable1=value1. *The first value is the variable name (*variable1*), and the value after the equal sign (=) is the value of that variable (*value1*). Flash will read these values and store them in the* _root *of the movie that is called in the URL.*

To tell your Flash navigation that you are on the Services page, you would modify your Flash call as shown in Listing 4-7.

Listing 4-7. Flash Call with QueryString Data

```
<OBJECT classid="clsid:D27CDB6E-AE6D-11cf-96B8-444553540000"
    codebase=
    "http://download.macromedia.com/pub/shockwave/cabs/flash/swflash. ↵
cab#version=6,0,0,0"
  WIDTH="150"
  HEIGHT="300"
  id="dynamicNav- "
  ALIGN="">
  <PARAM NAME=movie VALUE="dynamicNav-.swf?activeOpt=3">
  <PARAM NAME=loop VALUE=false>
  <PARAM NAME=menu VALUE=false>
  <PARAM NAME=quality VALUE=high>
  <PARAM NAME=bgcolor VALUE=#CCCCCC>
  <EMBED
    src="dynamicNav-.swf?activeOpt=3"
    loop=false
    menu=false
```

```
        quality=high
        bgcolor=#CCCCCC
        WIDTH="150"
        HEIGHT="300"
        NAME="dynamicNav- "
        ALIGN=""
        TYPE="application/x-shockwave-flash"
        PLUGINSPAGE="http://www.macromedia.com/go/getflashplayer">
    </EMBED>
</OBJECT>
```

In this example, you simply passed the value of activeOpt to the Flash movie as 3. This tells Flash that menu option three (the number is set in the XML file) is the active menu option. When the Flash navigation parses the XML and it gets to option three in the loop, it will know (from this QueryString value) that option three is the active option and will show any suboptions that might be there for that option. Figure 4-3 shows what you should get when you run your movie.

Figure 4-3. Finished navigation

Summary

In this chapter, you finished building a dynamic Flash navigation using the basic techniques that will be required in all of your Flash applications in this book. After the previous chapter and this chapter, you should have a good base from which to create more complex and interesting applications. In the next chapter, you will build a database-driven online poll engine with Flash doing all of the front-end work of displaying both the poll and results.

Part Two

Creating Sample Solutions

CHAPTER 5

Building a Flashy
Online Poll Engine

FOR THE FIRST of the full-featured sample applications, you will build a Flash poll that is directly driven from a database. You often see polls on Web sites covering topics from your favorite sports team to whether Joe Schmo should become the country's next teen idol. These polls can be dynamically created using Flash and database technology.

The example solution in this chapter demonstrates standard poll features including tracking voters to minimize multiple votes, providing full administration to create and define polls, and of course providing a Flash interface for displaying the poll. In the first part of the chapter, you will build the database and associated Active Server Pages (ASP). In the second half of the chapter, you will implement the Flash interface.

Building the ASP and SQL Server Foundation

This chapter utilizes Microsoft SQL Server and ASP to build the data-driven foundation of the poll. You can utilize either Windows 2000 or Windows XP with Internet Information Services (IIS) 5.0 or 6.0. As mentioned in Chapter 2, "Setting Up the Web Server and Database Environment," you can use the .NET Framework and still run ASP.

This example was specifically built with Visual Interdev 6.0. We utilized Microsoft's SQL Server Enterprise Manager to create the database. If you are running the Microsoft SQL Server Desktop Engine (MSDE) version of SQL Server and using Visual Studio .NET, refer to the instructions for setting up a database in Chapter 2, "Setting Up the Web Server and Database Environment." If you are not running MSDE, then you need to have access to the Enterprise Manager tools.

NOTE *You can use Microsoft Access for this solution. The only required change is that you need to set up the connection string to the database to point to the .mdb file. See Chapter 2, "Setting Up the Web Server and Database Environment," for an example.*

Designing the Database

The poll engine database consists of four tables that define the poll data and that define who can manage the poll data via the ASP administration interface. Polls have questions and answers that will be stored in the database. The poll will track the Internet Protocol (IP) addresses of people who have voted. Figure 5-1 shows the four required tables and their relationships.

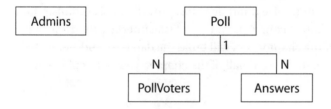

Figure 5-1. The poll engine's four tables

The Admins table defines usernames and passwords for accessing the administrative interface. The Poll and Answers tables define the questions and answers for each of the polls. Note there is one poll related to multiple (N) answers. The PollVoters table tracks the IP address for each vote in each poll. Thus, one poll has many (N) voters.

Let's now dissect each table starting with Poll. Table 5-1 defines the fields for the Poll table.

Table 5-1. Poll Table Definition

FIELD NAME	DATA TYPE	DESCRIPTION
intPollID	int/identity	The primary key of the table and autoincrements. Be sure and set the field to be an identity column.
strQuestion	nvarchar (500)	Stores the text of the question.

That is all you need to define the basic poll-level data. Listing 5-1 defines the SQL script for creating the table.

Listing 5-1. Poll Table SQL Create Script

```
if exists (select * from dbo.sysobjects where id = object_id(N'[dbo].[Poll]')
and OBJECTPROPERTY(id, N'IsUserTable') = 1)
drop table [dbo].[Poll]
GO

if not exists (select * from dbo.sysobjects where id = object_id(N'[dbo].[Poll]')
and OBJECTPROPERTY(id, N'IsUserTable') = 1)
 BEGIN
CREATE TABLE [dbo].[Poll] (
    [intPollID] [int] IDENTITY (1, 1) NOT NULL ,
    [strQuestion] [nvarchar] (500)
                  COLLATE SQL_Latin1_General_CP1_CI_AS NULL
) ON [PRIMARY]
END
GO
```

The Answers table defines the answers that will be displayed for each poll question and tracks the responses. Table 5-2 defines the Answers table.

Table 5-2. Answers Table Definition

FIELD NAME	DATA TYPE	DESCRIPTION
intAnswerID	int/identity	The primary key of the table and autoincrements. Be sure and set the field to be an identity column.
intPollID	int	Foreign key that relates each answer to a specific poll.
strAnswer	nvarchar (255)	Stores the answer text.
intResponseCount	int	A counter that is incremented when the answer is selected as a response.

The Poll and Answers table are related by the intPollID foreign key field. Each answer response has a record entry in the Answers table, and the intPollID field is set to the ID value of the associated poll. Listing 5-2 shows the SQL script to create the Answers table.

Listing 5-2. Answsers Table SQL Create Script

```
if exists (select * from dbo.sysobjects where id = object_id(N'[dbo].[Answers]')
and OBJECTPROPERTY(id, N'IsUserTable') = 1)
drop table [dbo].[Answers]
GO


if not exists (select * from dbo.sysobjects where id =
object_id(N'[dbo].[Answers]')
and OBJECTPROPERTY(id, N'IsUserTable') = 1)
 BEGIN
CREATE TABLE [dbo].[Answers] (
    [intAnswerID] [int] IDENTITY (1, 1) NOT NULL ,
    [intPollID] [int] NULL ,
    [strAnswer] [nvarchar] (255) COLLATE SQL_Latin1_General_CP1_CI_AS NULL ,
    [intResponseCount] [int] NULL
) ON [PRIMARY]
END
GO
```

The last poll-related table, PollVoters, stores the IP addresses of the poll respondents. This allows you to track respondents and limit a user's ability to respond multiple times. Table 5-3 defines the PollVoters table.

Table 5-3. PollVoters Table Definition

FIELD NAME	DATA TYPE	DESCRIPTION
intVoterID	int/identity	The primary key of the table and autoincrements. Be sure and set the field to be an identity column.
intPollID	int	Foreign key that relates each voter to a specific poll.
strVoterIP	nvarchar (50)	Stores the IP address of the poll voter.

The Poll and PollVoters table are related by the intPollID foreign key field. Each voter's IP address has a record entry in the PollVoters table, and the intPollID field is set to the ID value of the poll. Listing 5-3 shows the SQL script to create the PollVoters table.

Listing 5-3. PollVoters Table SQL Create Script

```
if exists (select * from dbo.sysobjects where id = object_id(N'[dbo].[PollVoters]')
and OBJECTPROPERTY(id, N'IsUserTable') = 1)
drop table [dbo].[PollVoters]
GO
```

```
if not exists (select * from dbo.sysobjects where id =
object_id(N'[dbo].[PollVoters]')
and OBJECTPROPERTY(id, N'IsUserTable') = 1)
 BEGIN
CREATE TABLE [dbo].[PollVoters] (
    [intVoterID] [int] IDENTITY (1, 1) NOT NULL ,
    [intPollID] [int] NULL ,
    [strVoterIP] [nvarchar] (50) COLLATE SQL_Latin1_General_CP1_CI_AS NULL
) ON [PRIMARY]
END
GO
```

NOTE *Some Internet Service Providers (ISPs) and corporate users appear to the general Internet as one IP address even though they have multiple active users. If those multiple users each hit a poll that tracks IP addresses, they collectively will only be able to vote one time. If this is a major issue, consider issuing cookies to track who has voted vs. IP filtering as implemented in this example. The downside is that the user can easily delete the cookie and vote again to try and skew the results.*

The last table, Admins, stores usernames and passwords for accessing the poll administration features. When an administrative user attempts to log in, their information will be authenticated against the Admins data. Table 5-4 defines the Admins table.

Table 5-4. Admins Table Definition

FIELD NAME	DATA TYPE	DESCRIPTION
intAdminID	int/identity	The primary key of the table and autoincrements. Be sure and set the field to be an identity column.
UserName	nvarchar (20)	The user name for the administrator.
Password	nvarchar (20)	The password for the administrator.

The example developed for the chapter assumes that any administrator can modify any poll. Thus, the Admins table does not relate to any of the poll-related tables. (You could define specific relationships between certain administrators and certain polls, and you could have a "super" administrator who could set up the relationships.) Listing 5-4 shows the SQL script to create the Admins table.

Listing 5-4. Admins Table SQL Create Script

```
if exists (select * from dbo.sysobjects where id = object_id(N'[dbo].[Admins]')
and OBJECTPROPERTY(id, N'IsUserTable') = 1)
drop table [dbo].[Admins]
GO

if not exists (select * from dbo.sysobjects where id = object_id(N'[dbo].[Admins]')
and OBJECTPROPERTY(id, N'IsUserTable') = 1)
 BEGIN
CREATE TABLE [dbo].[Admins] (
    [intAdminID] [int] IDENTITY (1, 1) NOT NULL ,
    [UserName] [nvarchar] (20) COLLATE SQL_Latin1_General_CP1_CI_AS NULL ,
    [Password] [nvarchar] (20) COLLATE SQL_Latin1_General_CP1_CI_AS NULL
) ON [PRIMARY]
END

GO
```

These four database tables are all that is required to implement the data portion of the poll engine. Next, you will build the ASP portion of the poll engine that supports creating, defining, and managing polls.

Developing the Poll Engine Administrator

The poll administrator provides a secure set of tools for managing polls. The administrators can add, update, and delete polls and their associated answers. We wrote all of the administration pages in ASP with VBScript, and they all interface with the database created in the previous section.

The basic functionality flow of the administrator is straightforward. Figure 5-2 shows a top-down flow of the administration functionality. The user logs in and has two options. They can either manage Admins or Polls. For Admins, they have add, update, and delete functionality. For Polls, they also have add, update, and delete functionality. Furthermore, for the update functionality, they can also add, update, and delete poll answers.

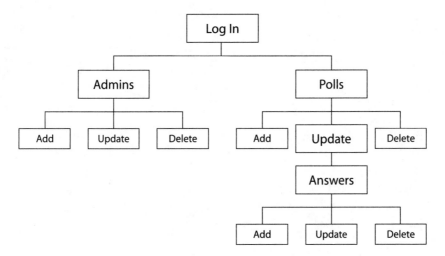

Figure 5-2. The poll administrator

Before development begins, you need to create the poll engine directory structure. On your development Web server, create a new folder called *PollEngine*. Create the Visual Studio project in that folder. Within that PollEngine folder, create an *Includes* folder. Also, create a folder called *Administration*. This is the folder where all of the administration pages will live.

The first step in building the functionality is to build the login and validation process for the administrators. This will encompass a login page where the administrator can enter a username and password. Create a new page in the Administration folder called *Login.asp*. Listing 5-5 shows the Hypertext Markup Language (HTML) for the page.

Listing 5-5. Login.asp

```
<%@ Language=VBScript %>
<%Option Explicit%>
<html>
<head>
<meta name="GENERATOR" Content="Microsoft Visual Studio.NET 7.0">
</head>
<body>
<title>Poll Engine Administration</title>

<!-- Build a form for the enter to log in and be validated -->
<form method="post" action="ValidateLogin.asp" ID="Form1">
```

```
<table cellpadding="4" cellspacing="4" align="center">
<tr>
    <td colspan="2" align="center">Poll Administration Log In<br> </td>
</tr>
<tr>
    <!--  Field to enter their username -->
    <td>Username:</td>
    <td><input type="text" size="29" value="" name="UserName"></td>
</tr>
<tr>
    <!--  Field to enter their password -->
    <td>Password:</td>
    <td><input type="password" size="25" value="" name="Password"></td>
</tr>
<tr>
    <td colspan="2" align="center">
        <input type="submit" value="Log In" name="Submit">
    </td>
</tr>

</table>

</form>

</body>
</html>
```

This page includes a simple HTML form for allowing the user to enter their username and password. The form posts to the ValidateLogin.asp page, which will validate the user to ensure they can have access. Before looking at the validation logic, let's first explore how you manage database connections, which will be required to validate the user.

The administration pages will be opening and utilizing databases frequently. Instead of copying the connection code across all of the .asp pages, you can place it in one file and include it on pages where you need to make a database connection. Create a file called *DBConnection.inc* in the Includes folder created earlier. Listing 5-6 shows the code for the page.

 NOTE *We used the .inc extension to differentiate these .asp pages from the main pages.*

Listing 5-6. DBConnection.inc

```
<%
dim sConn
dim objConn
dim objRS

' Define the connection string
sConn = "driver={SQL Server};server=SQLServer;database=PollEngine"

' Create the connection object
set ObjConn = Server.CreateObject("AdoDb.Connection")

' Open the connection
ObjConn.open sConn

%>
```

The first section of the code defines the connection string. Modify it as appropriate to connect to your database. See Chapter 2, "Setting Up the Web Server and Database Environment," for additional details on setting up a connection string. Next, the code creates a database Connection object and then opens the connection using the connection string.

Now that you have defined a method for connecting to the database, you can validate the user login. Create a new page called *ValidateLogin.asp* and save it in the Administration folder. Listing 5-7 shows the code for the page.

Listing 5-7. ValidateLogin.asp

```
<%@ Language=VBScript %>
<%Option Explicit%>
<!--#INCLUDE FILE="../includes/DBConnection.inc"-->
<%

dim sSQL
dim sUserName
dim sPassword

' Retrieve the posted username and password
sUserName = trim(request.form("UserName"))
sPassword = trim(request.form("Password"))
```

```
'  Double up any single quotes for a successful SQL query
sUserName = replace(sUserName, "'", "''")
sPassword = replace(sPassword, "'", "''")

' Build a query to see if there are any matching admin records
sSQL = "select username, password from Admins where username = '" & _
sUserName & "' and Password = '" & sPassword & "'"

'  Execute the query
Set objRS = objConn.Execute(sSQL)

'  Check the results
if objRS.eof then
    '  No matching admin - send the user to the login page
    response.Redirect("Login.asp")
    session("Validated") = False
else
    '  Maching admin - store the successful validation in a
    '  session variable and send the user to the main menu
    session("Validated") = True
    response.Redirect("menu.asp")
end if

%>
```

The first thing to note about the page is that it includes DBConnection.inc. Thus, when the page loads, it opens a database connection that can be utilized. After that, it retrieves the values entered in the username and password fields of the login page. Any single quotes used in the fields are doubled up (for example, *O'Conner* becomes *O''Conner*) so a successful SQL query can be executed.

Next, you created a SQL query to look up a user with a matching username and password. Note that case sensitivity (for example, *Smith* vs. *smith*) is not important when using the SQL where clause to find a match. The SQL statement then executes. If a result is returned, then there is a valid matching user, and the person is an administrator. In that case, a session variable, Validated, is set to indicate the person can have access. If not, then the person is not an administrator and is sent back to the login page.

To implement security throughout the site, you need to check the Validated session variable. To implement the checked code across multiple pages, you need to create an include file. Create a file in the Includes folder called *Validate.inc*. Listing 5-8 shows the code for the page.

NOTE *You need to manually add an administrator into the system using Enterprise Manager. This will allow an initial login. Another option is to not implement the validation check until you have entered a new administrator via the Web interface.*

Listing 5-8. Validate.inc

```
<%
'  Check for validation
if session("Validated") <> true then
    '  If not validated make the user log in
    response.Redirect("login.asp")
end if
%>
```

The page code does a check to see if the Validated variable is set to true. If not, then the user is redirected to the Login.asp page.

The menu page is the first page the user sees after logging into the administrator. It provides links to the two top-level administration options, as shown in Figure 5-2. Create a new file called *Menu.asp* and save it in the Administration folder. Listing 5-9 shows the code for the page.

Listing 5-9. Menu.asp

```
<html>
<head>
<meta name="GENERATOR" Content="Microsoft Visual Studio.NET 7.0">
</head>
<body>

<title>Poll Engine Administration Menu</title>

<!--  Build a menu for administrators and polls -->
<table border=1 align="center" cellpadding="2" cellspacing="2">
    <tr>
        <th>Poll Administrative Tools</th>
    </tr>
    <tr>
        <td align="center">
                <a href="MaintainAdmins.asp">Administrators</a>
            </td>
```

```
        </tr>
        <tr>
            <td align="center"><a href="MaintainPolls.asp">Polls</a></td>
        </tr>
    </table>


    </body>
    </html>
```

NOTE *We will not specifically review the functionality to add, update, and delete administrators. The .asp pages are similar to the code for managing poll questions and answers. The code for the user administration is included in the Downloads section of the Apress Web site (*http://www.apress.com*).*

The link to the poll administration goes to a page that displays the current polls in the database. It provides options to create a new poll, update existing polls, and delete an existing poll. Create a new page called *MaintainPolls.asp* and save it in the Administration directory. Listing 5-10 shows the code for the page.

Listing 5-10. MaintainPolls.asp

```
<%@ Language=VBScript %>
<%Option Explicit%>
<!--#INCLUDE FILE="../includes/validate.inc"-->
<!--#INCLUDE FILE="../includes/DBConnection.inc"-->
<html>
<head>
<meta name="GENERATOR" Content="Microsoft Visual Studio.NET 7.0">
</head>
<body>
<title>Maintain Polls</title>
<!--#INCLUDE FILE="../includes/navigation.inc"-->
<%

dim sSQL

' Retrieve the poll id and question
sSQL = "select intPollID, strQuestion from Poll order by intPollID"

'  Execute the query
```

```
Set objRS = objConn.Execute(sSQL)
%>


<!--  Build a table to display the option for managing the poll -->
<table border=1 cellspacing="3" cellpadding="4" align="center" ID="Table1">
<tr>
    <th colspan="4">Poll Maintenance</th>
</tr>
<tr>
    <!--  Add a new poll option -->
    <td colspan="4" align="center"><a href="AddNewPoll.asp">*Add New Poll*</a></td>
</tr>
<%
'  Loop through each poll
do until objRS.eof
%>

    <tr>
        <!--  Show the ID of the poll -->
        <td><%=objRS("intPollID")%></td>

        <!--  Show the question and link it to be updated -->
        <td>
            <a href="UpdatePoll.asp?idPoll=<%=objRS("intPollID")%>">↩
                <%=objRS("strQuestion")%></a>
        </td>

        <!--  Provide an option to manage the answers to the poll question -->
        <td>
            <a href="MaintainAnswers.asp?idPoll=<%=objRS("intPollID")%>">
                Manage Answers</a>
        </td>

        <!--- Provide an option to delete the poll -->
        <td>
            <a href="DeletePoll.asp?idPoll=<%=objRS("intPollID")%>">Delete</a>
        </td>
    </tr>

<%
'  Move to the next record in the record set
objRS.movenext
```

```
'   Loop back
Loop
%>

</table>

<%
objConn.close
%>

</body>
</html>
```

In the first part of the page, there are two include files for validating the user and opening the database connection. Following those includes is the navigation include. The code then uses the database connection to query the list of polls in the database. A SQL query retrieves all of the polls in the Poll table. The form and table headers display the list of polls. Note that the first entry in the table is a link to the AddNewPoll.asp page where a new poll can be set up.

For each poll record in the database, a table row is built that displays the poll ID, the poll question, a link to manage the poll answers, and a Delete option. Note that for each link, the ID of the poll is passed on the query string to the target page. That way, the target page can identify the appropriate poll with which to work. Once the table is complete, the database connection closes.

To add a new poll, you create a page with a form where the administrator will type in the poll question. To add this functionality, create a new page called *AddNewPoll.asp* and save it in the Administration directory. Listing 5-11 shows the code for the page.

Listing 5-11. AddNewPoll.asp

```
<%@ Language=VBScript %>
<%Option Explicit%>
<!--#INCLUDE FILE="../includes/validate.inc"-->

<html>
<head>
<meta name="GENERATOR" Content="Microsoft Visual Studio.NET 7.0">
</head>
<body>
<title>Add New Poll</title>
<!--#INCLUDE FILE="../includes/navigation.inc"-->
```

```
<%
'  Check for an error
if request.QueryString("Error") = 1 then
%>
<center>
<font color="red">You did not enter a valid question</font>
</center>
<%
end if
%>

<!--  Build a form to add the new poll -->
<form method="post" action="InsUpdPoll.asp" ID="Form1">

<!--  Indicate an insert of the new poll is to be performed -->
<input type="hidden" value="insert" name="Action" ID="Hidden1">

<!--  Build a table to display the data entry of the new poll -->
<table cellpadding="2" cellspacing="2" ID="Table1" align="center">
<tr>
    <td colspan="2" align="center">Add New Poll<br> </td>
</tr>
<tr>
    <td>Question:</td>
    <td>
        <textarea cols="50" name="Question"></textarea>
    </td>
</tr>
<tr>
    <td colspan="2" align="center">
        <input type="submit" value="Add" name="Submit">
    </td>
</tr>

</table>
</form>
</body>
</html>
```

The AddNewPoll.asp page builds a form that will allow the user to enter the poll question. Note the hidden field, Action, on the page. This field indicates to the target page, InsUpdPoll.asp, that the page should insert the results of the form post vs. trying to update an existing poll.

The page for updating a poll works similarly. Create a new .asp page called *UpdatePoll.asp* and save it in the Administration directory. Listing 5-12 shows the code for the page.

Listing 5-12. UpdatePoll.asp

```
<%@ Language=VBScript %>
<%Option Explicit%>
<!--#INCLUDE FILE="../includes/validate.inc"-->
<!--#INCLUDE FILE="../includes/DBConnection.inc"-->
<html>
<head>
<meta name="GENERATOR" Content="Microsoft Visual Studio.NET 7.0">
</head>
<body>
<title>Update Poll</title>
<!--#INCLUDE FILE="../includes/navigation.inc"-->

<%

dim sSQL

'  See if there is an error from a previous post
if request.QueryString("Error") = 1 then
%>
<center>
<font color="red">You did not enter a valid question.</font>
</center>
<%
end if

' Retrieve the question
sSQL = "select strQuestion from Poll where intPollID = " & _
       request.QueryString("idPoll")

'  Execute the SQL statement
Set objRS = objConn.Execute(sSQL)

%>

<!--  Build a form to display the poll question -->
<form method="post" action="InsUpdPoll.asp" ID="Form1">
```

```
<!-- Indicate to the post page that a poll is being updated -->
<input type="hidden" value="update" name="Action" ID="Hidden1">

<!-- Pass the ID of the poll that is being worked with -->
<input type="hidden" value="<%=request.querystring("idPoll")%>" name="PollID">

<table cellpadding="2" cellspacing="2" ID="Table1" align="center">
<tr>
    <td colspan="2" align="center">Update Poll<br> </td>
</tr>
<tr>
    <td>Question:</td>

    <!--  Show the question -->
    <td>
        <textarea cols="50" name="Question"><%=objRS("strQuestion")%></textarea>
    </td>

</tr>
<tr>
    <td colspan="2" align="center">
        <input type="submit" value="Update" name="Submit">
    </td>
</tr>

</table>

</form>

<%
objConn.close
%>

</body>
</html>
```

You set up the same form and table in this page as in the AddNewPoll.asp page. But, because the poll data is being updated, the poll question needs to be retrieved from the database. To do this, a SQL query is created to retrieve the data. The ID of the specific poll to update is retrieved from the query string for the page. The poll question data is then set as the value for the question textarea field.

Note at the beginning of the page there is a check to see if the query string ErrorCheck variable is set. The InsUpdPoll.asp page sets this when the user has not entered a valid question. This is pretty rudimentary error checking, but it provides a basic example and can be easily expanded. For example, you could set the value of the ErrorCheck variable to indicate the type of error and show the appropriate error message.

On this page, there are two hidden fields. The first is Action, which indicates that the InsUpdPoll.asp page should perform an update vs. an insert. The ID of the poll to update is stored in the second hidden field, PollID.

As noted, both the insert poll and update poll pages post to the same page. To build this page, create a new page called *InsUpdPoll.asp* and save it to the Administration folder. Listing 5-13 shows the code for the page.

Listing 5-13. InsUpdPoll.asp

```
<%@ Language=VBScript %>
<%Option Explicit%>
<!--#INCLUDE FILE="../includes/validate.inc"-->
<!--#INCLUDE FILE="../includes/DBConnection.inc"-->
<%

dim sSQL
dim sQuestion
dim sPassword

'  Retrieve the question from the posted form and ensure
'  any leading or trailing spaces are removed
sQuestion = trim(request.form("Question"))

'  Check to see if a value was entered at all
if len(sQuestion) = 0 then
    '  Check the value of the hidden action variable
    if request.Form("action") = "insert" then
        '  If an insert, send them to the add new poll page
        response.Redirect("AddNewPoll.asp?Error=1")
    else
        '  If an update, send them to the update poll page
        response.Redirect("UpdatePoll.asp?idPoll=" & _
                request.Form("PollID") & "&Error=1")
    end if
end if
```

```
'  Double up any single quotes for a successful insert into SQL
sQuestion = replace(sQuestion, "'", "''")

'  Check the value of the hidden action variable
if request.Form("action") = "insert" then
    ' Build a SQL insert for the new poll
    sSQL = "insert into Poll(strQuestion) values('" & sQuestion & "')"
else
    ' Build a SQL update for the existing poll
    sSQL = "update poll set strQuestion = '" & sQuestion & _
              "' where intPollID = " & request.Form("PollID")
end if

'  Execute the SQL statement
Set objRS = objConn.Execute(sSQL)

'  Send back to the poll maintance main pae
response.Redirect("MaintainPolls.asp")

objConn.close

%>
```

The purpose of this page is to make the appropriate data updates to the database. But, it is important to validate the data before the update is made. The page retrieves the question entry from the posted form and performs a check to see if question data was entered. If not, then the page sends the user back to the originating page. To figure out where to send the user, the page checks the Action variable to see if an insert or update is to be performed. If an insert, then it sends the user back to the AddNewPoll.asp page. If an update, then it sends the user back to the UpdatePoll.asp page.

Once the data has been validated, then the data can be applied to the database. Again, a check is done to see if an insert or updated should be performed. An appropriate SQL query is created. For the update, the ID of the poll to update is retrieved from the posted form. The SQL query is then executed, and the user is sent back to the poll maintenance page.

The poll deletion functionality is straightforward. Create a new .asp page called *DeletePoll.asp* and save it in the Administration folder. Listing 5-14 shows the code for the page.

Listing 5-14. DeletePoll.asp

```
<%@ Language=VBScript %>
<%Option Explicit%>
<!--#INCLUDE FILE="../includes/validate.inc"-->
<!--#INCLUDE FILE="../includes/DBConnection.inc"-->
<%

dim sSQL

' Build a SQL delete statement
sSQL = "delete from Poll where intPollID = " & request.QueryString("idPoll")

'  Execute the query
Set objRS = objConn.Execute(sSQL)

objConn.close

'  Send the user back to the main poll admin page
response.Redirect("MaintainPolls.asp")

%>
```

This code creates a SQL query string to the delete the poll. It retrieves the ID of the poll from the query string. It is important to also remove any associated answers with the question. A second query deletes all answers where the poll ID is set to the ID of the poll being deleted.

 CAUTION *This will also remove all of the response count information. If you want to simply archive the poll instead of actually deleting the rows, then consider adding an archive flag to the Poll and Answers tables that is set to true when the user chooses to delete the poll. Thus, the data is not deleted. You would also need to update the* select *queries to show polls and answers but not show archived data.*

The link to manage poll answers goes to the MaintainAnswers.asp page. Note that the ID of the poll is passed to the page so the right answers can display. The pages to add a new answer, update an answer, and delete an answer all work similarly to the poll maintenance pages reviewed in this chapter. The key difference is that when a new answer is inserted, the ID of the poll has to be tracked so the relationship can be set up properly. And, the ID of the poll is tracked on the update and delete pages to ensure that when the user is passed back to the answer maintenance page, and the proper answers are displayed.

All told, we created 21 pages for the administrative application. This chapter touched on a few key pages to explain how we developed the administrative functionality. Table 5-5 gives an overview of each page.

Table 5-5. Administrator ASP Page Reference

FIELD NAME	DESCRIPTION
Validate.inc	Include file that is used to determine if a user has been validated and can view the page
Navigation.inc	Include file that shows basic top-level navigation for the administrator
DBConnection.inc	Include file that sets and opens the connection to the database
AddAnswer.asp	Displays a form for the user to add a new answer to the selected poll
AddNewAdmin.asp	Displays a form for the user to add a new administrator
AddNewPoll.asp	Displays a form for the user to add a new poll
DeleteAdmin.asp	Deletes the specified administrator from the database
DeleteAnswer.asp	Deletes the specified answer from the database
DeletePoll.asp	Deletes the specified poll and associated answers from the database
InsUpdAdmin.asp	Either inserts a new administrator or updates an existing administrator
InsUpdAnswser.asp	Either inserts a new answer or updates an existing answer for the specified poll
InsUpdPoll.asp	Either inserts a new poll or updates an existing poll
Login.asp	Displays a login form to gain access to the administrator
MaintainAdmins.asp	Administrator management menu page
MaintainAnswers.asp	Answers management menu page for a specific poll
MaintainPolls.asp	Polls management menu page
Menu.asp	Initial menu displayed after login
UpdateAdmin.asp	Displays existing administrator data for update
UpdateAnswer.asp	Displays the existing answer for update
UpdatePoll.asp	Displays the existing poll question for update
ValidateLogin.asp	Validates the login data entered by the user

Utilizing the Poll Engine Administrator

At last, the administrator is ready to use. Be sure to download the rest of the files to run the administrator from the Downloads section of the Apress Web site (http://www.apress.com). The first step will be to log in to the site. Figure 5-3 shows the login page.

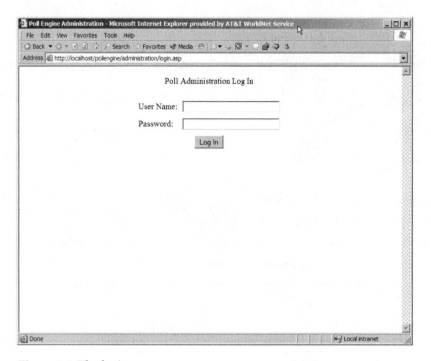

Figure 5-3. The login page

Enter the appropriate username and password to log in to the administrator. Once logged in, the menu page displays, as shown in Figure 5-4.

We will first go through the administration management functionality. Click the Administrators link. Figure 5-5 shows the administration menu. Note the navigation menu at the top of the page from Navigation.inc. The first option in the menu table is to add a new administrator to the database. Figure 5-5 shows several administrator entries. Click the Add New Admin link to add a new administrator.

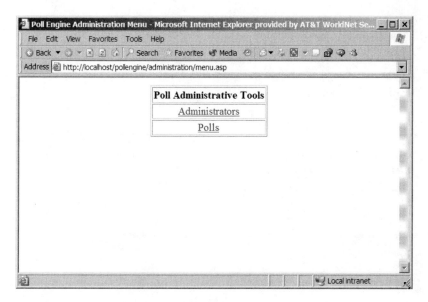

Figure 5-4. The administrator menu

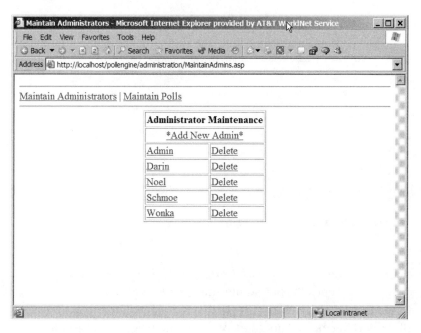

Figure 5-5. The administrator maintenance menu

The AddNewAdmin.asp page shows a form to enter the new administrator's username and password. Try entering a username with spaces in it (for example, *Waldo Wooskerowski*) and a password. You will be kicked back to the administrator page with an error message, as shown in Figure 5-6. The code does not allow usernames with spaces to be entered.

 NOTE *One potential upgrade to the functionality would be to retain the values entered into the data entry forms when there is an error.*

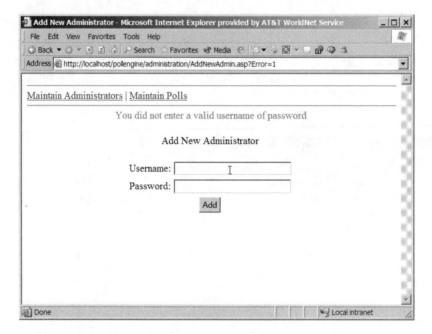

Figure 5-6. The new administrator entry error message

Correct the error and add a new user. Next, click the Maintain Polls link on the top navigation. This will open the poll administration menu, as shown in Figure 5-7.

You can add a new poll by clicking the Add New Poll link. You can update existing polls by clicking the poll question. And, you can delete existing polls by clicking the associated Delete link. To show the answers for a poll question, click the Manage Answers link. Figure 5-8 shows the answers for the sample question.

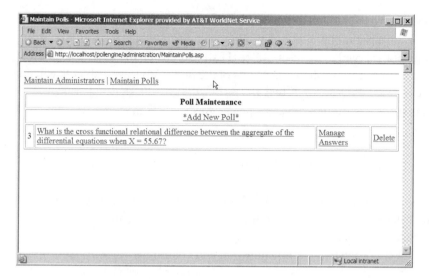

Figure 5-7. Poll maintenance

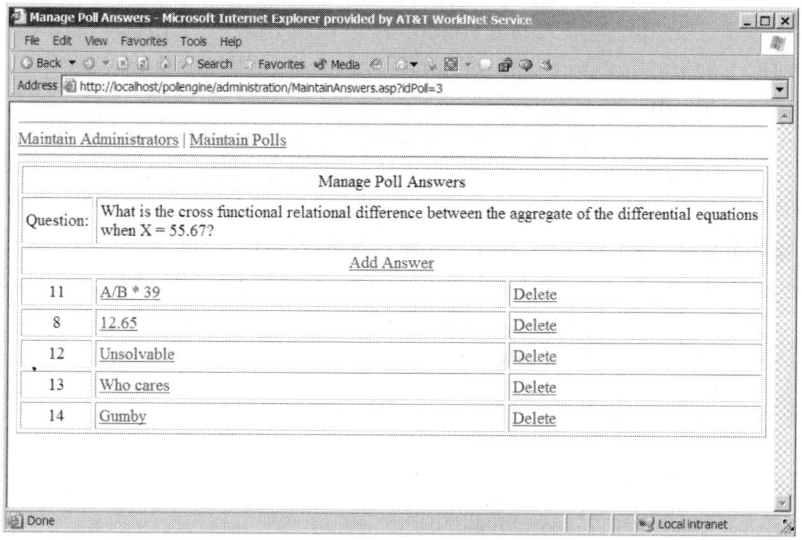

Figure 5-8. Answer maintenance

The answers display for the question with options to add additional answers, update existing answers, and delete existing answers.

That does it for building the database structure and administrative functionality of the poll engine. Next, you will build the user side of the poll engine and learn how you can display the poll in Flash and interface with the database.

Building the Flash User Interface

Most online polls served to the user utilize HTML, and when the user "votes," the entire page must refresh to show the results of the poll. With this Flash poll, you do *not* need to refresh the page to display the results because Flash can do the processing and display without requiring a page refresh.

Implementing the ASP Scripting

The first thing you need to do to get the Flash poll working is to write the ASP script that will call the database and retrieve the poll question, answers, and response counts (votes).

You know that each poll has one question and at least two answers (voting options). There is also the number of votes each answer has received. The questions reside in the Polls table, and the answers and vote counts reside in the Answers table. One other bit of information that you are interested in is whether the user has already voted. You want to keep users from voting multiple times and skewing the results. So, the table called PollVoters houses the IP addresses of those who have voted (see the first part of this chapter for more on the database setup for this poll application).

You also need an ASP script that will accept a vote and update the database with the new counts. After updating the counts, it should pass the counts back to Flash to display the results.

Knowing that you need all this information, you need to write an ASP script that will give the information to the Flash movie so you can display the information properly. So, in the root poll directory, create a new file and name it *PollRequest.asp*. Listing 5-15 shows the code for the page.

Listing 5-15. PollRequest.asp

```
<%@ Language=VBScript %>
<!--#INCLUDE FILE="includes/DBConnection.inc"-->

<%
'initializing variables for our script
Dim intPollID, strSQL, PollData, PollVote, strQuestion, intNumOpts, PollOptions
Dim strOptsOutput, strError, intCount, intNewCnt, intAnswerID, intTotalVotes
'defaulting the error string to nothing
strError = ""
'set total number of votes counted to zero to start
intTotalVotes = 0
```

```
if Request.QueryString("action") = "init" then
  'get poll data
  'if an ID is passed in the QueryString, use it
  If Request.QueryString("intPollID") > 0 Then
    intPollID = Request.QueryString("intPollID")
  'if no ID is passed set it to zero as a flag
  Else
    intPollID = 0
  End If


  'if ID > 0 then use the ID passed in
  If intPollID > 0 Then
    strSQL = "SELECT * FROM Poll WHERE intPollID=" & intPollID
  'if ID is 0 then retrieve first poll in the table
  Else
    strSQL = "SELECT TOP 1 * FROM Poll"
  End If


  PollData = objConn.Execute(strSQL)
  'grab question from retrieved poll
  strQuestion = trim(PollData("strQuestion"))
  'grab poll ID from retrieved poll
  intPollID = PollData("intPollID")


  'retrieve the answers/options that go with this poll
  set PollOptions = objConn.Execute("SELECT * FROM Answers WHERE intPollID=" & _
                           PollData("intPollID") & "ORDER BY intAnswerID")
  'if there are options found then
  if not PollOptions.EOF then
    'start counting from zero
    intCount = 0
    while not PollOptions.EOF
      ' add one to count
      intCount = intCount + 1
      'dim new incremented variable
      Execute("Dim strOpt" & intCount)
      'set new variable to answer
      Execute("strOpt" & intCount & "=" & chr(34)&PollOptions("strAnswer")&chr(34))
      'add new variable to the output string going to the Flash Applicataion
      Execute("strOptsOutput = " & chr(34)&strOptsOutput & "&opt" & intCount & _
                             "=" & eval("strOpt" & intCount)&chr(34))
```

```
                'Dim new incremented variable
                Execute("Dim intOptCnt" & intCount)
                'set new variable = number of votes for that answer
                Execute("intOptCnt" & intCount & "=" & chr(34) & _
                        PollOptions("intResponseCount") & chr(34))
                'add new variable to output string going to the Flash Application
                Execute("strOptsOutput = " & chr(34) & strOptsOutput & "&opt" & intCount & _
                                    "Cnt=" & eval("intOptCnt" & intCount) & chr(34))
                'add this answer's votes to the total number of votes
                intTotalVotes = intTotalVotes + PollOptions("intResponseCount")
                PollOptions.MoveNext
            wend
            'set the output number representing number of answers in this poll
            intNumOpts = intCount
        else
            'if there was an error
            strError = "Error pulling options."
        end if
        set PollOptions = nothing

        'check if this person's IP address is in the already voted table for this poll
        strSQL = "SELECT * FROM PollVoters WHERE strVoterIP='" & _
                    Request.ServerVariables("REMOTE_ADDR") & _
                    "' AND intPollID=" & PollData("intPollID")
        set PollVoted = objConn.Execute(strSQL)
        'set boolean flag whether they have voted already or not
        if PollVoted.EOF then
            voted = 0
        else
            voted = 1
        end if
        set PollVoted = nothing

        'output the strings to the Flash application
        Response.Write("dummy=1&question=" & strQuestion & "&numopts=" & intNumOpts & _
                            "&intTotalVotes=" & intTotalVotes & "&ID=" & intPollID)
        Response.Write(strOptsOutput)
        'if the error string has something in it, send it to the Flash application
        if len(strError) > 0 then
            Response.Write("&error=" & strError)
        end if
        Response.Write("&voted=" & voted & "&done=1")
```

```
      set PollData = nothing
elseif Request.QueryString("action") = "vote" then
   'add vote
   strSQL = "SELECT * FROM Answers WHERE intPollID=" & Request.QueryString("ID") & _
                                          " ORDER BY intAnswerID"

   set PollVote = objConn.Execute(strSQL)

   'if poll answers were found
   if not PollVote.EOF then
     'start counting at zero
     intCount = 0
     while not PollVote.EOF
       'add one to count
       intCount = intCount + 1
       'add new variable to hold the number of votes for this answer
       Execute("Dim intOptCnt" & intCount)
       'if this is the answer voted for
       if intCount = cint(Request.QueryString("select")) then
         'set the number of votes = the vote count plus one
         Execute("intOptCnt" & intCount & "=" & chr(34) & _
                 PollVote("intResponseCount") + 1 & chr(34))
         intNewCnt = PollVote("intResponseCount") + 1
         intAnswerID = PollVote("intAnswerID")
       else
         'set the number of votes = the vote count
         Execute("intOptCnt" & intCount & "=" & chr(34) & _
                    PollVote("intResponseCount") & chr(34))
       end if
       'add counts to output string going to Flash application
       Execute("strOptsOutput = " & chr(34) & strOptsOutput & "&opt" & intCount & _
                             "Cnt=" & eval("intOptCnt" & intCount) & chr(34))
       'add votes to vote total
       intTotalVotes = intTotalVotes + PollVote("intResponseCount")
       PollVote.MoveNext
     wend
     intTotalVotes = intTotalVotes + 1

     'update new vote total for voted for answer
     strSQL = "UPDATE Answers set intResponseCount=" & intNewCnt & _
          " where intPollID = " & cint(Request.QueryString("ID")) & _
                                " AND intAnswerID=" & intAnswerID
     objConn.Execute(strSQL)
```

```
   'add this voter to the already voted list
   strSQL = "INSERT INTO PollVoters (intPollID, strVoterIP) VALUES (" & _
                               Request.QueryString("ID") & ", '" & _
                          Request.ServerVariables("REMOTE_HOST") & "')"
  objConn.Execute(strSQL)
 else
   'if there was an error
   strError="There was an error tabulating votes"
 end if
 set PollVote = nothing

 'output the string to the Flash application
 Response.Write("dummy=1" & strOptsOutput & "&intTotalVotes=" & intTotalVotes & _
                                "&ID=" & Request.QueryString("ID"))
 'if there was an error, output that to the Flash
 if len(strError) > 0 then
   Response.Write("&error=" & strError)
 end if
 Response.Write("&done=1")
end if
%>
```

The first step is to check the QueryString for a poll ID value. If there is not one, you pull the first poll in the table. If there is an ID specified, you query the table for the poll with that ID.

NOTE *This is not the best way to retrieve a default poll when no ID is specified. You could add a flag to the Polls table that tells whether the poll is active. If no poll ID is specified, then you retrieve the first active poll. In the previous code, this will pull the first poll in the table, most likely the first poll you ever entered. This is really meant to be called using an ID. Pulling the first poll in the table in the absence of an ID is just to keep the application from crashing because of no data.*

You then query the database for the answers that go with that poll. Because the poll administration you built earlier in this chapter allows for any number of options, you do a little dynamic variable creation using the Execute and Eval methods in ASP.

The Eval function evaluates an expression and returns the result. An expression is a regular expression in string format. For example:

```
Dim strExp, intResult
strExp = "1 + 1"
intResult = Eval(strExp)
```

The previous code would set intResult = 2.

The Execute function is similar to the Eval function except that it executes a statement rather than evaluating it:

```
Dim strVar
Execute("strVar=1")
```

This code would simply set strVar to one. Using Eval and Execute allows you to programmatically set dynamic variable names to dynamic values. This is necessary because you do not always know how many answers there are going to be with each poll.

You then check the PollVoters table to see if you find the current user's IP address for this poll.

NOTE *Some ISPs and corporate users appear to the general Internet as one IP address even though they have multiple active users. If those multiple users each hit a poll that tracks IP addresses, they collectively will only be able to vote one time. If this is a major issue, consider issuing cookies to track who has voted vs. IP filtering as implemented in this example. The downside is that the user can easily delete the cookie and vote again to try and skew the results.*

You do all of that to send the data back to the Flash poll. Notice that there are no HTML header tags in this page. This is *not* meant to be a page with standard HTML output. You do not want to have <HEAD>, <TITLE>, or <BODY> tags at all. If you were to put those or any other HTML tags in the page, Flash would not accept the output you are going to send. Instead, it would cause an error because of those tags. The output must be exactly what it would look like if you were creating a text file with the variables in it for Flash to call and load (see Chapter 4, "Adding ActionScript to Your Flash Application"). So, instead of headers or tags, you will just use the ASP method of Response.Write to send the variables to Flash in plain-text format.

When this page is called with `PollRequest.asp?action=init[&id=`*n*`]`, the code will send a string to Flash that includes the variables in Listing 5-16.

NOTE *We always send* dummy=1 *as the first variable in our scripts. We do this because, in the past, Flash would occasionally "eat" the first variable sent in a string of variables. We found that sending a "dummy" variable first solves that problem. We have never stopped this practice with newer versions of Flash to see if the problem still exists.*

Listing 5-16. Poll Initialization Variables

```
dummy=1
id
question
opt1
opt2
etc. for as many options as there are in that particular poll
opt1Cnt
opt2Cnt
etc. for as many options as there are in that particular poll
numopts
intTotalVotes
voted (equals either a 1 if true or 0 if false)
done=1
```

Listing 5-17 shows some sample output with real poll data. There is a question along with four options.

NOTE *If the user's IP address was found in the PollVoters table, the script would return* voted=1 *to Flash, letting the application know that this person (or someone using that IP address) has already voted in this poll. The Flash would then take necessary steps to skip the option to vote and go directly to displaying the current results.*

Listing 5-17. Sample Initialization Output

```
dummy=1&ID=1000&question=Does this thingwork?&numopts=↵
4&opt1=yes&opt1Cnt=67&opt2=no&opt2Cnt=0&opt3=what?&opt3Cnt=0&opt4=Can't tell↵
yet&opt4Cnt=20&voted=0&done=1
```

NOTE *In our scripts,* done=1 *is always the last variable in the string. We use this to tell the Flash application when all the variables have been received so the application can move on to the processing/parsing of those variables. In the Flash scripting, when you load the data from this ASP script, the Flash movie will go into a loop looking for the* done=1 *value to be set. When the entire set of values is passed back to the Flash movie,* done=1 *is the last variable sent; when the Flash movie receives that value, it knows all the data has been received and moves out of the waiting loop.*

In this same .asp page, you include the script to receive a vote from the Flash poll, increment the counts in the database, and send the current results back to the Flash. When this page is called with `PollRequest.asp?action=vote&id=`_n_`&select=`_n_, the code will send a string to Flash that includes the variables in Listing 5-18.

Listing 5-18. Poll Vote Variables

```
dummy=1
ID
opt1Cnt
opt2Cnt
etc. for as many options as there are for that poll
intTotalVotes
done=1
```

Listing 5-19 shows some sample output using the previous example.

Listing 5-19. Poll Vote Sample Output

```
dummy=1&ID=1000&opt1Cnt=67&opt2Cnt=0&opt3Cnt=0&opt4Cnt=20&done=1
```

That is all you need the ASP to do. With the database set up and the code written to pass this data to the Flash interface, you will now build the Flash interface to finish out the poll application.

Planning the Poll Application

Open Flash MX and get a new movie started. Figure 5-9 shows a basic flow of what you want the poll to do. You will call your ASP script, which will pull the poll data from the database and send it back to Flash as a string of variables. You will parse through those variables, display the poll questions, duplicate enough poll options to hold the number of options in that particular poll, set the text for each option, and display that text. If the user has not voted yet, you will make the option voting buttons available and be ready to accept a vote from that user. If the user has already voted, you will go straight to the display of the current poll results without making the voting buttons available.

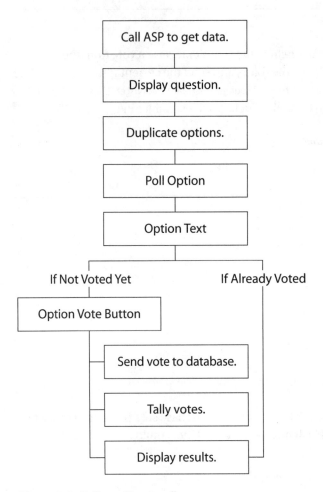

Figure 5-9. Poll application flow

The Flash poll will use MovieClips to hold each poll option, and you will create one option clip and duplicate it to match the number of options in the poll. You will place each clip on the poll and display each option for voting and displaying results.

To make the poll do these things, you need to create a few objects and variables within the movie. Let's get started.

Setting the Movie Properties

As you did with the dynamic navigation bar, you will first set the basic movie properties. In the Properties Panel, click the movie size and set the movie width to *168* pixels and the movie height to *300* pixels. Next, set the background color to *FFFFCC*, which is a pale yellow. Set the frames per second (fps) to *20*. Now click OK.

NOTE *You can choose whatever colors you would like while creating this Flash application. Feel free to choose colors that will fit into your own site or colors that you prefer.*

From the Toolbox, choose the Rectangle tool. You are going to give your poll an outline. In the Properties Panel, set the Stroke Color to black and the Fill Color to none. Draw a rectangle anywhere within the poll Stage. Again, you will use the Properties Panel to position and size the outline to fit the movie perfectly. Choose the Arrow tool and double-click any side of the outline. Double-clicking should select the entire outline. In the Properties Panel, enter *168* for the width, enter *300* for the height, enter *0* for X, enter *0* for Y, and enter *2* for the stroke height (see Figure 5-10). Double-click the layer name and change it to *outline*.

TIP *To set the Fill Color or Stroke Color to none, simply choose the color chip that is white with a red diagonal line through it.*

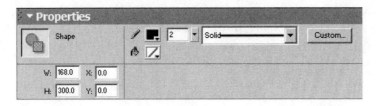

Figure 5-10. Poll outline properties

Building the Poll

You are going to add new frames to your Timeline because there is only one right now. On the top of the Timeline there are numbers representing the frame number on which you are located. That pinkish-red rectangle is the playhead marker, which shows the frame you are currently viewing. Click Frame 1 (most likely the playhead is already there, but click it anyway to make sure that not just one layer is selected but the entire frame). Now press F5 (or choose Insert ➤ Frame) two times. This should make the movie three frames long.

Now add a layer above the outline layer. Double-click the new layer's name and change it to *control*. This is going to be a layer with few objects or shapes; instead, it will have mostly ActionScript commands to control the movie (thus the name). Click in Frame 2 of the control layer and press F6 (or select Insert ➤ Keyframe). With that frame still selected, open the Actions Panel and type *stop()*; or choose the Stop command from the Actions Toolbox if you are using Normal mode. This simply tells the Flash movie to stop at Frame 2 and wait for further instructions.

TIP *We recommend using Expert mode in your Actions Panel while working through this chapter so you can follow along with our instructions.*

Select the keyframe in Frame 1 of the control layer. In the Actions Panel, type the following:

```
_root.done = 0;
_root.done2 = 0;
```

You use the variable done as a Boolean (True or False) flag so your Flash application will know when certain parts of the code or loading of variables is done. In this case, the done variable is telling Flash whether the data has been successfully loaded from the ASP yet, and the done2 variable is telling Flash when the results are tallied after a vote has been initiated. Both are set to False (or zero) initially because neither has been completed thus far.

Next, you need to create the textbox that will display the question. Select the outline layer by clicking its name and then use the Insert Layer button to add a new layer above the outline layer and below the control layer. Name this layer *question*. Add a keyframe to Frame 2 of the question layer. With that frame selected, choose the Text tool from the Toolbox, and in the Properties Panel set it to Dynamic Text. Set the font to Verdana, the size to 9, the color to black, and the alignment to left justified. Also, choose Multiline, toggle the selectable button off, and click the Character button (see Figure 5-11). Choose Include All Characters and then click Done.

 NOTE *Because you have set the question textbox to include all characters for the Verdana font, you will not have to set this option for any other textbox that uses the Verdana font in this Flash movie. It will already be embedded in the movie, and all other textboxes using the font will be able to access the embedded font that this textbox uses.*

Figure 5-11. Question textbox properties

Draw a textbox on the Stage, making sure you only drag straight to the right and not down or up. This will make sure the textbox is only one-line tall. With your new textbox selected, go to the Properties Panel, enter *50* for X, and enter *6* for Y. This should place the textbox toward the top of the poll. Now double-click the textbox. This should select it and place a blinking cursor in the textbox. Hit the Enter key three times. This will make the textbox four lines high. Figure 5-12 shows what it should look like so far. If you need to adjust the width of the textbox to get it aligned with the right edge of the poll, just double-click the textbox and use the little white square at the bottom-right corner as a handle for resizing the textbox. Click and drag that corner to the right or left. Be sure not to move it up or down, or it will resize the height of the textbox. If that happens by accident, simply double-click in the box and hit Enter until it is four lines high again.

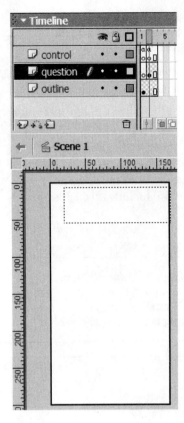

Figure 5-12. Poll movie with question textbox

With the Arrow tool, select the textbox again. In the Properties Panel, enter *question* for its instance name and enter *strQuestion* for its variable name (refer to Chapter 3, "Creating Your First Flash Application," for where and how you set those settings).

Next, let's add a little label-like thing to the question to make it clear that it is a poll question. First, make sure that you are still in Frame 2 of the question layer and that the question textbox is *not* selected. Second, using the Text tool again, use the Properties Panel and select Static Text. Next, set the font to Verdana and the size to 14. Toggle bold and italic on, and make it left justified. Click anywhere on the Stage. Type *Q:* and then select the Arrow tool from the Toolbox. Select the newly created text, and in the Properties Panel enter *-1.1* for X and enter *1.9* for Y. This will place the label next to the question textbox.

To keep from accidentally selecting or changing something in the finished layers, you can lock them. There are two small black dots next to each of the layer's names. The left is the visibility toggle, hiding or showing that layer within the authoring environment, and the other is the layer lock. Next to the outline and question layers, click the dots, and a padlock icon will appear. This will keep you from being able to select anything within those layers so you cannot accidentally mess them up. Go ahead try to select the textboxes or outlines. If they are correctly locked, you should not be able to select anything on the Stage at this point.

Set the playhead to Frame 2 by clicking above Frame 2 on the Timeline numbers. Press F5 (or select Insert ➤ Frame) three times. Click Frame 3 of the control layer and press F7 (or select Insert ➤ Blank Keyframe). In the Properties Panel, enter *vote* for the Frame Label option. Click Frame 4 of the control layer and press F7 (or select Insert ➤ Blank Keyframe). In the Properties Panel, enter *results* for the Frame Label option. Click Frame 5 of the control layer and press F7 (or select Insert ➤ Blank Keyframe). In the Properties Panel, enter *error* for the Frame Label option. Click Frame 5 of the control layer and drag down to the question layer, selecting Frame 5 in both layers. Press F7 (or select Insert ➤ Blank Keyframe). Set the playhead to Frame 2 by clicking above Frame 2 on the Timeline numbers. Press F5 (or select Insert ➤ Frame). Click Frame 3 of the control layer and press F7 (or select Insert ➤ Blank Keyframe). The movie now has all the frames and labels needed for processing the poll data in the main Timeline.

NOTE *You use frame labels to specify a certain area in the Timeline for a certain process. For example, if there was an error in the ASP script while trying to retrieve the poll data, you would send the Flash application to the error frame label to display the error. Frame labels are used in ActionScript in conjunction with the* goto *command.*

If the question layer is still locked (a padlock will be showing next to the layer name), click the padlock to unlock it. Click Frame 2 of the question layer. Using the Arrow tool, click anywhere on the Stage where there is not an object or shape. This is to deselect anything on that layer because clicking the frame will select everything on that layer within the frame clicked. Choose the Text tool from the Toolbox, and in the Properties Panel set it to Dynamic Text. Then, set the font to Verdana, the size to 8, and the color to black. Make it right justified, choose Single Line, toggle selectable to off, and, if bold and italic are still toggled on, toggle them off. Click just inside the left edge of the poll Stage and drag straight to the right until just inside the right edge of the Stage and release. In the Properties Panel, enter *2* for X and enter *284* for Y. That should place the textbox at the bottom of the poll. If your textbox overlaps any edge, adjust it so that it is just within the left, right, and bottom edges of the poll Stage. Using the Arrow tool, select the textbox, and in the Properties Panel set the instance name to *votes* and the variable name to *totalVotes*. This will display the total number of voters that the results reflect.

Now it is time to create the options. Create a new layer above the question layer and below the control layer (select the question layer and click the New Layer button). Rename the layer to *option*. Select Frame 2 of the option layer and create a new keyframe (press F6 or select Insert ➤ Keyframe). With the new keyframe selected (Frame 2 of the option layer), select the Text tool from the Toolbox, and in the Properties Panel set it to Dynamic Text. Then set the font to Verdana, set the size to 9, make it left justified, and set it to Multiline. Click the left edge of the question textbox and drag straight to the right edge of the question textbox and release. This should make a one-line textbox about the same width as the question textbox. Double-click the new textbox and press Enter once to make it two lines high. Choose the Arrow tool from the Toolbox and make sure the new textbox is selected. Then, go to the Properties Panel, enter *option* for the instance name, and enter *strOption* for the variable name.

That textbox will display the text for voting options, so you just need a button that will allow someone to vote for that option. Choose the Oval tool from the Toolbox. In the Properties Panel for the Oval tool, set the Fill Color to white and the Stroke Color to black and then draw a circle on the Stage (in Frame 2 of the option layer). Size is not important because you will resize it using the Properties Panel in a minute. Using the Arrow tool, double-click the center of this shape to select both the fill and the outline. In the Properties Panel, enter *10* for the width and enter *10* for the height. Then, set the stroke height to 1. With the shape still selected, press F8 (or select Insert ➤ Convert to Symbol). For the name, enter *voteButton*. Enter *button* for the behavior and click OK.

You are going to place these two objects in a new position on the Stage. Using the Arrow tool, select the voteButton. In the Properties Panel, enter *2* for X and enter *-40* for Y. Using the Arrow tool, select the option textbox. In the Properties Panel, enter *16* for X and enter *-44* for Y. This should place the textbox and button above the actual poll Stage by a little bit. This is just like the dynamic navigation in that this option will be a MovieClip that is never seen but only used as the original to duplicate new clips onto the Stage.

 NOTE *Remember that throughout this book we refer to the use of the Control key in "shortcut" key combinations. Obviously, this is a key found on PCs. In most cases, the same shortcut keys work on Macs by substituting the Command key for the Control key.*

Using the Arrow tool, click and drag a box around both the button and textbox to select both. You can also select multiple items by holding the Control key and clicking on each item to add to the selection. Once both items are selected, press

F8 (or select Insert ➤ Convert to Symbol) and enter *optionClip* for the name. For the behavior, choose the Movie Clip option. With the new MovieClip selected, go to the Properties Panel and enter *option* for the instance name. This is going to be the master MovieClip from which all other option clips will be duplicated.

Double-click the optionClip to open it in symbol-editing mode (or select it and press Control+E). The first thing you want to do is add a layer above the only layer in this clip so far. So, click the Insert Layer button. Rename the new layer to *vote button*. Rename the other layer to *option text*. Using the Arrow tool, select the round voting button and press Control+X (or select Edit ➤ Cut). Click in Frame 1 of the vote button layer and press Control+Shift+V (or select Edit ➤ Paste in Place). This should successfully move your voting button to a new layer in the same position that it was before.

Place the playhead in Frame 1 by clicking the one on the top of the Timeline (even if the playhead, the pinkish rectangle, is already there, click it anyway because it deselects any active layers or objects that would cause the Insert Frames command to malfunction). Now press F5 (or select Insert ➤ Frame). Next, click Frame 2 of the vote button layer and press F7 (or select Insert ➤ Blank Keyframe). What that does is create a blank keyframe in Frame 2 of the vote button layer. Because you are using this same clip to display both the voting option with a vote button and the results after the voting option is chosen, you need to only show the vote button before any voting has been done by the current user. Because you have now removed the vote button from Frame 2, after the voting has been activated by the current user, you can send the option clip to Frame 2, and the vote button will no longer be visible.

In addition to this, you are going to add a progress graphic to this clip to show the percentage of votes the option has received. When all the options in a poll have a percent bar graphically representing their vote percentages, it will be a mini bar chart.

You now want to add a layer below the option text layer. Click the Insert Layer button, click and drag the new layer to the bottom of the layers list, and release it. It should pop down to the bottom of the list. Rename the layer to *percent bar*. Click in Frame 2 of the percent bar layer and press F6 (or select Insert ➤ Keyframe). You are only going to place the percent bar in Frame 2 so it will only be visible when the vote button is not.

Select the Rectangle tool from the Toolbox, and in the Properties Panel set the Fill Color to 0000FF and the Stroke Color to black. The stroke height should be 1. Draw a rectangle anywhere on the Stage in Frame 2 of the percent bar layer. Select the Arrow tool and double-click the rectangle to select the entire shape including outlines. In the Properties Panel, set W to 156.8, H to 4.2, X to -78.4, and Y to 4.7. This should resize the shape and place it right under the option textbox.

Make sure the entire shape is selected including outlines and press F8 (or select Insert ➤ Convert to Symbol). For the name, enter *percentBar* and set the behavior to Movie Clip. Double-click the percent bar to edit it.

You now want to create two new layers below the current layer in this clip. Click the Insert Layer button twice and drag both new clips to the bottom of the layers list. Now click the blue fill of the shape and press Control+X (or select Edit ➤ Cut). Click Frame 1 of the bottom layer and press Control+Shift+V (or select Edit ➤ Paste in Place). With the fill still selected, use the Properties Panel to change the Fill Color to white. Now click in Frame 1 of the middle layer and press Control+Shift+V (or select Edit ➤ Paste in Place). White will be the background color for when the percent bar is less than 100 percent, and blue will be the actual percent bar.

Using the horizontal scrollbar at the bottom of the Timeline, scroll the Timeline to where you can see Frame 100. Click in Frame 100 of the top layer and drag straight down through all three layers. This should select Frame 100 in all three layers. Press F5 (or select Insert ➤ Frame). The MovieClip is now 100 frames long. You have done this because you are going to create a tweened animation of the percent bar going from 0 percent (at Frame 1) to 100 percent (at Frame 100). When you want to display the percent bar at 26 percent, you will simply tell the percent bar MovieClip to go to Frame 26 and stop.

Click on Frame 100 of the middle layer (the blue shape layer). Press F6 (or select Insert ➤ Keyframe). Scroll your Timeline back to Frame 1. Lock the top and bottom layers by clicking the lock toggles for each of them. Click Frame 1 of the middle layer (the blue shape layer). Using the Arrow tool, click the blue shape. Do this whether it looks selected or not. Sometimes the shape will be highlighted as if it is selected, but the focus is actually on the frame instead. Using the Properties Panel, set the width to 1. The shape should be a tiny sliver of blue all the way to the left.

Click on Frame 1 of the middle layer again and look at the Properties Panel. Set Tween to Shape using the drop-down selector. The middle layer should be green through all 100 frames. This green represents a shape tween. Set the playhead on Frame 1 and press the Enter key (or select Control ➤ Play). The blue percent bar will slowly grow from the sliver to full width.

You have one more element to add to this percent bar: a textbox that displays the numeric representation of the percent. For example, if the option has 26 percent of the vote, you want to display *26%* somewhere on the option as well as have the bar display 26 percent of the way across. Click the Insert Layer button and drag the new layer to the top of the layers. Lock all other layers except this new layer. Choose the Text tool from the Toolbox, and in the Properties Panel set Dynamic Text. Then set the font to Verdana, the size to 8, the color to black, and the alignment to left justified. Then choose Single Line, and toggle off selectable. Now just click and release anywhere on the Stage. Choose the Arrow tool and double-click the new textbox to add some text to it. Type *100%* in the box. Using the white square (handle) in the lower-right corner of the textbox, drag it until you can get the box to be just wide enough to fit the *100%* text in it and still have it be a single-line text box. You might have to play with it a little to get the feel for resizing the box this way. When you get the size right, delete the text in the textbox (it was only for sizing the text box) and choose the Arrow tool again. Select the textbox (click), and in the Properties Panel, enter *-84.3* for X, enter *-14.3* for Y, enter *percent* for Instance Name, and enter *strPercent* for Var. That should move the textbox just above the percent bar.

There is only one more thing to do to finish the internal workings of the percent bar clip. Click Frame 1 of the top layer. In the Actions Panel, add stop(); to the frame. This will stop the percent bar at the beginning frame until you tell it to continue. At this point, the movie should look like Figure 5-13.

Figure 5-13. Percent bar clip

Move back to the option clip by clicking the optionClip name below the layers list. That is essentially a link to the parent MovieClip. If somehow you have gotten lost within the movie, click on the Scene 1 name below the layers list and then double-click the option clip to edit it again.

Using the Arrow key, select the percent bar clip (single click), and in the Properties Panel enter *percentBar* for the instance name.

With the playhead in Frame 1, use the Arrow tool to select the circular vote button (single click). In the Actions Panel, enter the code in Listing 5-20.

Listing 5-20. Vote Button Code

```
on (release) {
    _root.vote = optNum;
    _root.gotoAndStop("vote");
}
```

This tells the button to set what option was voted for and then to go to the vote processing section of the application.

Click Frame 1 of the percent bar layer. This should be a blank keyframe. In the Actions Panel, enter stop(); for the frame. This will stop the option on the vote button display until you tell it to continue. Move back to the main Timeline (press Control+E or select Edit ➤ Edit Document).

Select Frame 6 of the control layer. Using the Text tool, go to the Properties Panel, choose the Static Text option, set the font to Verdana, set the size to 10, set the color to black, and select center justified. Click the Stage and type *ERROR:*. Using the Arrow tool, click the Stage to deselect anything selected. Activate the Text tool again, and in the Properties Panel select Dynamic Text. Then, set the font to Verdana, the size to 12, and the color to black. Select left justified, choose Multi-line, and toggle off selectable. Click about 10 or so pixels from the left edge of the Stage and drag down and to the left until the textbox is about 10 pixels from the right edge and is pretty much square (in other words, so the height is about the same at the width). In the Properties Panel, enter *optionText* for Instance Name and enter *strError* for Var. See Figure 5-14 for the placement of the two textboxes in the error frame.

Select Frame 2 of the control layer. You are going to create a MovieClip here that is used to load the poll data. Using the Text tool, set the properties to Static Text, the font to Verdana, the size to 12, the color to black, and the alignment to center justified. Click in the middle of the poll Stage and type *INITIALIZING POLL . . .*

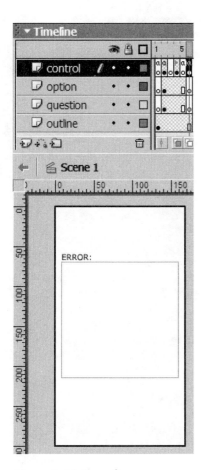

Figure 5-14. Error frame

Next, choose the Arrow tool and select the new textbox with a single click. Press F8 (or select Insert ➤ Convert to Symbol), name it *initClip,* and set its behavior to the Movie Clip option. Using the Align Panel, toggle Align to Stage on and center the clip vertically and horizontally (refer to Chapter 3, "Creating Your First Flash Application," for more details on how to use the Align Panel to do this).

Now you need to start writing your ActionScript to get this poll functioning. With the initClip selected, open the Actions Panel. You will utilize clip events to load and parse your data from the ASP script you have written. Attach the code in Listing 5-21 to the initClip.

Listing 5-21. Poll Initialization Script

```
onClipEvent(load) {
  //if a poll ID was passed to the Flash originally
  if (_root.intPollID > 0) {
    //call script to load poll data
    loadVariables("PollRequest.asp?action=init&id=" + _root.intPollID,_root);
  } else {
    loadVariables("PollRequest.asp?action=init",_root);
  }
  //start timer for how long data is taking to load
  startTime = getTimer();
}

onClipEvent (enterFrame) {
  //if timer is 10 seconds or greater
  if ((getTimer() - startTime)/1000 > 10) {
    //time out the poll and go to error frame
    _root.strError = "The poll timed out connecting to the server."
    _root.gotoAndStop("error");
  }

  //if data retrieval is complete
  if (_root.done == "1") {
    //if error string was passed in
    if(length(_root.error) > 1) {
      //set error to string and go to error frame
      _root.strError = _root.error;
      _root.gotoAndStop("error");
    }

    //display question
    _root.strQuestion = _root.question
    //parse through answers
    for (i=1;i<=_root.numopts;i++) {
      //duplicate answer clip for this answer
      duplicateMovieClip(_root.option,"option" + i,i+10);
      //set the option number of this answer
      set("_root.option" + i + ".optNum",i);
      //set answer text
      set("_root.option" + i + ".strOption",eval(["_root.opt" + i]));
      //move answer clip to where it needs to be displayed
      setProperty("_root.option" + i, _y ,int(69+((i-1)*30)));
      //make the option clip and initClip invisible
      _root.option._visible = false;
```

```
    _root.initClip._visible = false;
    //reset the done var to zero for future use
    _root.done = 0
  }
  //if they have not already voted, move to display of options
  if (_root.voted != "1") {
    _root.nextFrame();
  //if they have already voted, move to display of results
  } else {
    _root.gotoAndStop("vote");
  }
 }
}
```

The `load` clip event calls the `PollRequest.asp?action-init` script and waits for a response. If a response is not received within 10 seconds, an error is generated and the application is sent to the error frame label.

The `enterFrame` clip event continuously checks for `done=1`. When it evaluates to true, if there was no error in the script, the option clips are duplicated and spaced evenly on the Stage, and all the variables are set.

You are almost finished. Using the Arrow tool, select the option clip (single click). You need to add the code in Listing 5-22 to the clip.

Listing 5-22. Option Clip Code

```
onClipEvent(enterFrame) {
  //if done2 has been set meaning we are ready to process this clip
  if (_root.done2 == 1) {
    //if this clip is not processed yet
    if (this.done != 1) {
      //move clip to frame 2
      this.gotoAndStop(2);
      //check for two line answer
      if (this.option.textHeight < 20) {
        //move percent bar down if answer is two lines
        this.percentBar._y = this.percentBar._y - 12;
      }
      //move percent bar to proper percent display
      this.percentBar.gotoAndStop(this.percentage);
      //set this flag to say this clip is processed
      this.done=1;
    }
  }
}
```

This code utilizes the `enterFrame` clip event to continuously check for results data, and when it finds that the results are in, it processes its option results and displays the percent bar at the correct size. It even adjusts the vertical positioning of the percent bar for the occasion of the option text being two lines high.

Click Frame 4 of the control layer. Using the Text tool, set the properties to Static Text, the font to Verdana, the size to 12, the color to black, and the alignment to center justified. Click in the middle of the poll Stage and type *REGISTERING VOTE...*

Choose the Arrow tool and select the new text with a single click. Press F8 (or select Insert ➤ Convert to Symbol), name it *voteClip*, and set its behavior to the Movie Clip option.

You are going to use this clip to process the vote and call the ASP script to update the database and to retrieve the most current poll results to display.

Using the Align Panel, toggle Align to Stage on and center the clip vertically and horizontally (refer to Chapter 3, Creating Your First Flash Application," for more details on how to use the Align Panel to do this). Attach the code in Listing 5-23 to the voteClip using the Actions Panel.

Listing 5-23. Vote Code

```
onClipEvent(load) {
  //if they have not voted already
  if (_root.voted == "0") {
    //call ASP script to vote
    loadVariables("PollRequest.asp?action=vote&ID="+_root.ID+"&select=" ↵
+_root.vote,_root);
  } else {
    //if already voted don't call vote, just display results
    _root.done = 1;
  }
  //make all answer clips invisible while we process results
  for (i=1;i<=_root.numopts;i++) {
    setProperty(["_root.option"+i],_visible,false);
  }
  //start timer for how long data is taking to load
  startTime = getTimer();
}

onClipEvent(enterFrame){
  //if timer is greater than 10 seconds
  if ((getTimer() - startTime)/1000 > 10) {
    //time out poll and send to error frame
    _root.strError = "The poll timed out connecting to the server."
```

```
    _root.gotoAndStop("error");
  }


  //if poll data was successfully received
  if (_root.done==1) {
    //if error string was passed in set error and go to error frame
    if(length(_root.error) > 1) {
      _root.strError = _root.error;
      _root.gotoAndStop("error");
    }

    for (i=1;i<=_root.numopts;i++) {
      //calculate percentage of votes for each answer
      set("_root.option" + i + ".percentage",Math.round((eval(["_root.opt" + i +
                                 "Cnt"])/_root.intTotalVotes)*100));
      set("_root.option" + i + ".strPercent",eval(["_root.option" + i +
                                 ".percentage"]) + "%");
      //set flag so answer clips know to process individual results
      _root.done2 = 1;
      //make clip visible again
      setProperty(["_root.option"+i],_visible,true);
    }
    //go to results frame
    _root.gotoAndStop("results")
  }
}
```

This script calls the PollRequest.asp?action=vote&id=*n*&select=*n* Uniform Resource Identifier (URL), with id being the poll ID and select being the option that was picked in this vote cast. The ASP script adds the vote to the proper tally and sends back a string with updated and current tallies for all options. The Flash movie then does a little math to figure percentages—(number of votes/total votes)*100—and moves the option clips to Frame 2 to display the percent bars that represent the amount of the vote that each option has received.

Believe it or not, that's it. After you get the database set up, the ASP scripts in place, and the Flash published (see Chapter 4, "Adding ActionScript to Your Flash Application," for more information on publishing Flash movies), upload the published SWF file (Poll.swf) and HTML file (Poll.html) to the same directory that the PollRequest.asp file is in. Use the poll administration pages to create a poll and answers (if you have not already) and call the Poll.html page to see it work. Figure 5-15 shows the poll in action.

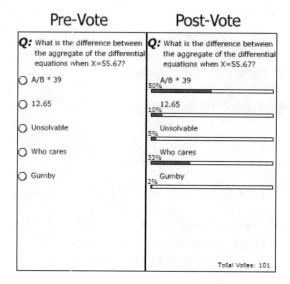

Figure 5-15. Live poll sample

To place the poll on another existing page, just copy the Flash call from the HTML (everything between and including the `<OBJECT></OBJECT>` tags) and paste it into the page desired. If the page receiving the pasted code is in a different directory, be sure to change the path that the code is using to call the Flash movie to reflect the proper path to the .swf file.

 CAUTION *In the code that calls the .swf file and loads it into a page, there are two sets of tags that are important to know:* `<OBJECT>` *and* `<EMBED>`. *The* `<OBJECT>` *tags are for Microsoft Internet Explorer (and similar) browsers, and the* `<EMBED>` *tags are specifically for Netscape browsers. To change the path to the .swf file, you* must *change it in both sets of tags. If you only change it in the* `<OBJECT>` *tag and not the* `<EMBED>` *tags, Netscape users will not see the Flash at all (and visa versa).*

Summary

In this chapter, you built the foundation for creating Flash polls that interface via ASP with SQL Server. You can even expand the example in this chapter into a more powerful poll engine. For example, you could modify the user side to string together multiple polls to build an interactive survey and optionally not display results.

In the next chapter, you will explore building a full-featured trivia game using ASP.NET, SQL Server, and of course Flash. The Flash application, ASP.NET code, database, and integration with Flash will take the interactive question and answer format up a level.

CHAPTER 6

Building a Nontrivial Trivia Game

IN THIS CHAPTER, you are going to take the level of complexity of your projects up a notch. Although the trivia game may be similar to a poll in that they both follow a question and answer format, you will see that the trivia game requires significantly more work to implement.

This example will use ASP.NET and SQL Server for implementation. The data interaction will take on some new dimensions and get more complicated than the poll engine. The Flash side of the application will also get more complex. You will create a full Flash application with input and output data as well as a path that the application (Flash) will take depending on the data variables.

Creating the Trivia Game Business Rules

Before getting down and dirty into the technical details, let's quickly look at the business rule requirements for the trivia game. The trivia game has players. Players will be able to register and log in. When they log out and back in again, they will be able to continue the game from where they last left off. When they complete the game, they will see a recap of their responses and their final score.

Furthermore, the trivia game consists of a series of questions that are organized into levels and categories. Levels define how complicated the questions are and how many points the questions in the levels are worth. Questions are also organized into topical categories such as Sports or History. So, a question could be in level 1, could be worth two points, and could be in the Sports category. Questions are displayed to the user as defined by a level order value. Within the level, the questions are sequenced by an order value as well.

From an administrative perspective, you want to be able to maintain players, questions, and answers. For players, you need to be able to review their playing history and reset their status. Furthermore, the administrator needs to support defining level names, defining their display order, and defining question point values.

For question data, questions need to appear in levels and categories. They also need to be sequenced for display order within the level. You also need to be able to define answers for each question.

 NOTE *For the purposes of this exercise, you can assume that each question will consist of four answers. In the previous chapter, we demonstrated the Flash techniques for showing a variable number of answer options. Refer to that chapter for details on how to implement that technique.*

Figure 6-1 shows the logical flow of the levels and questions.

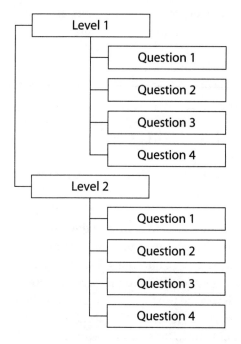

Figure 6-1. Levels and questions

The question display order to the player does *not* have to correspond to the order in which you enter the levels and questions. The administration tools allow you to update the display order as required.

Finally, you need a way for players to gain access to the trivia game. The system needs to provide the ability for a player to register, start the game, log out, log back in, and continue. The player needs to access their game by using a player name and password login process.

Given all of these business rules, there are some requirements that were intentionally left out that would make great enhancements to the provided functionality. We will note these throughout the chapter as you review the functionality.

Building the ASP.NET and SQL Server Foundation

This chapter will utilize Microsoft SQL Server and ASP.NET pages to build the data-driven foundation of the trivia game. You can use either Windows 2000 or Windows XP with Internet Information Services (IIS) 5.0 or 6.0. The programming language will be Visual Basic .NET.

The database was specifically built with Visual Studio .NET, and Microsoft's SQL Server Enterprise Manager was utilized to create the database. If you are running the Microsoft SQL Server Desktop Engine (MSDE) version of SQL Server and using Visual Studio .NET, refer to the instructions for setting up a database in Chapter 2, "Setting Up the Web Server and Database Environment." If you are not running MSDE, then you need to have access to the Enterprise Manager tools.

 NOTE *You can also use Microsoft Access for this solution. The primary change is that you need to set up the connection string to the database to point to the .mdb file. See Chapter 2, "Setting Up the Web Server and Database Environment," for an example.*

Designing the Database

The trivia game database consists of six tables that define the trivia and player data that will support the business requirements outlined in the previous section. These tables will store the players, questions, levels, categories, and response data.

Figure 6-2 shows the six tables and their relationships to each other.

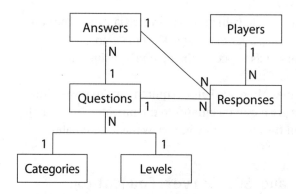

Figure 6-2. The six tables and their relationships

Players will have multiple responses as they go through the game. Responses will relate to one answer and one question. Each answer relates to one question, and each question relates to one category and one level.

Let's now dissect each table starting with Players. Table 6-1 defines the fields for the Players table.

Table 6-1. Players Table Definition

FIELD NAME	DATA TYPE	DESCRIPTION
idPlayer	int/identity	The primary key of the table and auto increments. Be sure and set the field to be an identity column.
PlayerName	varchar (20)	The name entered by the player at registration.
Password	varchar (20)	The password entered by the player at registration.
LastQuestion	int	The ID of the last question for which the player has a response.

A player has a name and password. Both of these are used for accessing the trivia game. You also store the last question they viewed, which is used to start them back up in the trivia game later. In other words, when they return, it determines the next question they should see in the sequence and ensures they do not see a question more than once. Technically, you could figure out what question in the display order they last responded to by looking at the responses and then tracking the data relationships to the answer, the level, and the question display order. However, storing it here makes the startup logic a bit simpler (and, as you will see, it is complicated enough as it is). Listing 6-1 shows the SQL script to create the table.

Listing 6-1. Players Table SQL Create Script

```
if exists
(select * from dbo.sysobjects where id = object_id(N'[dbo].[Players]')
and OBJECTPROPERTY(id, N'IsUserTable') = 1)
drop table [dbo].[Players]
GO

if not exists
(select * from dbo.sysobjects where id = object_id(N'[dbo].[Players]')
and OBJECTPROPERTY(id, N'IsUserTable') = 1)
BEGIN
CREATE TABLE [dbo].[Players] (
    [idPlayer] [int] IDENTITY (1, 1) NOT NULL ,
    [PlayerName] [varchar] (20) COLLATE SQL_Latin1_General_CP1_CI_AS NULL ,
    [Password] [varchar] (20) COLLATE SQL_Latin1_General_CP1_CI_AS NULL ,
    [LastQuestion] [int] NULL
) ON [PRIMARY]
END
GO
```

The Levels table defines the levels for the questions. Each level will have a color for display in the Flash front end (a hex value), the order of the level, and the number of points awarded for correct question responses. Table 6-2 shows the fields for the Levels table.

Table 6-2. Levels Table Definition

FIELD NAME	DATA TYPE	DESCRIPTION
idLevel	int/identity	The primary key of the table and auto increments. Be sure and set the field to be an identity column.
LevelName	varchar (100)	The name of the level.
LevelColor	varchar (20)	The Flash display color of the level.
LevelOrder	int	The order setting for when questions assigned to this level should be displayed.
QuestionPoints	int	The points to be awarded for correct responses of questions assigned to this level.

Listing 6-2 shows the script for creating the table.

Listing 6-2. Levels Table SQL Create Script

```
if exists
(select * from dbo.sysobjects where id = object_id(N'[dbo].[Levels]')
and OBJECTPROPERTY(id, N'IsUserTable') = 1)
drop table [dbo].[Levels]
GO


if not exists (select * from dbo.sysobjects where id = object_id(N'[dbo].[Levels]')
and OBJECTPROPERTY(id, N'IsUserTable') = 1)
BEGIN
CREATE TABLE [dbo].[Levels] (
    [idLevel] [int] IDENTITY (1, 1) NOT NULL ,
    [LevelName] [varchar] (100) COLLATE SQL_Latin1_General_CP1_CI_AS NULL ,
    [LevelColor] [varchar] (20) COLLATE SQL_Latin1_General_CP1_CI_AS NULL ,
    [LevelOrder] [int] NULL ,
    [QuestionPoints] [int] NULL
) ON [PRIMARY]
END
GO
ALTER TABLE [dbo].[Levels] WITH NOCHECK ADD
    CONSTRAINT [DF_Levels_QuestionPoints] DEFAULT (1) FOR [QuestionPoints]
GO
```

Table 6-3 shows the fields for the Categories table. Questions are assigned to topic categories.

Table 6-3. Categories Table Definition

FIELD NAME	DATA TYPE	DESCRIPTION
idCategory	int/identity	The primary key of the table and auto increments. Be sure and set the field to be an identity column.
CategoryName	varchar (100)	The name of the category.

Categories are pretty simple, with each category having a name. Listing 6-3 shows the SQL script to create the table.

Listing 6-3. Categories Table SQL Create Script

```
if exists (select * from dbo.sysobjects where id = object_id(N'[dbo].[Categories]')
and OBJECTPROPERTY(id, N'IsUserTable') = 1)
drop table [dbo].[Categories]
GO
if not exists
(select * from dbo.sysobjects where id = object_id(N'[dbo].[Categories]')
and OBJECTPROPERTY(id, N'IsUserTable') = 1)
BEGIN
CREATE TABLE [dbo].[Categories] (
    [idCategory] [int] IDENTITY (1, 1) NOT NULL ,
    [CategoryName] [varchar] (100) COLLATE SQL_Latin1_General_CP1_CI_AS NULL
) ON [PRIMARY]
END
GO
```

The Questions table shows the fields for the question data. The Questions table is where all of the related game elements come together. Table 6-4 shows the fields.

Table 6-4. Questions Table Definition

FIELD NAME	DATA TYPE	DESCRIPTION
idQuestion	int/identity	The primary key of the table and auto increments. Be sure and set the field to be an identity column.
idCategory	int	The ID of the category to which the question is assigned.
idLevel	int	The ID of the level to which the question is assigned.
DisplayOrderNumber	int	The order in which the question should be displayed for the assigned level.
QuestionText	varchar (1024)	The text of the question.

Each question is assigned a level and a category. The DisplayOrderNumber field defines the order in which the question should be displayed for its assigned level. Note that this is not the display order for all of the questions. Listing 6-4 shows the SQL creation script.

Listing 6-4. Questions Table SQL Create Script

```
if exists
(select * from dbo.sysobjects where id = object_id(N'[dbo].[Questions]')
and OBJECTPROPERTY(id, N'IsUserTable') = 1)
drop table [dbo].[Questions]
GO
if not exists
(select * from dbo.sysobjects where id = object_id(N'[dbo].[Questions]')
and OBJECTPROPERTY(id, N'IsUserTable') = 1)
BEGIN
CREATE TABLE [dbo].[Questions] (
    [idQuestion] [int] IDENTITY (1, 1) NOT NULL ,
    [idCategory] [int] NULL ,
    [idLevel] [int] NULL ,
    [DisplayOrderNumber] [int] NULL ,
    [QuestionText] [varchar] (1024) COLLATE SQL_Latin1_General_CP1_CI_AS NULL
) ON [PRIMARY]
END
GO
```

The Answers table defines the answer options for each question. The user can select one of the answers as the correct response. Table 6-5 shows the fields.

Table 6-5. Answers Table Definition

FIELD NAME	DATA TYPE	DESCRIPTION
idAnswer	int/identity	The primary key of the table and auto increments. Be sure and set the field to be an identity column.
idQuestion	int	The ID of the related question.
AnswerText	varchar (1024)	The text of the answer.
Correct	bit	Flag indicating if the answer is correct.

Listing 6-5 shows the create SQL script for the Answers table.

Listing 6-5. Answers Table SQL Create Script

```
if exists
(select * from dbo.sysobjects where id = object_id(N'[dbo].[Answers]')
and
OBJECTPROPERTY(id, N'IsUserTable') = 1)
drop table [dbo].[Answers]
GO
if not exists
(select * from dbo.sysobjects where id = object_id(N'[dbo].[Answers]')
and OBJECTPROPERTY(id, N'IsUserTable') = 1)
BEGIN
CREATE TABLE [dbo].[Answers] (
    [idAnswer] [int] IDENTITY (1, 1) NOT NULL ,
    [idQuestion] [int] NULL ,
    [AnswerText] [varchar] (1024) COLLATE SQL_Latin1_General_CP1_CI_AS NULL ,
    [Correct] [bit] NULL
) ON [PRIMARY]
END
GO
ALTER TABLE [dbo].[Answers] WITH NOCHECK ADD
    CONSTRAINT [DF_Answers_Correct] DEFAULT (0) FOR [Correct]
GO
```

The Responses table stores the player responses to each question. The table stores the IDs for the player, question, and selected answer. Note that technically you do not need to store the ID of the question in the response. Because you know the ID of the answer, you can get the ID of the question. But, as you will see in the Visual Basic code, the queries get pretty ugly as it is. So, storing the question ID with the response makes things a bit easier. Table 6-6 shows the fields.

Table 6-6. Responses Table Definition

FIELD NAME	DATA TYPE	DESCRIPTION
idPlayer	int/identity	The primary key of the table and auto increments. Be sure and set the field to be an identity column.
idQuestion	int	The ID of the related question for the response.
idAnswer	int	The ID of the related answer for the response.

Listing 6-6 shows the SQL create script for the Questions table.

Listing 6-6. Questions Table SQL Create Script

```
if exists
(select * from dbo.sysobjects where id = object_id(N'[dbo].[Responses]')
and
OBJECTPROPERTY(id, N'IsUserTable') = 1)
drop table [dbo].[Responses]
GO
if not exists (select * from dbo.sysobjects where id =
object_id(N'[dbo].[Responses]')
and OBJECTPROPERTY(id, N'IsUserTable') = 1)
BEGIN
CREATE TABLE [dbo].[Responses] (
    [idPlayer] [int] NULL ,
    [idQuestion] [int] NULL ,
    [idAnswer] [int] NULL) ON [PRIMARY]
END
GO
```

If you reviewed the previous chapter, you may be wondering where the table is that holds the administrator's username and password for managing the trivia game data. We decided in this example to forgo the database and coding requirements for that functionality because we already demonstrated it in the previous chapter. It would certainly be easy enough to add to the project.

To set up the database, follow the steps outlined in Chapter 2, "Setting Up the Web Server and Database Environment," for the ASP.NET/SQL Server project example. Name the database *TriviaGame*. Ensure you have the proper permissions to access the database from your project and set them appropriately in the SQL connection string. That does it for the database. Now you are ready to dive into setting up the project.

Developing the Trivia Game Administrator

The trivia game administrator provides a secure set of tools for managing trivia games. The administrators can add, update, and delete players, levels, categories, questions, and their associated answers. All of the administration pages are written in ASP.NET with Visual Basic, and they interface with the database created in the previous section.

The basic functionality flow of the administrator is straightforward. Figure 6-3 shows a top-down flow of the administration functionality. All of the major data elements include add, update, and delete capabilities. For questions, you can define the relationships to levels and categories and define answers. For players, you can review and manage their game histories.

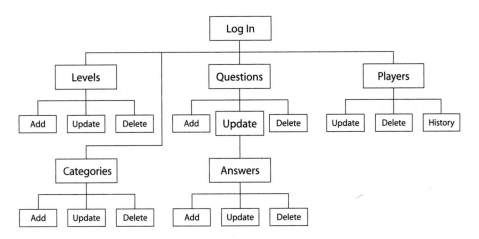

Figure 6-3. The administration functionality

Before development begins, you need to create the trivia game's directory structure. On your development Web server, create a new folder called *TriviaGame*. Create the Visual Studio ASP.NET project in that folder. Within the TriviaGame folder, create an *Admin* folder, which is where the administrative pages will live. Within that folder, create a folder called *Includes,* which will be used for creating common elements across the administrator pages.

After you have created the project, in the Global.aspx.vb file that is created, set up an application variable called *strConn* in the `Application_Start` subroutine. Set that variable to be the connection string used to connect to the database. In the following example, replace `YourServer` with the name of your database server. By making the connection globally available, you can set your SQL connection strings to this variable and not have to copy the connection string throughout the pages. It also makes it easier to manage changes to the connection string. An example of setting the variable is as follows:

```
Application("strConn") = "data source=YourServer;" & _
    "initial catalog=TriviaGame;integrated security=SSPI;" & _
    "persist security info=False;workstation id=Server size=4096"
```

Building the Login Functionality

The first step in building the functionality is to build the login and validation process for the administrator. As mentioned previously, for this project we have made it a simple process. In the Admin folder of the Visual Studio .NET project, create and save a new file called *Login.aspx*. To build the page, follow these steps:

1. Select the Web Forms tab on the Toolbox.

2. Drag two TextBox and two RequiredFieldValidator Web controls onto the form.

3. Name the first textbox *Username.*

4. Name the second textbox *Password* and set its `TextMode` property to *Password.*

5. For the two validators, have one validate the Username textbox and the other validate the Password textbox by setting the `ControlToValidate` property to the corresponding textbox. Also, set the `ErrorMessage` property for both controls. Set appropriate error messages to be displayed if the user does not enter data into the fields.

6. Next, drag a Button control onto the page and name it *SubmitLogin.* Set its `Text` property to *Log In.*

7. Finally, add some appropriate labels from the HTML tab to identify the textboxes and add instruction text to the page.

Your final page should look like Figure 6-4. Listing 6-7 shows the HTML code.

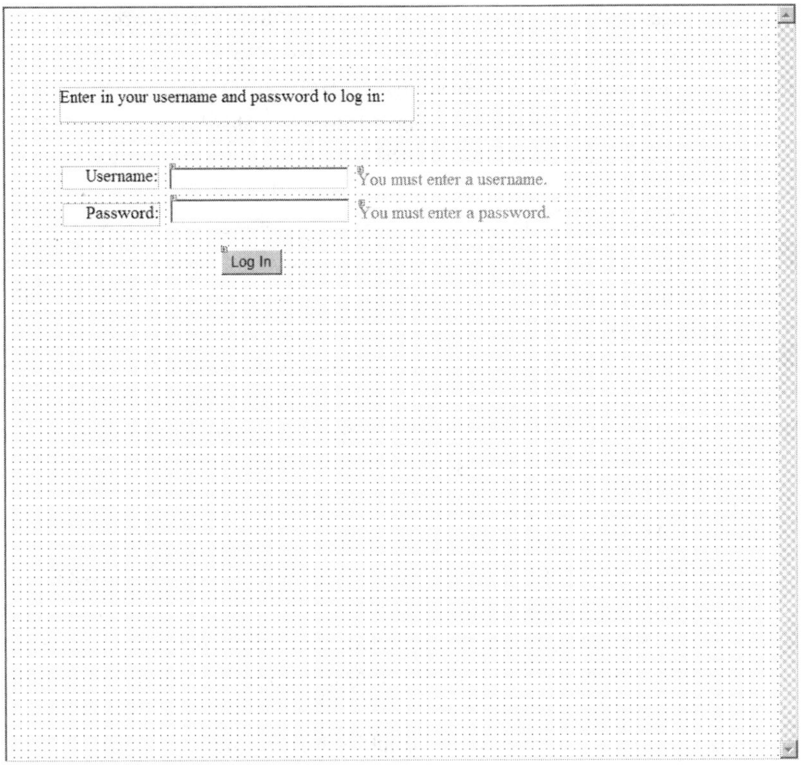

Figure 6-4. The Login.aspx page

Listing 6-7. Login.aspx

```
<%@ Page Language="vb" AutoEventWireup="false"
Codebehind="Login.aspx.vb" Inherits="TriviaGame.Login"%>
<!DOCTYPE HTML PUBLIC "-//W3C//DTD HTML 4.0 Transitional//EN">
<HTML>
    <HEAD>
        <title>WebForm1</title>
        <meta name="GENERATOR" content="Microsoft Visual Studio.NET 7.0">
        <meta name="CODE_LANGUAGE" content="Visual Basic 7.0">
        <meta name="vs_defaultClientScript" content="JavaScript">
        <meta name="vs_targetSchema"
                    content="http://schemas.microsoft.com/intellisense/ie5">
    </HEAD>
    <body MS_POSITIONING="GridLayout">
```

```
<form id="Form1" method="post" runat="server">
    <DIV style="DISPLAY: inline; Z-INDEX: 100;
        LEFT: 63px; WIDTH: 405px; POSITION: absolute;
        TOP: 88px; HEIGHT: 39px" ms_positioning="FlowLayout">Enter
        in your username and password to log in:</DIV>
    <asp:RequiredFieldValidator id="RequiredFieldValidator2"
        style="Z-INDEX: 108; LEFT: 404px; POSITION: absolute;
        TOP: 218px" runat="server" Width="232px"
        ErrorMessage="You must enter a password." Height="25px"
        ControlToValidate="Password"></asp:RequiredFieldValidator>
    <asp:TextBox id="Password" style="Z-INDEX: 102; LEFT: 190px;
        POSITION: absolute; TOP: 212px" runat="server" TextMode="Password"
        Width="204px"></asp:TextBox>
    <asp:TextBox id="UserName" style="Z-INDEX: 101; LEFT: 189px;
        POSITION: absolute; TOP: 177px" runat="server"></asp:TextBox>
        <DIV style="DISPLAY: inline; Z-INDEX: 103; LEFT: 65px; WIDTH: 112px;
            POSITION: absolute; TOP: 176px; HEIGHT: 26px; TEXT-ALIGN: right"
            ms_positioning="FlowLayout">User Name:</DIV>
        <DIV style="DISPLAY: inline; Z-INDEX: 104; LEFT: 66px; WIDTH: 112px;
            POSITION: absolute; TOP: 217px; HEIGHT: 26px; TEXT-ALIGN: right"
            ms_positioning="FlowLayout">Password:</DIV>
    <asp:Button id="SubmitLogin" style="Z-INDEX: 105; LEFT: 248px;
        POSITION: absolute; TOP: 269px" runat="server"
            Text="Log In"></asp:Button>
    <asp:RequiredFieldValidator id="RequiredFieldValidator1"
        style="Z-INDEX: 107; LEFT: 403px; POSITION: absolute; TOP: 181px"
        runat="server" Width="232px"
        ErrorMessage="You must enter a user name." Height="25px"
        ControlToValidate="UserName"></asp:RequiredFieldValidator>
    </form>
</body>
</HTML>
```

The Visual Studio .NET Web Form Designer automatically builds a form with the server-side Web controls. For this page, you do not need to make any additional modifications.

 NOTE *Visual Studio generates extensive style formatting to visually place the elements exactly where they are placed on the page. Depending on your point of view, this can be a help or a hindrance. It can be difficult to anticipate where dynamically created elements should be placed to ensure that items do not overlap.*

The code-behind module for the page is pretty simple. Double-click the button placed on the form to go to the SubmitLogin_click subroutine. Listing 6-8 shows the entire subroutine code for validating the user.

Listing 6-8. Login.aspx.vb

```
Private Sub SubmitLogin_Click(ByVal sender As System.Object, _
    ByVal e As System.EventArgs) Handles SubmitLogin.Click
    '  See if the proper user name and password was entered
    If LCase(username.Text) = "admin" And _
        LCase(Password.Text) = "password" Then

        '  If so then validate the user
        Session("Validated") = True

        '  Send the user to the manager menu
        Server.Transfer("ManagerMenu.aspx")

    Else
        '  Indicate the user was not validated
        Session("Validated") = False
    End If

End Sub
```

This click event fires when the user clicks on the submit button you placed on the form. A simple check is done to see if the user entered a preset player name and password. If so, then the user is validated by setting the Validated session variable to True, and the user is sent to the administration manager page.

NOTE *When the button is clicked and the form is submitted, the* page_load *subroutine still fires. You could have just as easily placed the validation code in that subroutine as well and checked to see if the page load was the result of a form post. You will see examples of this on the other pages.*

In order to implement security throughout the site, you need to have the code check the `Validated` session variable. To implement the checked code across multiple pages, create an include file. Create a file in the Includes folder under Admin called *ValidateCheck.inc*. Listing 6-9 shows the code for the page.

Listing 6-9. ValidateCheck.inc

```
<%
'   Check our session variable to see if the user has
'   been validated. This will help to ensure that
'   none of the admin pages are accessed without
'   authorization.
If Not Session("Validated") Then
'      ' Redirect back to the login page.
       'Server.Transfer("Login.aspx")
End If
%>
```

The code checks to see if the `Validated` variable is set to `True`. If not, then the user is redirected to the Login.aspx page.

Building the Menu Functionality

The menu page is the first page the user sees after logging into the administrator. We will not show the code for the page because it is essentially a series of links to the various administration pages. A top navigation menu will appear across all of the pages. You will also set this up as an include file. Create a new file called *Menu.inc* and save it in the Includes folder. Listing 6-10 shows the code for the page.

Listing 6-10. Menu.inc

```
<!--  Navigation menu for the administrator -->
<a href="ManagePlayers.aspx">Manage Players</a> |
<a href="ManageCategories.aspx">Manage Categories</a> |
<a href="ManageLevels.aspx">Manage Levels</a></TD> |
<a href="ManageQuestions.aspx">Manage Questions</a></TD>
```

Building the Player Management Functionality

First, you will look at player management. The first step is to create a page that lists all of the existing players in the system. To do this, create a new page in the Admin folder called *ManagePlayers.aspx*. To build the components of the page, follow these steps:

1. Select the Web Forms tab on the Toolbox. Drag a DataGrid control onto the page and name it *dgPlayers*. Make sure the AutoGenerateColumns property is *false*. To allow sorting of the grid data, set the AllowSorting flag to *true*.

2. Select the Data tab on the Toolbox. Drag a SQLConnection control onto the page and name it *cnnTriviaGame*. In the ConnectionString property, define the connection string to connect to your SQL server and the TriviaGame database (see Chapter 2, "Setting Up the Web Server and Database Environment").

3. Next, drag a SQLCommand control to the page and name it *cmdGetPlayers*.

4. In the CommandText property of the SQLCommand control, place the following query, which will return all of the players in the table:

```
select * from Players
```

5. Next, drag a Label control to the page from the HTML tab on the Toolbox and enter *Manage Players:* for the text.

> **NOTE** *In this example, you used the Web form controls for the SQL connection and the SQL command. In the rest of the administration pages, you will not use these controls and instead simply create the* Command *and* Connection *objects dynamically in the Visual Basic code.*

That builds the basic form and controls for the page. Now you need to modify the created HTML to have the DataGrid display the data you want and provide a couple of options. Figure 6-5 shows the layout of the page, and Listing 6-11 shows the code for the page.

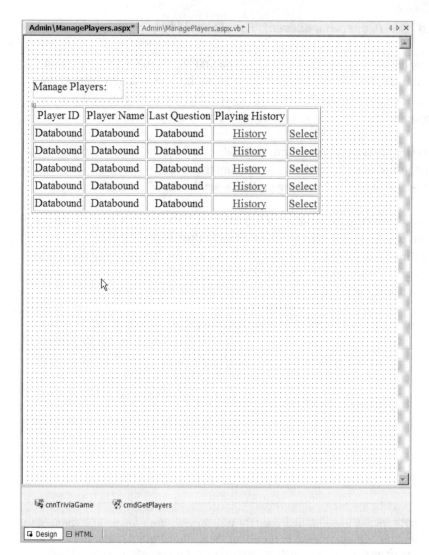

Figure 6-5. The ManagePlayers.aspx page

Listing 6-11. ManagePlayers.aspx

```
<%@ Page Language="vb" AutoEventWireup="false"
Codebehind="ManagePlayers.aspx.vb"
Inherits="TriviaGame.ManagePlayers"%>
<!DOCTYPE HTML PUBLIC "-//W3C//DTD HTML 4.0 Transitional//EN">
<HTML>
    <HEAD>
        <title>Manage Players</title>
```

```html
        <meta name="GENERATOR" content="Microsoft Visual Studio.NET 7.0">
        <meta name="CODE_LANGUAGE" content="Visual Basic 7.0">
        <meta name="vs_defaultClientScript" content="JavaScript">
        <meta name="vs_targetSchema"
                content="http://schemas.microsoft.com/intellisense/ie5">
    </HEAD>
    <body MS_POSITIONING="GridLayout">
        <!-- #Include File="includes/ValidateCheck.inc" -->
        <!-- #Include File="includes/menu.inc" -->

        <form id="Form1" method="post" runat="server">
            <DIV style="DISPLAY: inline; Z-INDEX: 102; LEFT: 16px;
                WIDTH: 162px; POSITION: absolute; TOP: 76px; HEIGHT: 31px"
                ms_positioning="FlowLayout">Manage Players:</DIV>
            <asp:DataGrid id="dgPlayers" style="Z-INDEX: 101; LEFT: 14px;
                POSITION: absolute; TOP: 119px" runat="server"
                AllowSorting="True"
                CellPadding="2" CellSpacing="2" AutoGenerateColumns="False">
                <Columns>
            <asp:BoundColumn DataField="idPlayer"
                ItemStyle-HorizontalAlign="Center"
                HeaderStyle-HorizontalAlign="Center"
                HeaderText="Player ID"></asp:BoundColumn>
            <asp:BoundColumn DataField="PlayerName"
                ItemStyle-HorizontalAlign="Center"
                HeaderStyle-HorizontalAlign="Center"
                HeaderText="Player Name"></asp:BoundColumn>
            <asp:BoundColumn DataField="LastQuestion"
                ItemStyle-HorizontalAlign="Center"
                HeaderStyle-HorizontalAlign="Center"
                HeaderText="Last Question"></asp:BoundColumn>
            <asp:ButtonColumn Text="History" CommandName="History"
                HeaderText="Playing History"
                HeaderStyle-HorizontalAlign="Center"
                ItemStyle-
                HorizontalAlign="Center"></asp:ButtonColumn>
            <asp:ButtonColumn Text="Select" CommandName="Select">
            </asp:ButtonColumn>
                </Columns>
            </asp:DataGrid>
        </form>
    </body>
</HTML>
```

189

In the first part of the page, there are two include files for validating the user and displaying the top-level menu. After that, the form for the page starts, and the HTML introductory text appears.

For the DataGrid, you define the columns of data you would like displayed. You use the `<Columns>` formatting and the `<asp:BoundColumn>` tags to define the columns to display. Specifically, the grid should show the ID, player name, and last question from the database. You add three column tags to the `<Columns>` section of the DataGrid with the `DataField` property set to the appropriate database fields.

NOTE *In the code-behind module, you will be connecting the DataGrid to the Players table using the SQL* Connection *and* Command *objects placed on the page.*

Finally, you also need to add two options for managing the player data. The first is a link to a page to see the player's game history. The second is a link to update the player's data. You implement these with the `<ASP:ButtonColumn>` tags. Set the `Text` and `CommandName` properties for each button column.

TIP *You can set all of the column properties using the property builder tool of the DataGrid. Right-click the DataGrid and select Property Builder.*

Now you are ready to look at the code-behind module for the page. Listing 6-12 shows the code for the page.

Listing 6-12. ManagePlayers.aspx.vb

```
Private Sub Page_Load(ByVal sender As System.Object, _
        ByVal e As System.EventArgs) Handles MyBase.Load

    ' First time the page is loaded (not a form postback)
    If Not IsPostBack Then

        ' Create a new SqlDataReader
        Dim objDR As SqlClient.SqlDataReader

        ' Open the connection placed on the aspx page
        cnnTriviaGame.Open()
```

```
    ' Get the data by executing the command on the aspx page
    objDR = cmdGetPlayers.ExecuteReader

    ' Set the grid data source
    dgPlayers.DataSource = objDR

    ' Show the data
    dgPlayers.DataBind()

    End If

End Sub

Private Sub dgPlayers_ItemCommand(ByVal source As Object, _
ByVal e As System.Web.UI.WebControls.DataGridCommandEventArgs) _
Handles dgPlayers.ItemCommand
    ' e.Item is the row of the DataGrid where the link was
    ' clicked.

    ' Check for what kind of action the user wants to take
    If LCase(Trim(e.CommandName)) = "select" Then

        ' update player
        Server.Transfer("UpdatePlayer.aspx?idPlayer=" & e.Item.Cells(0).Text)

    Else
        ' View the player's answer history
        Server.Transfer("ViewPlayerHistory.aspx?idPlayer=" & _
        e.Item.Cells(0).Text)

    End If

    End Sub

End Class
```

Two basic actions take place on the page. The first is when the page loads. If the page is loading for the first time and is not a postback to the page (for example, one of the DataGrid links is clicked), then you bind the DataGrid to the data sources placed on the page. This shows all of the players in the grid.

The second action is to handle when a user clicks the History or Select links in the DataGrid for a player. When that happens, the dgPlayers_ItemCommand event fires. To get to this event, click the left drop-down box on the top of the code editor and pick the dbPlayers control. In the right drop-down box, select the ItemCommand method.

In the ItemCommand method, you check the name of the command selected by looking at the CommandName property of the event arguments (e) passed into ItemCommand. If it is the History command, then the user is sent to the ViewPlayerHistory.aspx page. If it is the Select command, they are sent to the UpdatePlayer.aspx page. On both server transfers, the ID of the player is passed on the Uniform Resource Locator (URL).

Building the Update Player Functionality

Next, let's look at the update player functionality. The goal of this page is to allow the administrator to update the player name and password. You also want to provide an option to delete the player from the database. Create a new Web form called *UpdatePlayer.aspx* and save it in the Admin folder. To create the user interface part of the page, follow these steps:

1. Drag two TextBox and two RequiredFieldValidator Web controls to the form.

2. Name the first textbox *PlayerName.*

3. Name the second textbox *Password* and set its TextMode property to *Password.*

4. For the two validators, have one validate the PlayerName textbox and the other validate the Password textbox. Set appropriate error messages to be displayed if the user does not enter data into the fields.

5. Drag a Button control onto the page and name it *SubmitUpdatePlayer.* Set its Text property to *Update Player.*

6. Next drag a Web form Label control to the page. Name it *idPlayer* and set its Text property to blank.

7. To link to the delete functionality, add a LinkButton Web control to the page and name it *PlayerDelete.* Set its Text property to *Delete Player.*

8. Finally, add HTML labels to the page to provide instructions and field labels.

TIP *Because this page is similar to the login page, you can copy the controls from the login page to this page instead of creating the controls from scratch*

The final result looks like Figure 6-6; Listing 6-13 shows the code for the page.

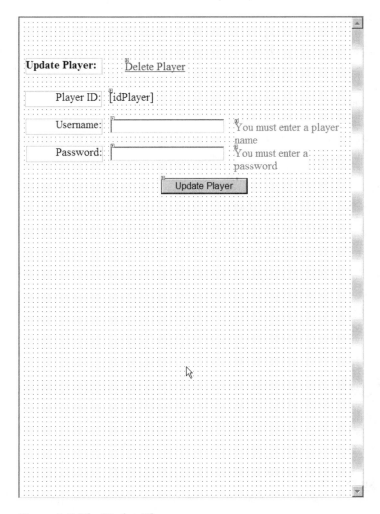

Figure 6-6. The UpdatePlayer.aspx page

Listing 6-13. UpdatePlayer.aspx

```
<%@ Page Language="vb" AutoEventWireup="false"
Codebehind="UpdatePlayer.aspx.vb"
Inherits="TriviaGame.UpdatePlayer"%>
<!DOCTYPE HTML PUBLIC "-//W3C//DTD HTML 4.0 Transitional//EN">
<HTML>
    <HEAD>
        <title>UpdatePlayer</title>
        <meta content="Microsoft Visual Studio.NET 7.0" name="GENERATOR">
        <meta content="Visual Basic 7.0" name="CODE_LANGUAGE">
        <meta content="JavaScript" name="vs_defaultClientScript">
        <meta content="http://schemas.microsoft.com/intellisense/ie5"
                    name="vs_targetSchema">
    </HEAD>
    <body MS_POSITIONING="GridLayout">
        <!-- #Include File="includes/ValidateCheck.inc" -->
        <!-- #Include File="includes/menu.inc" -->
        <form id="Form1" method="post" runat="server">
        <DIV style="DISPLAY: inline; FONT-WEIGHT: bold; Z-INDEX: 101; LEFT: 11px;
                    WIDTH: 138px; POSITION: absolute; TOP: 71px; HEIGHT: 28px"
                    ms_positioning="FlowLayout">Update Player:</DIV>

            <asp:requiredfieldvalidator id="RequiredFieldValidator2"
                style="Z-INDEX: 109; LEFT: 385px;
                POSITION: absolute; TOP: 226px"
                runat="server" ErrorMessage="You must enter a password"
                ControlToValidate="Password"></asp:requiredfieldvalidator>

            <asp:textbox id="Password" style="Z-INDEX: 107; LEFT: 164px;
                POSITION: absolute; TOP: 224px" runat="server"></asp:textbox>

            <asp:label id="idPlayer" style="Z-INDEX: 102; LEFT: 161px;
                POSITION: absolute; TOP: 128px" runat="server"></asp:label>

            <DIV style="DISPLAY: inline; Z-INDEX: 103; LEFT: 10px; WIDTH: 138px;
                POSITION: absolute; TOP: 128px; HEIGHT: 28px" align="right"
                ms_positioning="FlowLayout">Player ID:</DIV>
```

```
<DIV style="DISPLAY: inline; Z-INDEX: 104; LEFT: 11px; WIDTH: 138px;
        POSITION: absolute; TOP: 176px; HEIGHT: 28px" align="right"
        ms_positioning="FlowLayout">User Name:</DIV>

<DIV style="DISPLAY: inline; Z-INDEX: 105; LEFT: 12px; WIDTH: 138px;
        POSITION: absolute; TOP: 224px; HEIGHT: 28px" align="right"
        ms_positioning="FlowLayout">Password:</DIV>

    <asp:textbox id="PlayerName" style="Z-INDEX: 106; LEFT: 164px;
        POSITION: absolute; TOP: 176px"
        runat="server"></asp:textbox>

    <asp:requiredfieldvalidator id="RequiredFieldValidator1"
        style="Z-INDEX: 108; LEFT: 386px;
        POSITION: absolute; TOP: 181px"
        runat="server" ErrorMessage="You must enter a player name"
        ControlToValidate="PlayerName"></asp:requiredfieldvalidator>

    <asp:button id="SubmitUpdatePlayer"
        style="Z-INDEX: 110; LEFT: 255px;
        POSITION: absolute; TOP: 280px" runat="server"
        Text="Update Player"></asp:button>

    <asp:LinkButton id="PlayerDelete" style="Z-INDEX: 113; LEFT: 190px;
        POSITION: absolute; TOP: 75px" runat="server">Delete
        Player</asp:LinkButton>
    </form>
    </body>
</HTML>
```

Visual Studio has automatically added all of the Web form controls to the page. Note that it places the code to include the two validation and menu files in the page before the form tag. You do not have to make any additional modifications other than to add the include files.

The code-behind module for this page handles three primary functions. The first is to display the player data, the second is to update the player data, and the third is to delete the player. Listing 6-14 shows the Visual Basic code for UpdatePlayer.aspx.vb.

Listing 6-14. UpdatePlayer.aspx.vb

```vb
Private Sub Page_Load(ByVal sender As System.Object, _
    ByVal e As System.EventArgs) Handles MyBase.Load
    'Put user code to initialize the page here

    Dim objCMD As New SqlClient.SqlCommand()
    Dim objConn As New SqlClient.SqlConnection()
    Dim objDR As SqlClient.SqlDataReader
    Dim strSQL As String

    ' Open the connection
    objConn.ConnectionString = Application("strConn")
    objConn.Open()

    ' Set the command connection
    objCMD.Connection = objConn

    ' First time the page is displayed (not a form post)
    If Not IsPostBack Then

        ' Build a query to retrieve the player data
        strSQL = "select * from Players where idPlayer = " & _
        Request.QueryString("idPlayer")

        ' Set the command query
        objCMD.CommandText = strSQL

        ' Set the reader
        objDR = objCMD.ExecuteReader

        ' Get the data
        objDR.Read()

        ' Display the data
        idPlayer.Text = objDR.Item("idPlayer")
        PlayerName.Text = objDR.Item("PlayerName")
        Password.Text = objDR.Item("Password")

    End If

End Sub
```

```
Private Sub PlayerDelete_Click(ByVal sender As System.Object, _
    ByVal e As System.EventArgs) Handles PlayerDelete.Click
  Dim objCMD As New SqlClient.SqlCommand()
  Dim objConn As New SqlClient.SqlConnection()
  Dim strSQL As String

  ' Open the connection
  objConn.ConnectionString = Application("strConn")
  objConn.Open()

  ' Set the command connection
  objCMD.Connection = objConn

  ' Build the delete query
  strSQL = "Delete from Players where idPlayer = " & idPlayer.Text

  ' Set the command query
  objCMD.CommandText = strSQL

  ' Execute the query
  objCMD.ExecuteNonQuery()

  ' Send the user back to the player management page
  Server.Transfer("ManagePlayers.aspx")
End Sub

Private Sub SubmitUpdatePlayer_Click(ByVal sender As System.Object, _
    ByVal e As System.EventArgs) Handles SubmitUpdatePlayer.Click

  Dim objCMD As New SqlClient.SqlCommand()
  Dim objConn As New SqlClient.SqlConnection()
  Dim strSQL As String

  ' Open the connection
  objConn.ConnectionString = Application("strConn")
  objConn.Open()

  ' Build query to update the player
  strSQL = "Update Players set PlayerName = '" & _
  Replace(PlayerName.Text, "'", "''") & "', Password = '" & _
  Replace(Password.Text, "'", "''") & _
  "' where idPlayer = " & idPlayer.Text
```

```
'   Set the command connection
objCMD.Connection = objConn

'   Set the command query
objCMD.CommandText = strSQL

'   Execute the query
objCMD.ExecuteNonQuery()

'   Send the user back to the player management page
Server.Transfer("ManagePlayers.aspx")

End Sub
```

When the page is loaded for the first time (not a form post), the data for the player is pulled from the database. This happens by accessing the ID of the player off of the URL. Then, this code creates SQL Connection and Command objects. The SQL connection is set to the global application variable, which defines the connection string. A SQL query is created to retrieve the data for the specific player. A SQL DataReader object pulls the data from the table, and the text values of the idPlayer, PlayerName, and Password textboxes are set to the corresponding database table name values.

The second function is to delete the player when the Delete Player link is clicked. The click event of the PlayerDelete link button is where you place the delete functionality. Double-click the link button in the .aspx page, and the click event is created for you. As with displaying the player data, SQL Connection and Command objects are created and set up. A SQL query to delete the specified player is built and then executed. Then the user is sent back to the manage players page.

The final function is to update the player data with any entered changes. Note that the required field validators will ensure that user does not try to submit empty player names or passwords. You can create the SubmitUpdatePlayer click event by double-clicking the submit button on the .aspx page. In the click event, the appropriate SQL objects and SQL query string are created to update the player data. The new data is read from the text properties of the textboxes.

Creating the Player History Functionality

The final functionality for managing players is for viewing the player's game history. The goal is to show the questions, responses, and score for each player and then provide an option to reset the player's history so they can go through the game again. Create a new page called *ViewPlayerHistory.aspx* and save it in the Admin folder. To create the user interface for the page, follow these steps:

1. Drag a Web form Data control to the page and name it *dgAnswers.*

2. Drag a Web form Label control to the page, name it *Score,* and clear the Text Field property.

3. Drag a Web form LinkButton control to the page, name it *ResetPlayer,* and set the Text property to *Reset Player.*

4. Drag an HTML Label control to the page to label where the score will display.

NOTE *You might want to consider adding the ability to edit user responses for questions. This would be useful for cases where the user clicked the wrong response, there was a data entry error in entering an answer, and so on.*

The page should look like Figure 6-7. Listing 6-15 shows the code for the page.

Question	Points	Answer	Correct
Databound	Databound	Databound	☐
Databound	Databound	Databound	☐
Databound	Databound	Databound	☐
Databound	Databound	Databound	☐
Databound	Databound	Databound	☐

Score: [Score]   Reset Player

Figure 6-7. The ViewPlayerHistory.aspx page

Listing 6-15. ViewPlayerHistory.aspx

```
<%@ Page Language="vb" AutoEventWireup="false"
Codebehind="ViewPlayerHistory.aspx.vb"
Inherits="TriviaGame.ViewPlayerHistory"%>
<!DOCTYPE HTML PUBLIC "-//W3C//DTD HTML 4.0 Transitional//EN">
<HTML>
    <HEAD>
        <title>ViewPlayerHistory</title>
        <meta name="GENERATOR" content="Microsoft Visual Studio.NET 7.0">
        <meta name="CODE_LANGUAGE" content="Visual Basic 7.0">
        <meta name="vs_defaultClientScript" content="JavaScript">
        <meta name="vs_targetSchema"
                  content="http://schemas.microsoft.com/intellisense/ie5">
    </HEAD>
    <body MS_POSITIONING="GridLayout">
        <!-- #Include File="includes/ValidateCheck.inc" -->
        <!-- #Include File="includes/menu.inc" -->
        <form id="Form1" method="post" runat="server">
            <asp:label id="Score" style="Z-INDEX: 101; LEFT: 86px;
                      POSITION: absolute; TOP: 60px" runat="server"></asp:label>
            <asp:datagrid id="dgAnswers" style="Z-INDEX: 102; LEFT: 8px;
                      POSITION: absolute; TOP: 125px" runat="server"
                      Width="800" AutoGenerateColumns="False" CellSpacing="2"
                      CellPadding="2" AllowSorting="True">
            <Columns>
              <asp:BoundColumn ItemStyle-HorizontalAlign="left"
                        HeaderStyle-HorizontalAlign="center"
                         DataField="QuestionText"
                          HeaderText="Question"></asp:BoundColumn>
              <asp:BoundColumn HeaderStyle-HorizontalAlign="center"
                        DataField="QuestionPoints" HeaderText="Points">
                    </asp:BoundColumn>
                    <asp:BoundColumn HeaderStyle-HorizontalAlign="center"
                        DataField="AnswerText" HeaderText="Answer">
                    </asp:BoundColumn>
                <asp:TemplateColumn HeaderText="Correct"
                        HeaderStyle-HorizontalAlign="center"
                        ItemStyle-HorizontalAlign="Center">
                <ItemTemplate>
                        <asp:CheckBox runat="server" ID="Correct"
                              Checked=
                        '<%# DataBinder.Eval(Container.DataItem, "Correct") %>'>
```

```
                    </asp:CheckBox>
                 </ItemTemplate>
          </asp:TemplateColumn>
       </Columns>
     </asp:datagrid>

          <DIV style="DISPLAY: inline; Z-INDEX: 103; LEFT: 8px;
             WIDTH: 70px; POSITION: absolute; TOP: 60px; HEIGHT: 15px"
             align="right" ms_positioning="FlowLayout">Score:</DIV>

          <asp:LinkButton id="ResetPlayer" style="Z-INDEX: 104; LEFT: 237px;
             POSITION: absolute; TOP: 57px" runat="server">
             Reset Player</asp:LinkButton>
     </form>
   </body>
</HTML>
```

The question, points, and answer columns of the DataGrid are pretty straightforward; you can set them up with the property builder. The column that will be challenging to build is the Correct field checkbox column to show which responses of the player are correct. There are a couple of different ways to approach building the column. The first is to add the column in the visual property builder and indicate it is a template column. Then go to the edit template functionality of the DataGrid and drag a CheckBox Web form control into the ItemTemplate section of the template editor. Then go to the DataBindings property of the checkbox and put in a custom binding for the Checked property as follows:

```
DataBinder.Eval(Container.DataItem, "Correct")
```

This indicates that the column should be bound to the correct column of the table. Now, this is all pretty complicated to get right. An easier method may be to build the HTML directly instead of using the Graphical User Interface (GUI) control properties. The HTML is as follows:

```
<asp:TemplateColumn HeaderText="Correct"
    HeaderStyle-HorizontalAlign="center"
    ItemStyle-HorizontalAlign="Center">
    <ItemTemplate>
          <asp:CheckBox runat="server" ID="Correct"
             Checked='<%# DataBinder.Eval(Container.DataItem, "Correct") %>'>
          </asp:CheckBox>
    </ItemTemplate>
</asp:TemplateColumn>
```

Although this may seem complicated, if you follow the tagging through, it is actually quite easy. You have an <asp:TemplateColumn> tag that starts the column as a template. Next, you indicate that it uses an item template with the <ItemTemplate> tags. Finally, you have the <asp:checkbox> field that builds the checkbox, and you bind the Checked property to the Correct field from the data bound to the DataGrid.

 NOTE *Microsoft provides excellent references for the DataGrid control and working with its various capabilities. For more information, refer to the following page on the Microsoft site:* http://msdn.microsoft.com/ library/default.asp?url=/library/en-us/cpref/html/ frlrfSystemWebUIWebControlsDataGridClassTopic.asp.

Once you have the DataGrid set up, you are ready to build the Visual Basic code to wire up the page and make everything work. Listing 6-16 shows the code for the ViewPlayerHistory.aspx.vb module.

Listing 6-16. ViewPlayerHistory.aspx.vb

```
Private Sub Page_Load(ByVal sender As System.Object, ByVal e As System.EventArgs) _
      Handles MyBase.Load
      Dim objCMD As New SqlClient.SqlCommand()
      Dim objConn As New SqlClient.SqlConnection()
      Dim strSQL As String
      Dim blnReturn As Boolean
      Dim objDR As SqlClient.SqlDataReader

      ' Open the connection
      objConn.ConnectionString = Application("strConn")
      objConn.Open()

      ' Build a query to get the score by looking
      ' at the correct responses and get the
      ' corresponding level and point value
      strSQL = "SELECT Sum(Levels.QuestionPoints) FROM (Questions INNER " & _
      "JOIN (Responses INNER JOIN Answers ON Responses.idAnswer = " & _
      "Answers.idAnswer) ON Questions.idQuestion = Answers.idQuestion) " & _
      "INNER JOIN Levels ON Questions.idLevel = Levels.idLevel WHERE " & _
      "Responses.idPlayer=" & Request.QueryString("idPlayer") & _
      " and answers.correct = 1"
```

```
' Open the connection
objCMD.Connection = objConn

' Set the command query
objCMD.CommandText = strSQL

' Set the reader
objDR = objCMD.ExecuteReader

' Get the data and ensure something is returned (there may be no correct
' responses)
blnReturn = objDR.Read()

' If data was returned (any answers at all)
If blnReturn = True Then
    ' Display the score if not NULL
    If Not objDR.IsDBNull(0) Then
        Score.Text = objDR.Item(0)
    Else
        Score.Text = 0
    End If

Else
    ' Else score of 0
    Score.Text = 0
End If

' Close the reader for reuse
objDR.Close()

' Build a query to get the responses of the user and the corresponding
' question text, answer text, and point value
strSQL = "SELECT questions.questiontext, Levels.QuestionPoints, " & _
"Answers.AnswerText, Answers.Correct FROM (Questions INNER JOIN " & _
"(Responses INNER JOIN Answers ON Responses.idAnswer = " & _
"Answers.idAnswer) ON Questions.idQuestion = Answers.idQuestion) " & _
"INNER JOIN Levels ON Questions.idLevel = Levels.idLevel WHERE " & _
"(((Responses.idPlayer)=" & Request.QueryString("idPlayer") & ")) " & _
"order by levels.levelorder, questions.displayordernumber"

' Set the command query
objCMD.CommandText = strSQL
```

```vb
'  Set the reader
objDR = objCMD.ExecuteReader

'  Set the grid data source
dgAnswers.DataSource = objDR

'  Show the data
dgAnswers.DataBind()

End Sub

Private Sub ResetPlayer_Click(ByVal sender As System.Object, _
    ByVal e As System.EventArgs) Handles ResetPlayer.Click

    Dim objCMD As New SqlClient.SqlCommand()
    Dim objConn As New SqlClient.SqlConnection()
    Dim strSQL As String
    Dim objDR As SqlClient.SqlDataReader

    '  Open the connection
    objConn.ConnectionString = Application("strConn")
    objConn.Open()

    '  Open the connection
    objCMD.Connection = objConn

    '  Delete all of the responses
    strSQL = "delete FROM responses where idPlayer = " & _
    Request.QueryString("idPlayer")

    '  Set the command query
    objCMD.CommandText = strSQL

    '  Execute the query
    objCMD.ExecuteNonQuery()

    '  Reset the last question
    strSQL = "update players set LastQuestion = NULL where idPlayer = " & _
    Request.QueryString("idPlayer")

    '  Set the command query
    objCMD.CommandText = strSQL
```

```
'  Execute the query
objCMD.ExecuteNonQuery()

Server.Transfer("ManagePlayers.aspx")
```

```
End Sub
```

The first thing that happens when the page loads is that the score is calculated and displayed. If you are not a SQL jockey, that big query might scare you a bit given that is has a triple inner join. In order to get the score, you need to know the question point values for each correct response. In order to get that, you have to get the level point value for each player response that is the correct answer. Get all that? Let's break down the FROM part of the query, which is as follows:

```
FROM
    (Questions INNER JOIN
        (Responses INNER JOIN Answers ON Responses.idAnswer = Answers.idAnswer)
            ON Questions.idQuestion = Answers.idQuestion)
    INNER JOIN Levels ON Questions.idLevel = Levels.idLevel
```

The first nested inner join is as follows:

```
Responses INNER JOIN Answers ON Responses.idAnswer = Answers.idAnswer
```

That combines the Response and Answers tables based on the linked answer ID. This determines if a response is correct. The next inner join takes the data returned from the first inner join and joins it with the Questions table on the ID of the question related to the answer:

```
(Questions INNER JOIN
 (Responses INNER JOIN Answers ON Responses.idAnswer = Answers.idAnswer)
    ON Questions.idQuestion = Answers.idQuestion)
```

Finally, the results of all that are joined with the Levels table to get the question point values:

```
(Questions INNER JOIN
    (Responses INNER JOIN Answers ON Responses.idAnswer = Answers.idAnswer)
        ON Questions.idQuestion = Answers.idQuestion)
INNER JOIN Levels ON Questions.idLevel = Levels.idLevel
```

The where clause then specifies only responses for the player you are working with and the correct responses. And, voila, you have all of the correct responses from the player and their corresponding point values. The Sum function of SQL then totals the score. The SQL is a bit tricky but not too hard if you break it down.

That query executes using a SQLDataReader object. If the result of executing the read method of the object is True, then data was returned. If no data is returned, then there are no correct responses for the player. There may be responses for the player, but none of them may be correct; therefore, the resulting score value may be NULL, which is checked for, and the score displays as zero. If there is a score value, then it is displayed in the Score Label control.

The next section of the page fills out the DataGrid to show the question, point value, answer, and correct check for each of the player's responses. Again, you see a pretty ugly query staring you in the face. The good news is that the FROM clause is the same as the FROM clause for the score query. The main differences in this query are that you are pulling back the columns of data you need to display, and you are ordering the data by level and question display order within the level. The data is then bound to the DataGrid control.

The other primary function in the code executes when the Reset Player link is clicked. The click event of the link fires. Double-click the link to create the Reset-Player_Click method of the control.

In that method, you are going to delete the responses of the player and update the last question viewed by the player. You use SQLConnection, SQLCommand, and SQLDataReader objects for accessing the database. The response delete query removes all responses for the specified user. Once that is done, then the LastQuestion field of the Players record for the player is set to NULL to indicate there are no responses.

Building the Question Management Functionality

Next, you will look at the question management process. The first step is to list the existing questions in the database. The key is you want to list them in level order and display order within the level—just as the trivia game player would see them. You also want to display the associated level and category for each question. From this one page view, the administrator can see all questions, their associations (for example, category and level), and the order in which they are displayed. In order to manage the questions, you need to be able to update the question data as well as supply answers for each question.

Create a new page called *ManageQuestions.aspx*. On that page, add a DataGrid control named *dgQuestions*. Then add a LinkButton control named *NewQuestion* and set the Text property to *New Question*. Finally, add an HTML label and set it to *Manage Questions:*. The resulting page will look like Figure 6-8; Listing 6-17 shows the HTML code.

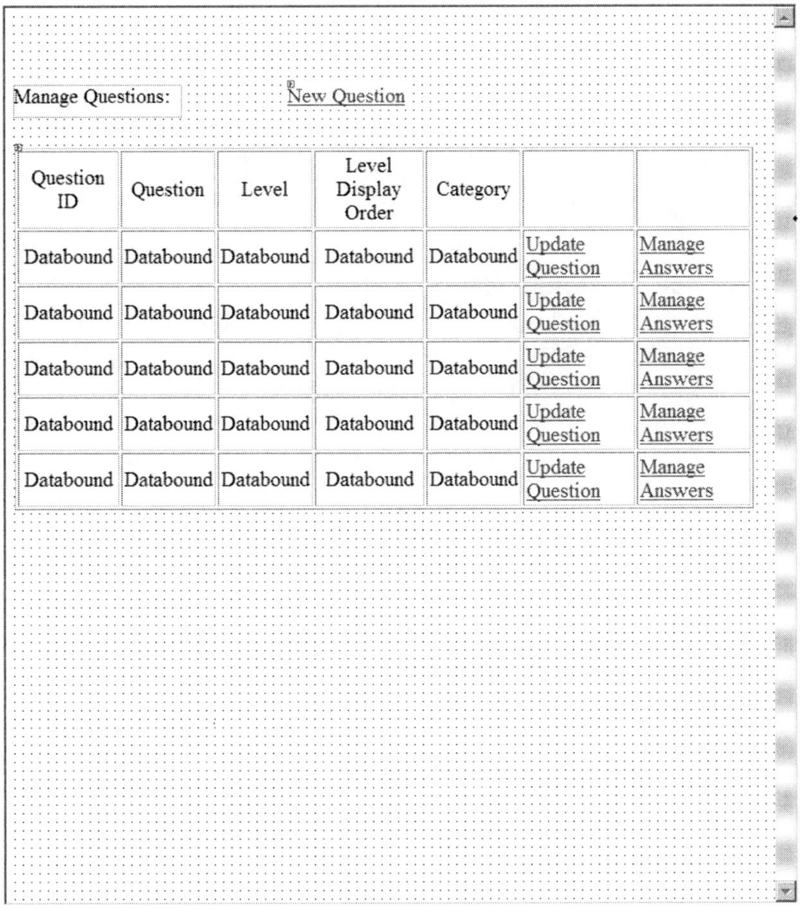

Figure 6-8. The ManageQuestions.aspx page

Listing 6-17. ManageQuestions.aspx

```
<%@ Page Language="vb" AutoEventWireup="false"
        Codebehind="ManageQuestions.aspx.vb"
        Inherits="TriviaGame.ManageQuestions"%>
<!DOCTYPE HTML PUBLIC "-//W3C//DTD HTML 4.0 Transitional//EN">
<HTML>
    <HEAD>
        <title>ManageQuestions</title>
        <meta name="GENERATOR" content="Microsoft Visual Studio.NET 7.0">
        <meta name="CODE_LANGUAGE" content="Visual Basic 7.0">
        <meta name="vs_defaultClientScript" content="JavaScript">
        <meta name="vs_targetSchema"
                content="http://schemas.microsoft.com/intellisense/ie5">
```

```
        </HEAD>
    <body MS_POSITIONING="GridLayout">
        <!-- #Include File="includes/ValidateCheck.inc" -->
        <!-- #Include File="includes/menu.inc" -->
        <form id="Form1" method="post" runat="server">
            <DIV style="DISPLAY: inline; Z-INDEX: 105; LEFT: 8px; WIDTH: 162px;
                    POSITION: absolute; TOP: 72px; HEIGHT: 31px"
                    ms_positioning="FlowLayout">
                    Manage Questions:</DIV>
                <asp:DataGrid id="dgQuestions" style="Z-INDEX: 102;
                    LEFT: 9px; POSITION:
                    absolute; TOP: 131px" runat="server"
                    AutoGenerateColumns="False"
                    CellSpacing="2" CellPadding="2" AllowSorting="True">
            <Columns>
                <asp:BoundColumn ItemStyle-HorizontalAlign="Center"
                        HeaderStyle-HorizontalAlign="center" DataField="idQuestion"
                        HeaderText="Question ID"></asp:BoundColumn>
                <asp:BoundColumn HeaderStyle-HorizontalAlign="center"
                        DataField="QuestionText" HeaderText="Question">
                </asp:BoundColumn>
                    <asp:BoundColumn HeaderStyle-HorizontalAlign="center"
                        DataField="LevelName" HeaderText="Level"></asp:BoundColumn>
                        <asp:BoundColumn ItemStyle-HorizontalAlign="Center"
                            HeaderStyle-HorizontalAlign="center"
                            DataField="DisplayOrderNumber"
                            HeaderText="Level<BR>Display Order"></asp:BoundColumn>
                        <asp:BoundColumn HeaderStyle-HorizontalAlign="center"
                            DataField="CategoryName"
                            HeaderText="Category"></asp:BoundColumn>
                        <asp:ButtonColumn Text="Update Question"
                                CommandName="Update">
                            </asp:ButtonColumn>
                        <asp:ButtonColumn Text="Manage Answers"
                                CommandName="Answers">
                            </asp:ButtonColumn>
            </Columns>
        </asp:DataGrid>
        <asp:LinkButton id="NewQuestion" style="Z-INDEX: 104; LEFT: 271px;
                POSITION: absolute; TOP: 72px" runat="server">
                New Question</asp:LinkButton>
        </form>
    </body>
</HTML>
```

The DataGrid in this case is pretty standard and does not require any item-level templates. You do need two custom CommandName columns to provide options for the player to update the question or manage answers for the question.

The code behind the page is pretty straightforward. It retrieves the question data and handles the link request for the questions. Listing 6-18 shows the code for the page.

Listing 6-18. ManageQuestions.aspx.vb

```
Private Sub Page_Load(ByVal sender As System.Object, _
        ByVal e As System.EventArgs) Handles MyBase.Load

    Dim objCMD As New SqlClient.SqlCommand()
    Dim objConn As New SqlClient.SqlConnection()
    Dim strSQL As String
    Dim objDR As SqlClient.SqlDataReader

    ' See if first time page is displayed (not a form postback)
    If Not IsPostBack Then

        ' Set up the connection
        objConn.ConnectionString = Application("strConn")
        objConn.Open()

        ' Query for all questions and the related levels and categories
        ' ordered by level display order and then question
        ' displayordernumber - so it shows all of the
        ' question detail in the order the player will see them
        strSQL = "SELECT Questions.idQuestion, Questions.QuestionText, " & _
        "Questions.DisplayOrderNumber, Levels.LevelName, " & _
        "Categories.CategoryName FROM Levels INNER JOIN (Categories " & _
        "INNER JOIN Questions ON Categories.idCategory = " & _
        "Questions.idCategory) ON Levels.idLevel = Questions.idLevel " & _
        "order by levelorder, DisplayOrderNumber"

        ' Set up the command object
        objCMD.Connection = objConn
        objCMD.CommandText = strSQL

        ' Set up the reader
        objDR = objCMD.ExecuteReader

        ' Set the grid data source
```

```
            dgQuestions.DataSource = objDR

            ' Show the data
            dgQuestions.DataBind()

        End If


    End Sub

    Private Sub dgQuestions_ItemCommand(ByVal source As Object, _
     ByVal e As System.Web.UI.WebControls.DataGridCommandEventArgs) _
    Handles dgQuestions.ItemCommand
        ' e.Item is the row of the DataGrid where the link was
        ' clicked.

        ' Based on the option selected, send the user to the appropriate page
        If LCase(Trim(e.CommandName)) = "update" Then
            ' Update the question
            Server.Transfer("UpdateQuestion.aspx?idQuestion=" & _
                                            e.Item.Cells(0).Text)
        Else
            ' manage the question answers
            Server.Transfer("ManageAnswers.aspx?idQuestion=" & _
                                            e.Item.Cells(0).Text)
        End If

    End Sub

    Private Sub NewQuestion_Click(ByVal sender As System.Object, ByVal e As _
    System.EventArgs) Handles NewLevel.Click, NewQuestion.Click

        ' Send the user to add a new question
        Server.Transfer("NewQuestion.aspx")

    End Sub
```

The first step in the page is to bind the DataGrid to the question data. Once again you see a fairly long query to retrieve the appropriate data. The good news is that there is one less inner join than before because you do not need any player response data. The query joins together the question, category, and level for each question. Then a SQLDataReader object retrieves the results and binds them to the DataGrid.

The `ItemCommand` method of the DataGrid is once again used to handle the link click for the questions. If the Update Question link is clicked, the user is sent to the UpdateQuestion.aspx page. If the Manage Answers link is clicked, the user is sent to the ManageAnswers.aspx page. In both cases, the ID of the selected question is passed on the URL.

Building the Update Question Functionality

Next, you will take a look at the update question process. The goal of this page is to display the question data. This includes showing the current selection for levels and categories. You will use drop-down list boxes to list the available levels and categories to choose from with the current setting defaulted.

NOTE *We will not specifically cover the capability to add a new question. The logic is simple and similar to the update logic except that the question is inserted into the table instead of updated and no existing data needs to be retrieved.*

To build the page, follow these steps:

1. Add a Web form Label control to the page and name it *idQuestion*. Clear the `Text` value of the Label control.

2. Add a Web form TextBox control to the page and name it *QuestionText*. Set the `TextMode` property to *MultiLine* and clear the `Text` property.

3. Add two DropDownList Web form controls to the page, name one *Levels*, and name the other *Categories*.

4. Add a Web form TextBox control to the page (between the two drop-down boxes) and name it *DisplayOrderNumber*. Clear the `Text` property.

5. For each of the TextBox and DropDownList controls, add a corresponding required field validator to ensure an error message is entered for each.

6. Add a LinkButton Web form control and name it *DeleteQuestion*. Set its `Text` property to *Delete Question*.

7. Add a Button Web form control to the page, name it *SubmitUpdateQuestion*, and set its `Text` property to *Update Question*.

8. Finally, add a HTML Label control to the page and set it to *Update Question:*.

Your page should look like Figure 6-9. Listing 6-19 shows the code for the page.

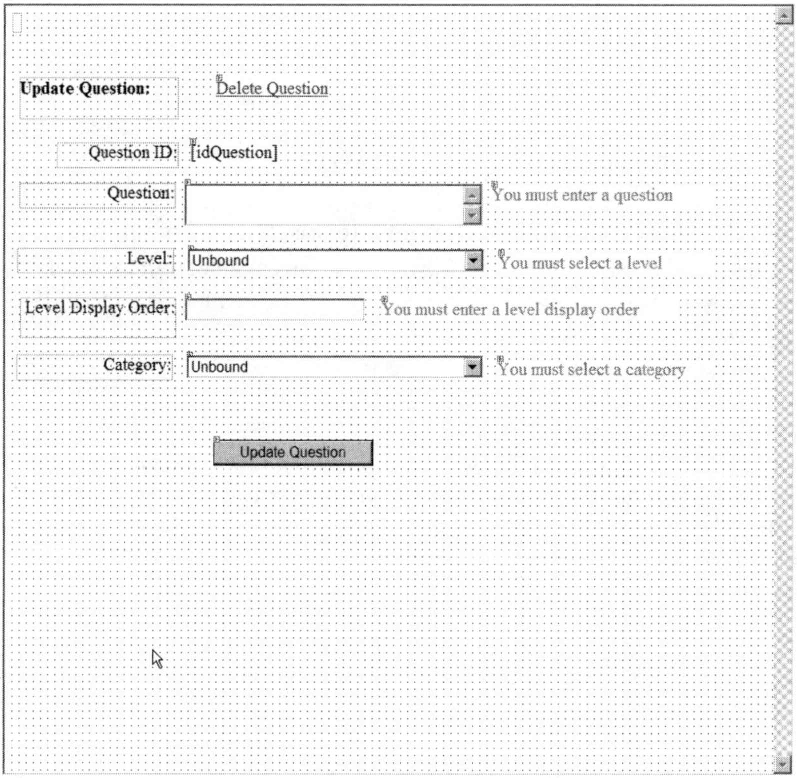

Figure 6-9. The UpdateQuestions.aspx.vb page

Listing 6-19. UpdateQuestions.aspx.vb

```
<%@ Page Language="vb" AutoEventWireup="false" Codebehind="UpdateQuestion.aspx.vb"
Inherits="TriviaGame.UpdateQuestion"%>
<!DOCTYPE HTML PUBLIC "-//W3C//DTD HTML 4.0 Transitional//EN">
<HTML>
    <HEAD>
        <title>UpdateQuestion</title>
        <meta name="GENERATOR" content="Microsoft Visual Studio.NET 7.0">
        <meta name="CODE_LANGUAGE" content="Visual Basic 7.0">
        <meta name="vs_defaultClientScript" content="JavaScript">
        <meta name="vs_targetSchema"
                content="http://schemas.microsoft.com/intellisense/ie5">
```

```
</HEAD>
<body MS_POSITIONING="GridLayout">
    <!-- #Include File="includes/ValidateCheck.inc" -->
    <!-- #Include File="includes/menu.inc" -->
    <DIV style="Z-INDEX: 100; LEFT: 8px; WIDTH: 10px; POSITION: absolute;
                TOP: 8px; HEIGHT: 10px" ms_positioning="text2D">
        <FORM id="Form1" method="post" runat="server">
            <DIV style="DISPLAY: inline; FONT-WEIGHT: bold; Z-INDEX: 100;
                        LEFT: 8px; WIDTH: 180px;
                        POSITION: absolute; TOP: 70px;
                        HEIGHT: 46px"
                        ms_positioning="FlowLayout">
                        Update Question:</DIV>
            <asp:RequiredFieldValidator id="RequiredFieldValidator2"
                        style="Z-INDEX: 111; LEFT: 548px;
                        POSITION: absolute;
                        TOP: 261px" runat="server" Width="243px"
                        ControlToValidate="Levels"
                        ErrorMessage="You must select a  level">
                        </asp:RequiredFieldValidator>
            <asp:RequiredFieldValidator id="RequiredFieldValidator1"
                        style="Z-INDEX: 102; LEFT: 540px;
                        POSITION: absolute;
                        TOP: 187px" runat="server"
                        ControlToValidate="QuestionText"
                        ErrorMessage="You must enter a question"
                        Width="245px">
                        </asp:RequiredFieldValidator>
            <DIV style="DISPLAY: inline; Z-INDEX: 103; LEFT: 8px;
                        WIDTH: 177px; POSITION: absolute; TOP: 185px;
                        HEIGHT: 28px" align="right"
                        ms_positioning="FlowLayout">Question:</DIV>
            <asp:TextBox id="QuestionText" style="Z-INDEX: 104;
                        LEFT: 195px; POSITION: absolute; TOP: 185px"
                        runat="server" Width="336px"
                        TextMode="MultiLine"></asp:TextBox>
                <asp:Button id="SubmitUpdateQuestion"
                        style="Z-INDEX: 105;
                        LEFT: 229px; POSITION: absolute; TOP: 465px"
                        runat="server" Text="Update Question">
                 </asp:Button>
                <asp:RequiredFieldValidator id="RequiredFieldValidator3"
                        style="Z-INDEX: 106; LEFT: 418px;
```

```
                                POSITION: absolute;
                                TOP: 312px" runat="server"
                                ControlToValidate="DisplayOrderNumber"
                                ErrorMessage= _
                                     "You must enter a level display order"
                                Width="333px"></asp:RequiredFieldValidator>
            <DIV style="DISPLAY: inline; Z-INDEX: 107; LEFT: 9px;
                                WIDTH: 177px; POSITION: absolute; TOP: 310px;
                                HEIGHT: 44px" align="right"
                                ms_positioning="FlowLayout">
                                Level Display Order:</DIV>
                        <asp:TextBox id="DisplayOrderNumber"
                                style="Z-INDEX: 108; LEFT: 196px;
                                POSITION: absolute; TOP: 310px"
                                runat="server"></asp:TextBox>
                        <asp:DropDownList id="Levels" style="Z-INDEX: 109;
                                LEFT: 199px; POSITTION: absolute; TOP: 257px"
                                runat="server" Width="334px"></asp:DropDownList>
            <DIV style="DISPLAY: inline; Z-INDEX: 110; LEFT: 6px;
                                WIDTH: 177px; POSITION: absolute; TOP: 256px;
                                HEIGHT: 28px" align="right"
                                ms_positioning="FlowLayout">Level:</DIV>
                    </DIV>
                <asp:linkbutton id="DeleteQuestion" style="Z-INDEX: 111;
                        LEFT: 239px; POSITION: absolute; TOP: 79px"
                        runat="server">Delete Question</asp:linkbutton>
                <asp:label id="idQuestion" style="Z-INDEX: 102;
                        LEFT: 209px; POSITION: absolute; TOP: 149px"
                        runat="server"></asp:label>
            <DIV style="DISPLAY: inline; Z-INDEX: 103; LEFT: 58px;
                        WIDTH: 138px; POSITION: absolute; TOP: 149px;
                        HEIGHT: 28px" align="right"
                        ms_positioning="FlowLayout">Question ID:</DIV>
                    <asp:DropDownList id="Categories" style="Z-INDEX: 117;
                        LEFT: 206px; POSITION: absolute; TOP: 381px"
                        runat="server" Width="334px"></asp:DropDownList>
                    <DIV style="DISPLAY: inline; Z-INDEX: 118; LEFT: 13px;
                        WIDTH: 177px; POSITION: absolute; TOP: 380px;
                        HEIGHT: 28px" align="right"
                        ms_positioning="FlowLayout">Category:</DIV>
                    <asp:RequiredFieldValidator id="RequiredFieldValidator4"
                        style="Z-INDEX: 119; LEFT: 555px; POSITION: absolute;
                        TOP: 385px" runat="server"
```

```
                    ErrorMessage="You must select a category"
                    ControlToValidate="Categories"
                    Width="243px"></asp:RequiredFieldValidator>

       </FORM>
     </body>
</HTML>
```

No modifications or additional updates are required for the page as generated by Visual Studio. The code-behind module handles all of the logic to wire up the data to the form and manage the deletes and updates. Listing 6-20 shows the code for the page.

Listing 6-20. UpdateQuestion.aspx.vb

```
Private Sub Page_Load(ByVal sender As System.Object, _
    ByVal e As System.EventArgs) Handles MyBase.Load
    'Put user code to initialize the page here

    Dim objCMDLevels As New SqlClient.SqlCommand()
    Dim objCMDCat As New SqlClient.SqlCommand()
    Dim objCMDDR As New SqlClient.SqlCommand()
    Dim objConnLevels As New SqlClient.SqlConnection()
    Dim objConnCat As New SqlClient.SqlConnection()
    Dim objConnDR As New SqlClient.SqlConnection()
    Dim strSQL As String
    Dim intCnt As Integer
    Dim objDRLevels As SqlClient.SqlDataReader
    Dim objDRCat As SqlClient.SqlDataReader
    Dim objDR As SqlClient.SqlDataReader

    '  First time the page is loaded (not a form post)
    If Not IsPostBack Then

        '  Open several connections for getting the page data

        '  Open the connection
        objConnLevels.ConnectionString = Application("strConn")
        objConnLevels.Open()

        '  Set the command connection
        objCMDLevels.Connection = objConnLevels
```

```
'  Open the connection
objConnCat.ConnectionString = Application("strConn")
objConnCat.Open()


'  Set the command connection
objCMDCat.Connection = objConnCat


'  Open the connection
objConnDR.ConnectionString = Application("strConn")
objConnDR.Open()


'  Set the command connection
objCMDDR.Connection = objConnDR


'  Build query to get the level data
strSQL = "Select * from levels order by LevelOrder"


'  Set the command query
objCMDLevels.CommandText = strSQL


'  Set the reader
objDRLevels = objCMDLevels.ExecuteReader


'  Assign the drop-down list data source and fields to display
Levels.DataSource = objDRLevels
Levels.DataTextField = "LevelName"
Levels.DataValueField = "idLevel"
Levels.DataBind()


'  Build the query to get the categories
strSQL = "Select * from categories"


'  Set the command query
objCMDCat.CommandText = strSQL


'  Set the reader
objDRCat = objCMDCat.ExecuteReader


'  Assign the drop-down list data source and fields to display
Categories.DataSource = objDRCat
Categories.DataTextField = "CategoryName"
Categories.DataValueField = "idCategory"
Categories.DataBind()
```

```
        ' Build the query to get the question data
        strSQL = "select * from questions where idQuestion = " & _
        Request.QueryString("idQuestion")

        ' Set the command query
        objCMDDR.CommandText = strSQL

        ' Set the reader
        objDR = objCMDDR.ExecuteReader

        ' Get the data
        objDR.Read()

        ' Display the data
        idQuestion.Text = objDR.Item("idQuestion")
        QuestionText.Text = objDR.Item("QuestionText")
        DisplayOrderNumber.Text = objDR.Item("DisplayOrderNumber")

        ' Select the current level
        For intCnt = 0 To (Levels.Items.Count - 1)
            If Levels.Items(intCnt).Value = objDR.Item("idLevel") Then
                Levels.SelectedIndex = intCnt
            End If
        Next

        ' Select the current category
        For intCnt = 0 To (Categories.Items.Count - 1)
            If Categories.Items(intCnt).Value = objDR.Item("idCategory") Then
                Categories.SelectedIndex = intCnt
            End If
        Next

    End If

End Sub

Private Sub DeleteQuestion_Click(ByVal sender As System.Object, _
        ByVal e As System.EventArgs) Handles DeleteQuestion.Click

    Dim objCMD As New SqlClient.SqlCommand()
    Dim objConn As New SqlClient.SqlConnection()
    Dim strSQL As String
```

```
              '  Open the connection
              objConn.ConnectionString = Application("strConn")
              objConn.Open()


              '  Set the command connection
              objCMD.Connection = objConn


              '  Build the delete query
              strSQL = "Delete from Questions where idQuestion = " & idQuestion.Text


              '  Set the command text
              objCMD.CommandText = strSQL


              '  Execute the query
              objCMD.ExecuteNonQuery()


              '  You also need to delete any related answers
              strSQL = "Delete from Answers where idQuestion = " & idQuestion.Text


              '  Execute the query
              objCMD.ExecuteNonQuery()


              '  Send the user to the question management page
              Server.Transfer("ManageQuestions.aspx")

    End Sub

    Private Sub SubmitUpdateQuestion_Click(ByVal sender As System.Object, _
              ByVal e As System.EventArgs) Handles SubmitUpdateQuestion.Click

          Dim objCMD As New SqlClient.SqlCommand()
          Dim objConn As New SqlClient.SqlConnection()
          Dim strSQL As String

              '  Open the connection
              objConn.ConnectionString = Application("strConn")
              objConn.Open()

              '  Build the update query
              strSQL = "Update Questions set QuestionText = '" & _
                      Replace(QuestionText.Text, "'", "''") & _
                      "', DisplayOrderNumber = " & _
                      DisplayOrderNumber.Text & ", idLevel=" & _
```

```
            Levels.SelectedItem.Value & ", idCategory = " & _
            Categories.SelectedItem.Value & " where idQuestion = " & _
            idQuestion.Text

    ' Set the command connection
    objCMD.Connection = objConn

    ' Set the command query
    objCMD.CommandText = strSQL

    ' Execute the query
    objCMD.ExecuteNonQuery()

    ' Send the user to the question management page
    Server.Transfer("ManageQuestions.aspx")

End Sub
```

When the page loads for the first time, a number of actions need to take place in order to display the current question data. The first is to populate the levels and categories drop-down boxes with the data from the Levels and Categories tables. SQL Command and DataReader objects are created with appropriate queries to retrieve the data. Note that the level data is ordered by the display order. The DataTextField property and DataValueField property are set to the name and ID fields. Then the drop-down list data sources are set to the corresponding data reader.

The next step is to retrieve the question data. This will include the currently assigned level and category. The text fields for question text and display order number are set to the data field values. The question ID label is set to the ID of the question.

Next, you need to select the current level and category in the drop-down lists. You do this by looping through each item in the drop-down list and matching the current value to the drop-down list item. When there is a match, the SelectedIndex is set to the matching item.

The delete logic handles removing the question and corresponding answers for the question. You want to be sure to not leave any "dangling" answers in the database that are not assigned to questions. Two queries are built to delete the question and answers, and then the user is sent back to the manage questions page.

TIP *Because you are not using SQL stored procedures in the code examples to delete the questions and answers, theoretically something could happen (like a system shutdown) between the two deletes that would cause the second delete to not happen and have unlinked answers. Ideally, the two delete queries would be wrapped into one transaction in a stored procedure and executed. That way, both queries will have to be executed in order for the full transaction to be committed.*

The final function is to update the question data. A SQL query is built to update the question based on the data in the form. The IDs of the category and level are read from the drop-down lists using the `SelectedItem.value` property.

We are not going to review the remaining pages of the administrator. The answer, level, and category management pages are straightforward and follow the same code logic as reviewed. One note on the answer pages is that they also have to track the ID of the question for the answers.

NOTE *The rest of the files can be downloaded from the Downloads section of the Apress Web site (http://www.apress.com).*

Utilizing the Trivia Game Administrator

At last, the administrator is ready to use. Let's first look at the player management functionality. Figure 6-10 shows the page.

All of the current players are listed. When you click the history page, the full question and answer history displays along with the player's score. Figure 6-11 shows the page with sample data. Note that the correct responses are checked.

Next, let's look at the question management page. Figure 6-12 shows the page with sample questions set up for four levels with two questions in each level. Note the levels are in order, and the questions within the levels are in order. Also, the category for each question displays.

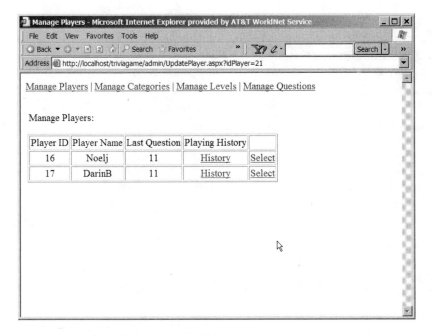

Figure 6-10. The administrator page

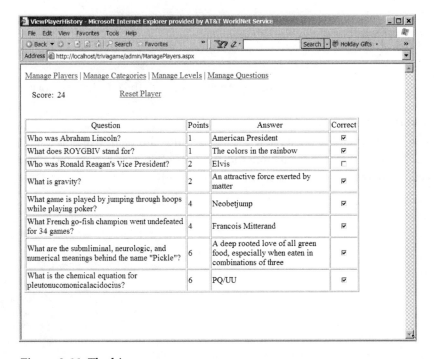

Figure 6-11. The history page

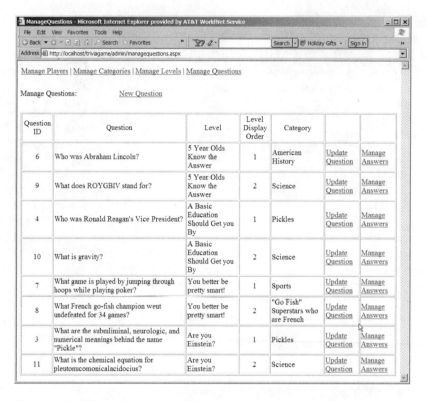

Figure 6-12. The question management page

Figure 6-13 shows the question management page with the current category and level data selected.

The rest of the pages work similarly.

That does it for building the database structure and administrative functionality of the poll engine. Next, you will build the user side of the trivia game and learn how you can display the game in Flash and interface with the database.

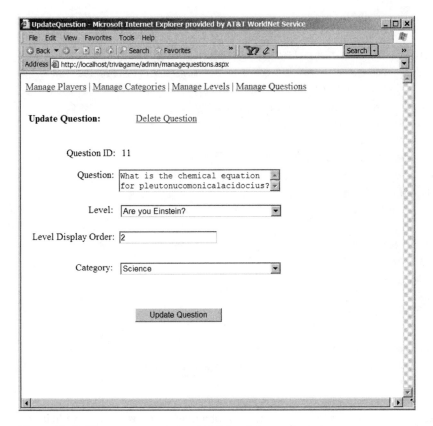

Figure 6-13. The current category and level data selected

Building the User .NET Pages

You need to build the pages that will pull the trivia game data and feed it to the Flash interface. These pages will take the user-provided data from the Flash interface and either register, log in, or show trivia game data to the user. They also will track the user's responses for the questions.

The first page to build is the default page that loads the Flash object. Create a new file in the project and save it as *Default.aspx*. Insert the Flash object as shown in Listing 6-21.

Listing 6-21. Flash Object Reference

```
<OBJECT classid="clsid:D27CDB6E-AE6D-11cf-96B8-444553540000" ↵
codebase="http://download.macromedia.com/pub/shockwave/cabs/flash/swflash.cab↵
#version=6,0,0,0" WIDTH="710" HEIGHT="430" id="triviaGame" ALIGN="" VIEWASTEXT>
    <PARAM NAME="movie" VALUE="triviaGame.swf">
    <PARAM NAME="loop" VALUE="false">
    <PARAM NAME="menu" VALUE="false">
    <PARAM NAME="quality" VALUE="best">
    <PARAM NAME="bgcolor" VALUE="#FFFFFF">
    <EMBED src="triviaGame.swf"
     loop="false"
     menu="false"
     quality="best"
     bgcolor="#FFFFFF"
     WIDTH="710"
     HEIGHT="430"
     NAME="triviaGame"
     ALIGN=""
     TYPE="application/x-shockwave-flash"
     PLUGINSPAGE="http://www.macromedia.com/go/getflashplayer"></EMBED>
</OBJECT>
```

Next, you need to handle the registration of a new user. Create a new file in the project and save it as *Register.aspx*. This page is called by the Flash interface when the user chooses to register vs. log in (see Listing 6-22).

Listing 6-22. Register.aspx

```
Private Sub Page_Load(ByVal sender As System.Object, _
        ByVal e As System.EventArgs) Handles MyBase.Load

    Dim objCMD As New SqlClient.SqlCommand()
    Dim objConn As New SqlClient.SqlConnection()
    Dim objDR As SqlClient.SqlDataReader
    Dim strSQL As String
    Dim blnResult As Boolean

    Response.Write("dummy=1")

    '  Set the connection
    objConn.ConnectionString = Application("strConn")
```

```vbnet
' Open the connection
objConn.Open()

' Set the command connection
objCMD.Connection = objConn

' See if an existing player with the same name exists
strSQL = "select idPlayer from Players where PlayerName= '" & _
Replace(Request.QueryString("PlayerName"), "'", "''") & "'"

' Set the command query
objCMD.CommandText = strSQL

' Set the reader
objDR = objCMD.ExecuteReader

' Get the data and see if anything is returned
blnResult = objDR.Read

' If no data returned
If blnResult = False Then

    ' Build a SQL statement to insert the new player
    strSQL = "insert into Players(PlayerName, Password) values('" & _
    Request.QueryString("PlayerName") & "', '" & _
    Request.QueryString("Password") & "')"

    ' Set the command query
    objCMD.CommandText = strSQL

    ' Close the reader
    objDR.Close()

    ' Execute the query
    objCMD.ExecuteNonQuery()

    strSQL = "select idPlayer from Players where PlayerName= '" & _
    Replace(Request.QueryString("PlayerName"), "'", "''") & _
    "' and Password = '" & _
    Replace(Request.QueryString("Password"), "'", "''") & "'"

    ' Set the command query
    objCMD.CommandText = strSQL
```

```
                              '  Set the reader
                              objDR = objCMD.ExecuteReader

                              '  Get the result of the read
                              blnResult = objDR.Read

                              '  If no results, then there is no player match
                              If blnResult = False Then
                                  Response.Write("&Error=There was an error registering " & _
                                            "your information.")
                              Else
                                  '  There is a match, store the player ID and
                                  '  send the user to the triva home page
                                  Session("idPlayer") = objDR.Item("idPlayer")
                              End If

                      Else

                          '  Indicate there is a user with the name already
                          Response.Write("&Error=The Player Name you selected " & _
                                        "has already been taken.")

                      End If

                      Response.Write("&done=1")

                  End Sub

          End Class
```

A couple of key things happen in this page. First, you need to ensure that the user registration is unique. An initial query executes that checks to see if there is a matching user. If there is, then you are going to indicate to the user that they need to pick a different login name.

If there is no matching user, then you insert the player's information into the database. After the insert is done, then you retrieve the ID of the newly inserted player from the database. Finally, you indicate to the Flash object an error or that you are ready to move to the question and answer process.

If the player is logging back in, the process to check and see if there is a valid user is similar to the subset of code for registration that does the same process. We are not going to explicitly show the login page logic here.

TIP *If you are using stored procedures, you can use the* @@Identity *SQL metavalue to get the new ID of the player after the insert instead of executing another query.*

Now you are ready to show the questions to the players. The Question.aspx page handles the logic of getting the next question and indicating the question data to the Flash object. Add Question.aspx to your project (see Listing 6-23 for the first part of the code for the page).

Listing 6-23. Question.aspx

```
Private Sub Page_Load(ByVal sender As System.Object, _
        ByVal e As System.EventArgs) Handles MyBase.Load
    Dim objCMD As New SqlClient.SqlCommand()
    Dim objConn As New SqlClient.SqlConnection()
    Dim strSQL As String
    Dim intLastQuestion As Integer
    Dim objDR As SqlClient.SqlDataReader
    Dim blnResult As Boolean

    Response.Write("dummy=1")

    ' Set the connection
    objConn.ConnectionString = Application("strConn")

    ' Open the connection
    objConn.Open()

    ' Set the command connection
    objCMD.Connection = objConn

    ' Get the last question for the player
    strSQL = "select LastQuestion from Players where idPlayer = " & _
    Session("idPlayer")

    ' Set the command query
    objCMD.CommandText = strSQL

    ' Set the reader
    objDR = objCMD.ExecuteReader()
```

```
'  Get the data
blnResult = objDR.Read()

'  See if the lastquestion field is null
If Not objDR.IsDBNull(0) Then

    '  Get the last question
    intLastQuestion = objDR.Item("LastQuestion")

    '  Get the last questions display order and level order
    strSQL = "SELECT Questions.DisplayOrderNumber, " & _
    "Levels.LevelOrder FROM Questions INNER JOIN Levels " & _
    "ON Levels.idLevel = Questions.idLevel where " & _
    "questions.idQuestion = " & intLastQuestion

    '  Close the reader for reuse
    objDR.Close()

    '  Set the command query
    objCMD.CommandText = strSQL

    '  Set the reader
    objDR = objCMD.ExecuteReader()

    '  Get the data
    objDR.Read()

    '  Store the starting level and the starting question display order
    Session("DisplayOrderNum") = objDR.Item("DisplayOrderNumber")

    Session("LevelOrder") = objDR.Item("LevelOrder")

    '  Get the next question and indicate that this isn't a new user
    GetNextQuestionFromDB(True)

Else

    '  Get the next question and indicate this is a new user
    GetNextQuestionFromDB(False)

End If
```

```
'   Always display the current score
DisplayScore()
Response.Write("&done=1")
```

```
End Sub
```

When the page loads, you need to perform a couple of checks. The first is to see if the player has seen a question. You do this by checking the LastQuestion field for the player. If the value is NULL, then they have not seen a question yet, and you need to retrieve the first question in the display order. If there is an existing question, then you retrieve the current level and display order. Then you call the GetNextQuestionFromDB subroutine to get the next question. Note the DisplayScore subroutine is also called to calculate the current score.

The GetNextQuestionFromDB subroutine handles getting the next question in the level/display order hierarchy. A flag is sent into it to indicate whether you should get the first question or the next question. The first question is retrieved when there is a new player. Listing 6-24 shows the GetNextQuestionFromDB subroutine.

Listing 6-24. Question.aspx, Continued

```
Private Sub GetNextQuestionFromDB(ByVal getnextflag As Integer)

    'Put user code to initialize the page here
    Dim objCMD As New SqlClient.SqlCommand()
    Dim objConn As New SqlClient.SqlConnection()
    Dim strSQL As String
    Dim intCnt As Integer
    Dim objDR As SqlClient.SqlDataReader
    Dim blnResult As Boolean

    '  Set up the connection

    objConn.ConnectionString = Application("strConn")
    objConn.Open()

    '  Set the command connection
    objCMD.Connection = objConn

    '  See if this is a new user or an in-process user
    If getnextflag = True Then

        '  Get the next question in the level for in process users
        strSQL = "SELECT Questions.idQuestion, Questions.QuestionText, " & _
        "Questions.DisplayOrderNumber, Levels.LevelName, " & _
```

```
                "Levels.LevelOrder, Levels.LevelColor, Categories.CategoryName " & _
                "FROM Levels INNER JOIN (Categories INNER JOIN Questions ON " & _
                "Categories.idCategory = Questions.idCategory) ON " & _
                "Levels.idLevel = Questions.idLevel where Levels.LevelOrder = " & _
                Session("LevelOrder") & " and Questions.DisplayOrderNumber > " & _
                Session("DisplayOrderNum") & _
                " order by levelorder, DisplayOrderNumber"

        Else

            ' Get all questions orderd by level and display order to start the user
            ' Note this is only executed when it is a new user who has not seen a
            ' question before
            strSQL = "SELECT Questions.idQuestion, Questions.QuestionText, " & _
                "Questions.DisplayOrderNumber, Levels.LevelName, " & _
                "Levels.LevelOrder, Levels.LevelColor, Categories.CategoryName " & _
                "FROM Levels INNER JOIN (Categories INNER JOIN Questions ON " & _
                "Categories.idCategory = Questions.idCategory) ON " & _
                "Levels.idLevel = Questions.idLevel order by levelorder, " & _
                "DisplayOrderNumber"

        End If

        ' Set the query
        objCMD.CommandText = strSQL

        ' Set the reader
        objDR = objCMD.ExecuteReader()

        ' Get data and see if there is a result
        blnResult = objDR.Read()

        ' check to see if there is a next question
        ' If not then you may be moving to a new level
        ' or may be at the last level and question
        If blnResult = False Then

            ' Query for the next higher level and the first question
            strSQL = "SELECT Questions.idQuestion, Questions.QuestionText, " & _
                "Questions.DisplayOrderNumber, Levels.LevelName, " & _
                "Levels.LevelOrder, Levels.LevelColor, Categories.CategoryName " & _
                "FROM Levels INNER JOIN (Categories INNER JOIN Questions ON " & _
                "Categories.idCategory = Questions.idCategory) ON " & _
```

```
        "Levels.idLevel = Questions.idLevel where Levels.LevelOrder > " & _
        Session("LevelOrder") & " order by levelorder, DisplayOrderNumber"

        ' Close the reader for reuse
        objDR.Close()

        ' Set the command query
        objCMD.CommandText = strSQL

        ' Set the reader
        objDR = objCMD.ExecuteReader()

        ' Get the data and see if there is a result
        blnResult = objDR.Read()

        ' If there is no result then there are no more questions
        ' Send the user to the game over page
        If blnResult = False Then
            Response.Write("&GameOver=1")
            blnGameOver = True
        End If
    End If
End If
If blnResult Then

    ' Save the current display order and level for future queries
    Session("DisplayOrderNum") = objDR.Item("DisplayOrderNumber")
    Session("LevelOrder") = objDR.Item("LevelOrder")

    ' Save the question for future queries
    Session("idQuestion") = objDR.Item("idQuestion")

    ' Show the level with the appropriate color
    Response.Write("&Level=" & objDR.Item("LevelName"))
    Response.Write("&LevelColor=" & _
            Replace(objDR.Item("LevelColor"), "#", ""))

    ' Show the question category
    Response.Write("&Category=" & objDR.Item("CategoryName"))

    ' Show the question
    Response.Write("&Question=" & objDR.Item("QuestionText"))
```

```
    ' Get the answers for the question
    strSQL = "SELECT idAnswer, AnswerText FROM Answers where " & _
    "idQuestion = " & objDR.Item("idQuestion")

    ' Close the reader for reuse
    objDR.Close()

    ' Set the query
    objCMD.CommandText = strSQL

    ' Set the reader
    objDR = objCMD.ExecuteReader()

    Dim i As Integer = 0
    While objDR.Read
        i = i + 1
        Response.Write("&Answer" & i & "ID=" & objDR("idAnswer") & _
        "&Answer" & i & "Text=" & objDR("AnswerText"))
    End While
    Response.Write("&numAnswers=" & i)
  End If
End Sub
```

The logic in this subroutine gets a little complicated. Because you are moving through levels of questions, you have to get the next question in the current level. If there is no next question, then you move to the next higher level and get the first question. You do all this with a series of SQL queries that will look familiar to the ones used in the administrator. Finally, you retrieve the question details, and you create the query string with the question and answer data for the Flash object. You also have to see if there are no more questions, and if not, you indicate to the Flash object that the GameOver.aspx page should be called.

The last subroutine in the page calculates the current score (see Listing 6-25). It executes a query that sums up all of question points for the current set of questions answered. Note that you have to account for the fact that there could be no score yet. The final score is written out for the Flash object to read.

Listing 6-25. Questions.aspx, Continued

```
  Private Sub DisplayScore()

    Dim objCMD As New SqlClient.SqlCommand()
    Dim objConn As New SqlClient.SqlConnection()
    Dim strSQL As String
```

```
        Dim objDR As SqlClient.SqlDataReader
        Dim blnResult As Boolean

        ' Set up the connection
        objConn.ConnectionString = Application("strConn")
        objConn.Open()

        ' Set the command connection
        objCMD.Connection = objConn

        ' Get the total points by combining responses, questions, and levels
        strSQL = "SELECT Sum(Levels.QuestionPoints) FROM (Questions INNER " & _
        "JOIN (Responses INNER JOIN Answers ON Responses.idAnswer = " & _
        "Answers.idAnswer) ON Questions.idQuestion = Answers.idQuestion) " & _
        "INNER JOIN Levels ON Questions.idLevel = Levels.idLevel WHERE " & _
        "Responses.idPlayer=" & Session("idPlayer") & " and answers.correct = 1"

        ' Set the command query
        objCMD.CommandText = strSQL

        ' Set the reader
        objDR = objCMD.ExecuteReader

        ' Read the data and see if results are returned
        blnResult = objDR.Read()

        ' If results are returned
        If blnResult = True Then
            ' If the score is no NULL
          If Not objDR.IsDBNull(0) Then
                ' Show score
                Response.Write("&Score=" & objDR.Item(0))
          Else
                ' Show 0 score
                Response.Write("&Score=0")
          End If
        Else
            ' Show 0 score
            Response.Write("&Score=0")
        End If

    End Sub
End Class
```

The next page handles processing an answer provided by the player. The page is called from the Flash object when the user gives a response. Create a new page in your project and save it as *Answer.aspx*. Listing 6-26 shows the code for the page.

Listing 6-26. Answer.aspx

```
Private Sub Page_Load(ByVal sender As System.Object, _
ByVal e As System.EventArgs) _
Handles MyBase.Load

        Response.Write("dummy=1")

        'check for answer sent from Flash
        'if not one, send error back
        'else process answer
        If Not Request.QueryString("Answers") <> "" Then
        Response.Write("&Error=ANSWER NOT RECEIVED BY SERVER" & Chr(13) & _
            Chr(13) & "(i.e. You probably didn't choose one.)")
        Else
            Dim objCMD As New SqlClient.SqlCommand()
            Dim objConn As New SqlClient.SqlConnection()
            Dim strSQL As String
            Dim objDR As SqlClient.SqlDataReader

            '  Set up the connection
            objConn.ConnectionString = Application("strConn")
            objConn.Open()

            '  Set the command connection
            objCMD.Connection = objConn

            '  Update the player's last question
            strSQL = "update Players set LastQuestion = " & _
            Session("idQuestion") & _
            " where idPlayer = " & Session("idPlayer")

            '  Set the command query
            objCMD.CommandText = strSQL

            '  Execute the query
            objCMD.ExecuteNonQuery()
```

```
' Insert the player's response for the question
strSQL = "insert into Responses(idPlayer, idQuestion, idAnswer) " & _
"values(" & Session("idPlayer") & ", " & Session("idQuestion") & _
", " & Request.QueryString("Answers") & ")"

' Set the command query
objCMD.CommandText = strSQL

' Execute the query
objCMD.ExecuteNonQuery()

' Get the correct setting for the answer
strSQL = "select answers.correct from responses inner join answers "&_
"on responses.idAnswer = Answers.idAnswer where responses.idAnswer = " & _
Request.QueryString("Answers")

' Set the command query
objCMD.CommandText = strSQL

' Set the reader
objDR = objCMD.ExecuteReader

' Get the data
objDR.Read()

' If it was the correct answer, then say so; otherwise indicate incorrect
If objDR.Item("Correct") = True Then
    Response.Write("&Feedback=1")
Else
    Response.Write("&Feedback=0")
End If
End If

Response.Write("&done=1")
End Sub
```

The first thing you do is update the LastQuestion field of the player data. This ensures you know the last question viewed. Then, you store the response to the question as well. Finally, you check to see if the player's response is correct. You create an appropriate query string parameter for the Flash object to indicate if the response is correct.

The final .aspx page handles recapping the player's session. This will display to the user in the Flash object. Add the GameOver.aspx page to your project (see Listing 6-27).

Listing 6-27. GameOver.aspx

```
Private Sub Page_Load(ByVal sender As System.Object, ByVal e As System.EventArgs) _
Handles MyBase.Load

        Dim objCMD As New SqlClient.SqlCommand()
        Dim objConn As New SqlClient.SqlConnection()
        Dim strSQL As String
        Dim blnResult As Boolean
        Dim objDR As SqlClient.SqlDataReader
        Dim score As String
        Dim cnt As Integer

        ' Set the DB connection
        objConn.ConnectionString = Application("strConn")
        objConn.Open()

        ' Get the score
        strSQL = "SELECT Sum(Levels.QuestionPoints) FROM " & _
        "(Questions INNER JOIN " & _
        "(Responses INNER JOIN Answers ON Responses.idAnswer = " & _
        "Answers.idAnswer) ON Questions.idQuestion = Answers.idQuestion) " & _
        "INNER JOIN Levels ON Questions.idLevel = Levels.idLevel WHERE " & _
        "Responses.idPlayer=" & Session("idPlayer") & " and answers.correct = 1"

        ' Set the command connection
        objCMD.Connection = objConn

        ' Set the command query
        objCMD.CommandText = strSQL

        ' Set the reader
        objDR = objCMD.ExecuteReader

        ' Read the data
        blnResult = objDR.Read()

        ' if there is a result
        If blnResult = True Then
            ' Show the score
```

```
        If Not objDR.IsDBNull(0) Then
            score = objDR.Item(0)
        Else
            score = score + 0
        End If

    Else
        '  Show a score of 0
        score = 0
    End If


'  Close the reader for future use
objDR.Close()


'  Get the question responses and join with the level of the
'  question to get the point score and the answer text
strSQL = "SELECT questions.questiontext, Levels.QuestionPoints, " & _
"Answers.AnswerText, Answers.Correct FROM (Questions INNER JOIN " & _
"(Responses INNER JOIN Answers ON Responses.idAnswer = " & _
"Answers.idAnswer) ON Questions.idQuestion = Answers.idQuestion) " & _
"INNER JOIN Levels ON Questions.idLevel = Levels.idLevel WHERE " & _
"(((Responses.idPlayer)=" & Session("idPlayer") & ")) order by " & _
"levels.levelorder, questions.displayordernumber"


'  Set the query
objCMD.CommandText = strSQL


'  Set the reader
objDR = objCMD.ExecuteReader
Response.Write("dummy=1&strSummary=")
Response.Write("<b><u>FINAL SCORE: " & score & "</u></b><br><br>")
While objDR.Read
    Response.Write("<b>Question: </b><u>" & objDR("QuestionText") & _
    "</u> - was worth <b>" & objDR("QuestionPoints") & _
    "</b> Points<br><b>You Answered:</b> " & objDR("AnswerText") & _
    "<br>You answered this question ")
    If objDR("Correct") Then
        Response.Write("<b>correctly</b>.<br><br>")
    Else
        Response.Write("<b>incorrectly</b>.<br><br>")
    End If
End While
Response.Write("&done=1")
End Sub
```

The steps in this page are pretty straightforward. The first thing is to get the score so you can display it to the user. This follows the same logic as the `DisplayScore` subroutine reviewed previously. Then you retrieve all of the questions and responses for that player from the database using a SQL query that joins the levels, questions, answers, and responses for the player.

Next, you are going to build a query string parameter that actually contains limited HTML. That HTML can then be displayed in the Flash object, as you will see in the next section.

That does it for the .NET user pages. Most of the logic is straightforward. Perhaps the most complex, as with the administrator, is understanding the SQL queries and what is being returned. Following the same steps to break down the query, as you did in the administrator section, will help to make them more understandable. Futhermore, many of the queries repeat the same logic as those in the administrator.

Next, you will start building the Flash user interface and see all of this hard work come together.

Building the Flash User Interface

You are going to use a few new techniques and some new capabilities of Flash MX in this project. You are also going to use many of the same methods you used in projects from previous chapters—there will just be more of them in this game. Let's start where you have in all of the other projects. . . .

Planning the Trivia Game Interface

Again, you will ask yourself the same questions: What does this interface need to do? What should it to look like? How do you get it to do what it is supposed to do?

When finished, this interface will display a login/registration screen, display questions and answers, receive user input on those answers, display the correctness (or not) of the chosen answers, display the score, inform the user of all applicable information related to the current game, be the go-between of the database and the game user passing data back and forth between the two. Piece of cake, right?

As far as what it needs to look like, you know that this game is going to be a Web-based game, so it should fit within a browser window. You typically standardize what sizes you are considering when designing applications such as this. Most Internet users use a screen resolution of at least 800-pixels wide by 600-pixels high. So, to design keeping that in mind, you generally choose to create Web sites and Flash interfaces somewhere around 750 × 425. This should fit within most browser windows. You will build the trivia game to be at 710 × 430.

You can create the graphics for any sort of game within Flash itself or in an external program, such as Adobe Photoshop, Adobe Illustrator, Macromedia Free-Hand, and so on, and then import them into Flash. For this game, we created the graphics using Photoshop and saved them as .png files. We did this because Flash can read the *alpha*, or transparency, channels that are saved within .png files and make whatever should be transparent in the image actually transparent in the Flash. We have included all the graphics used in the trivia game in the Downloads section of the Apress Web site (`http://www.apress.com`).

The last issue is getting Flash to do what you need it to do. You are going to set up several different areas, or *stations*, within the Flash movie, and each will have its own purpose within the interface. Each station will provide some sort of processing that will drive the interface to do what is needed. Some stations will process and display some data and send Flash to another station. Some will call ASP.NET scripts, which will send or receive data to or from the database. It is a easy way to organize your necessary actions and create a functional interface.

Building the Trivia Game Interface

Let's jump right in and start building the interface.

Creating the Interface and Initialization Objects

Open Flash MX and use the Properties Panel to set your movie size to 710 × 430, the frames per second (fps) to 30, and make sure the background color is white. Save the file as *trivia.swf*.

Rename the only layer in your movie to *control*.

 TIP *Rename a layer by double-clicking the layer name and typing the new name.*

On the Timeline for the control layer, click keyframe 10, selecting that frame. Press F6 (or choose Insert ➤ Keyframe). Using the Properties Panel, type *initialize* in the frame label textbox.

Use the same method as previously to create blank keyframes on the control layer in Frame 20 (name it *initialize2*), Frame 30 (name it *login*), Frame 40 (name it *register*), Frame 50 (name it *question*), Frame 60 (name it *question2*), Frame 70 (name it *answer*), Frame 80 (name it *continue*), Frame 90 (name it *gameover*), and Frame 100 (name it *error*). Now click Frame 110 and press F5 (or choose Insert ➤ Frame). The only reason you have left 10 frames between each keyframe is to make it easy to see the label names on the Timeline. This will make it much easier to find the stations as you build this interface.

Click Frame 10 again (the *initialize* station). Enter the code from Listing 6-28 into the Actions Panel for this frame. This code simply initializes some global variables used as settings for the game. You can change the first two variables, fadeRate and TimeoutLength, to fit your personal preferences, but the defaults work fine.

Listing 6-28. The Initialize Station

```
stop();
_root.fadeRate = 5; //how fast things fade in and out
_root.TimeoutLength = 10; //seconds to keep trying to contact server
_root.error=""; //initialize error variable and set it to nothing
```

Creating Interface Layers

Next, you are going to create all the layers that will hold the elements of your interface. Click the Insert Layer button on the Timeline. Now click it six more times, creating a total of seven layers in addition to the control layer. Now rename them starting with the layer just above the control layer, moving upwards in this order: *interface png, greenLight, redLight, level/score, cat/quest/answ, content1, content2.* Your finished layers list should look like Figure 6-14.

Figure 6-14. The layers

On the content1 layer, click Frame 1. To create the splash screen graphic, we just used some of the drawing tools, scribbled on the screen, and then typed some text over it. Feel free to take liberty with the splash graphic and create whatever you like here. When finished creating the graphic, select everything in the frame and press F8 (or choose Insert ➤ Convert to Symbol). Name the new symbol *splash* and make sure the Movie Clip option is selected. Click OK. Using the Properties Panel, give it an instance name of *splash*. In that same layer, click Frame 20 on the Timeline and press F7 (or choose Insert ➤ Blank Keyframe).

On the interface png layer, click Frame 10 and press F6 (or choose Insert ➤ Keyframe). Now press Control+R (or choose File ➤ Import) and find the triviaGame.png file in the files you downloaded from the Web site. If you need to use the Align Panel to make sure the image is centered, do so now. With the image selected, Press F8 (or choose Insert ➤ Convert to Symbol). Name the new symbol *interface* and make sure the Movie Clip option is selected. Click OK. With the new MovieClip selected, use the Properties Panel to give it an instance name of *interface*. Also, in the Properties Panel, click the Color drop-down list and select Alpha from the list. Set the value to 0% (zero). The interface graphic should be invisible now.

Open the Actions Panel, make sure the interface MovieClip is selected, and enter the code from Listing 6-29 into the Actions Panel for the clip. This simply fades the interface into view at the rate set in the global variable of fadeRate (which you set in the initialize station) and then sends the Flash to the initialize2 station. The fade is just sort of a fancy extra to make the game seem that much cooler. It is easy to accomplish yet effective.

Listing 6-29. Interface Clip

```
onClipEvent(enterFrame) {
  //if the alpha level of the interface object is less than 100, slowly fade it up
  if (_root.interface._alpha < 100) {
    _root.interface._alpha = _root.interface._alpha + _root.fadeRate;
    _root.splash._alpha = _root.splash._alpha - _root.fadeRate;
  } else {
    //if the interface is fully visible, fire up the game
    if (!interfaceFaded) {
      _root.gotoAndStop("initialize2");
      interfaceFaded = true;
    }
  }
}
```

Now you are going to add the login/registration station. On the content1 layer, click Frame 20 in the Timeline. There should be a blank keyframe already there (signified by a hollow circle). To import the graphic we have provided for this station, press Control+R (or choose File ➤ Import), browse to the directory where you saved the downloaded files, and find the login-registerBox.png file. Using the Align Panel, center this image both vertically and horizontally.

NOTE *We discussed the Align Panel and how to use it in Chapter 3, "Creating Your First Flash Application." Please refer to that chapter if you do not remember how to use it.*

Press F8 (or choose Insert ➤ Convert To Symbol), name it *loginBox*, and make sure the Movie Clip option is selected. Click OK. In the Properties Panel, give this new clip an instance name of *loginBox*.

Still on the content1 layer, you need to add some text to let the user know what to do and where to do it. Figure 6-15 shows what the text labels should look like. Using the Text tool and the Static Text setting, create labels that look as similar to Figure 6-12 as you can. We used Arial font, but as long as the font is readable, any will do. Be sure to leave space at the bottom of the login/register window for the buttons you are going to add a little later.

Figure 6-15. Login/registration text labels (outlines are for size and placement purposes only)

Now you must create two user input (form) fields where the user can enter their username and password. Using the same Text tool, in the Properties Panel set the tool to Input Text, make sure the Show Borders Around Text button is toggled down (on), and create two textboxes about the same size and placement as shown in Figure 6-16.

NOTE *The Selectable and Show Borders Around Text buttons were discussed in Chapter 1, "Introducing Flash MX." Please refer to that chapter if you do not remember how to use them.*

LOGIN/REGISTER

Login or Register to play
If you have registered before, fill in the fields and click LOGIN
If you have not registered before, fill in the fields and click REGISTER

Username:

Password:

Figure 6-16. Login/registration input text

After creating and placing the input boxes, use the Arrow tool and select the username input box. In the Properties Panel, enter an instance name of *username* and a variable name of *strUsername*. Do the same for the password input box, giving it an instance name of *password* and a variable name of *strPassword*. Also, for the password input box, make sure to choose Password in the Format drop-down selector.

TIP *The Format drop-down selector lets you choose the format of the input text such as Single Line, Multiline, Multiline No-Wrap, Password, and so on. By default, input text is Single Line when Flash first starts; when you change this value, your setting remains until you change it again.*

Now let's move to the content2 layer and click Frame 20. Press F6 (or choose Insert ➤ Keyframe), press Control+R (or choose File ➤ Import), browse to the directory where you saved the downloaded files, and find the registerButtonSM.png image. Place it in the lower-left corner of the login/register window. Do the same for the loginButtonSM.png image except place it in the lower-right corner of the window. See Figure 6-17 for the exact placement.

Figure 6-17. Login/registration button placements

Click the Register image, press F8 (or choose Insert ➤ Convert to Symbol), give it a name of *buttonRegisterSM,* choose the Button option, and click OK. With the button still selected, add the code from Listing 6-30 into the Actions Panel for that button.

Listing 6-30. Register Button

```
on(release){
    _root.gotoAndStop("register")
}
```

Click the Login image, press F8 (or choose Insert ➤ Convert to Symbol), give it a name of *buttonLoginSM,* choose the Button option, and click OK. With the button still selected, add the code from Listing 6-31 into the Actions Panel for that button.

Listing 6-31. Login Button

```
on(release){
    _root.gotoAndStop("login")
}
```

In the content2 layer, click Frame 30 and press F7 (or choose Insert ➤ Blank Keyframe). Do the same thing for the content1 layer on Frame 30.

Keeping Frame 30 selected on the content1 layer, choose the Text tool from the Toolbox and click somewhere on the Stage. Type *VERIFYING...* using 15-point Arial font. Choose the Arrow tool from the Toolbox and click the new text. Press F8 (or choose Insert ➤ Convert to Symbol). Name the new symbol *loginClip,* choose the Movie Clip option, and click OK. With the new clip selected, use the Align Panel to center the clip both vertically and horizontally. With the clip still selected, use the Actions Panel to enter the code from Listing 6-32. This code simply calls the Login.aspx page with the username and password that were entered, and the page will check the database for a match. This script also times itself, and in the event that it takes longer than the global TimoutLength setting, it will error. If the .aspx page returns a login error, this script sends the Flash movie to the error display with the error that was returned from the .aspx page. If everything processed without errors and the login information matched, the Flash movie moves on to the question station of the game.

Listing 6-32. Login Code

```
onClipEvent(load) {
  _root.done = 0;
  _root.loadVariables("Login.aspx?PlayerName="+_root.strUsername+"&Password="↵
+_root.strPas
  sword);
  startTime = getTimer();
}

onClipEvent(enterFrame) {
  if ((getTimer() - startTime)/1000 < _root.TimeoutLength) {
    if (_root.done=="1") {
      if (_root.Error != "") {
        _root.strReturn = "initialize2";
```

```
      _root.gotoAndStop("error");
    } else {
      _root.gotoAndStop("question");
    }
  }
} else {
  _root.error = "The server timed out while trying to verify↩
your login information. Please press OK below to try again.";
  _root.strReturn = "login";
  _root.gotoAndStop("error");
  }
}
```

Now you will do the same thing for the register station as you just did for the login station. In the content1 layer, click Frame 40 and press F7 (or choose Insert ➤ Blank Keyframe). Using the Text tool and the same font settings you used for the *VERIFYING* text, type *REGISTERING...* on the Stage. Choose the Arrow tool from the Toolbox and click the new text. Press F8 (or choose Insert ➤ Convert to Symbol). Name the new symbol *registeringClip,* choose the Movie Clip option, and click OK. With the new clip selected, use the Align Panel to center the clip both vertically and horizontally.

With the clip still selected, use the Actions Panel to enter the code from Listing 6-33. This code simply calls the Register.aspx page with the username and password that were entered. The page will check the database for exiting username and add the new one if it does not exist. This script also times itself, and in the event that it takes longer than the global TimeoutLength setting, it will error. If the .aspx page returns a registration error, this script sends the Flash movie to the error display with the error that was returned from the .aspx page. If everything processed without errors, the Flash moves on to the question station of the game.

Listing 6-33. Registration Code

```
onClipEvent(load) {
  _root.done = 0;
  //call aspx page to register new player
  _root.loadVariables("Register.aspx?PlayerName="+_root.strUsername+"&Password="↩
+_root.str
  Password);
  startTime = getTimer();
}


onClipEvent(enterFrame) {
    //check for timeout
```

```
  if ((getTimer() - startTime)/1000 < _root.TimeoutLength) {
    if (_root.done=="1") {
      //if aspx returned an error send to error screen
      if (_root.Error != "") {
        _root.strReturn = "initialize2";
        _root.gotoAndStop("error");
      } else {
        //if all is successful sent to question
        _root.gotoAndStop("question");
      }
    }
  } else {
    _root.error = "The server timed out while trying to register your↵
 information. Please press OK below to try again.";
    _root.strReturn = "register";
    _root.gotoAndStop("error");
  }
}
```

Now that you have the login/registration stations done, you are going to build the question station, which is where the game will call the database to get the next question, display it for the user to see, and choose an answer. On the control1 layer, click Frame 50 and press F7 (or choose Insert ➤ Blank Keyframe). Using the Text tool and the same font settings you used for the *VERIFYING* text, type *LOADING…* on the Stage. Choose the Arrow tool from the Toolbox and click the new text. Press F8 (or choose Insert ➤ Convert to Symbol). Name the new symbol *loadingClip*, choose the Movie Clip option, and click OK.

With the new clip selected, use the Align Panel to center the clip both vertically and horizontally. With the clip still selected, use the Actions Panel to enter the code from Listing 6-34. This code calls the Question.aspx page, which will query the database for the next question and pass it back to the Flash. The same timeout checking has been placed in this code as you used previously. If all the questions have been answered, the Flash movie moves to the game over screen. If there was an error, the Flash moves to the error screen. If a new question was returned, the Flash moves to the question2 station.

Listing 6-34. Load Question

```
onClipEvent(load) {
  _root.done = 0;
  dteNow = new Date()
  //call aspx to get next question
  _root.loadVariables("Question.aspx?" + dteNow.getHours + dteNow.getMinutes +↵
```

```
        dteNow.getSeconds + dteNow.getMilliseconds);
      startTime = getTimer();
   }


onClipEvent(enterFrame) {
   //check for timeout
   if ((getTimer() - startTime)/1000 < _root.TimeoutLength) {
     if (_root.done=="1") {
        //if no more questions, go to game summary
        if (_root.GameOver == "1") {
          _root.gotoAndStop("gameover");
        }
        //if aspx returns error, send to error screen
        if (_root.Error != "") {
          _root.strReturn = "question";
          _root.gotoAndStop("error");
        } else {
          _root.gotoAndStop("question2");
        }
     }
   } else {
     _root.error = "The server timed out while trying to retrieve the next↵
   question. Please press OK below to try again.";
     _root.strReturn = "question";
     _root.gotoAndStop("error");
   }
}
```

You will now build the question2 station, which is where the display of the question will actually take place. On the content2 layer, click Frame 60 and press F7 (or choose Insert ➤ Blank Keyframe). Do the same thing in Frame 60 of the content1, cat/quest/answ, level/score, redLight, and greenLight layers. Go back to the content2 layer in Frame 60 and press Control+R (or choose File ➤ Import) and browse to the image submitButton.png in the directory where you saved the downloaded files.

With the new image selected, use the Properties Panel to enter *332* for its X position and enter *386* for its Y position. With the image still selected, press F8 (or choose Insert ➤ Convert to Symbol), give it a name of *submitButtonClip,* choose the Movie Clip option, and click OK. In the Properties Panel, give this clip an instance name of *submitButton*. Double-click the new clip to open it in edit mode. Click the submit button image to select it, press F8 (or choose Insert ➤ Convert to

Symbol), give it a name of *buttonSubmit,* choose the Button option, and click OK. With the new button selected, use the Actions Panel to enter the code from Listing 6-35 for the button.

Listing 6-35. Submit Button

```
on(release){
  _root.gotoAndStop("answer");
}
```

The reason you put the submitButton inside of a MovieClip instead of just putting the button directly on the Stage is because you want to be able to dynamically move the submitButton vertically based on how long the question and answer texts are. If it is a short question with shorter answers, you do not want a big gap between the last answer and the submitButton. So you will determine the _y value (vertical position) of the last answer choice and move the submitButton to a certain distance below that using ActionScript. But first you need to build the question and answer objects to display.

To make it a little easier to place your display objects on the game interface, you can make the background interface image visible because it is not at this point. Click the white Stage somewhere that there is not some other object. This should select the interface background image. To know if you have selected the correct object or not, look at the Properties Panel. It should have an instance name of *interface,* and it should say *instance of: interface* next to the instance name. Using that same Properties Panel, set the alpha to *100%.* You will change this back later, but for now it will help with placement.

Showing the Score

On the level/score layer, click Frame 60. You are going to add a couple of textboxes to show the level for the questions and the current score. Choose the Text tool from the Toolbox and use the Properties Panel to set the text to Dynamic Text, Arial, 11 points, and bold. Also, choose white for the text color. Using Figure 6-18 as a guide as to where to place your textbox, click and drag to draw a textbox. Using the Properties Panel, give this textbox an instance name of *levelTxt* and a variable name of *strLevel.*

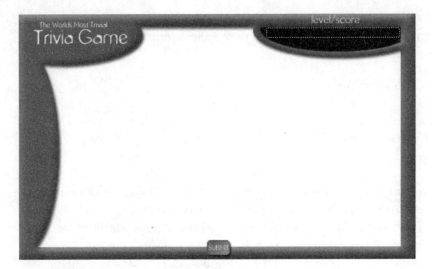

Figure 6-18. Level textbox placement

Choose the Text tool from the Toolbox again if it is not still chosen. Make sure the level textbox is not still selected; then, use the Properties Panel and set the type to Dynamic Text, the font to Arial, and the size to 15 points. Using Figure 6-19 as a guide, draw another textbox. Using the Properties Panel, give this textbox an instance name of *scoreTxt* and a variable name of *strScore*.

Figure 6-19. Score textbox placement

Choose the Text tool from the Toolbox again if it is not still chosen. Make sure the score textbox is not still selected; then, use the Properties Panel and set the type to Dynamic Text, the font to Arial, the size to 15 points, and the color to black. Using Figure 6-20 as a guide, draw another textbox. Using the Properties Panel, give this textbox an instance name of *categoryTxt* and a variable name of *strCategory*. Click the textbox itself and type *Category:* into it. Also, set the text mode to Multiline in the Properties Panel for this textbox.

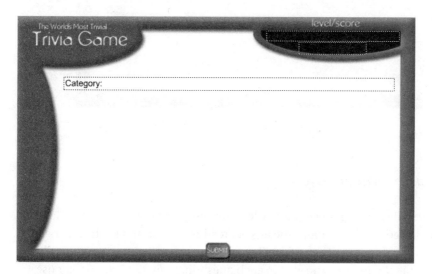

Figure 6-20. Category textbox placement

All of the next textboxes will be created on the cat/quest/answ layer in Frame 60. So, click there now and make sure as you create each of the following textboxes that you remain in the correct layer and frame.

Creating the Question Object

Choose the Text tool from the Toolbox again if it is not still chosen. Make sure the category textbox is not still selected; then, use the Properties Panel and set the type to Dynamic Text, the font to Arial, the size to 15 points, and the color to black. Using Figure 6-21 as a guide, draw another textbox. Using the Properties Panel, give this textbox an instance name of *questionTxt* and a variable name of *strQuestion*. Click the textbox itself and type *Question:* into it. Also, set the text mode to Multiline in the Properties Panel for this textbox.

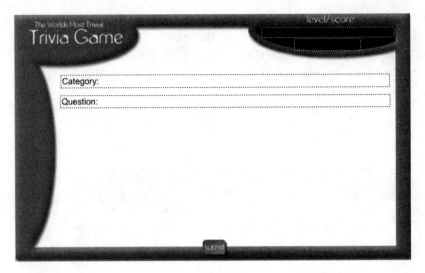

Figure 6-21. Question textbox placement

Creating the Answer Object

The answers display is going to be a little more complex because you need to create a MovieClip that contains the answer textbox and button to choose that answer during the game. Then you will write some ActionScript to dynamically duplicate this clip for every answer in each question. From the Toolbox, choose the Text tool. In the Properties Panel, set the type to Static Text, the font to Arial, the size to 15 points, and the color to black. Click the Stage and type *Answers:* and choose the Arrow tool from the Toolbox after typing. Use Figure 6-22 as a guide to move the answer text to the proper place.

With the answers textbox still selected, press F8 (or choose Insert ➤ Convert to Symbol). Give it a name of *answerTitle* and choose the Movie Clip option. Click OK. In the Properties Panel, give this new clip an instance name of *answerTitle*.

Now you will create the textbox that will display the answers. Choose the Text tool from the Toolbox again, and in the Properties Panel set the options to Dynamic Text, the font to Arial, the size as 13 point, and the color to black. Using Figure 6-23 as a guide, draw a new textbox on the Stage. In the Properties Panel again, give this textbox an instance name of *AnswerTxt* and a variable name of *strAnswer*. Using the Arrow tool, make sure this new textbox is selected and press F8 (or choose Insert ➤ Convert to Symbol). Give it a name of *answerClip*, select the Movie Clip option, and click OK. In the Properties Panel, give this clip an instance name of *answerClip0* (the 0 is a zero).

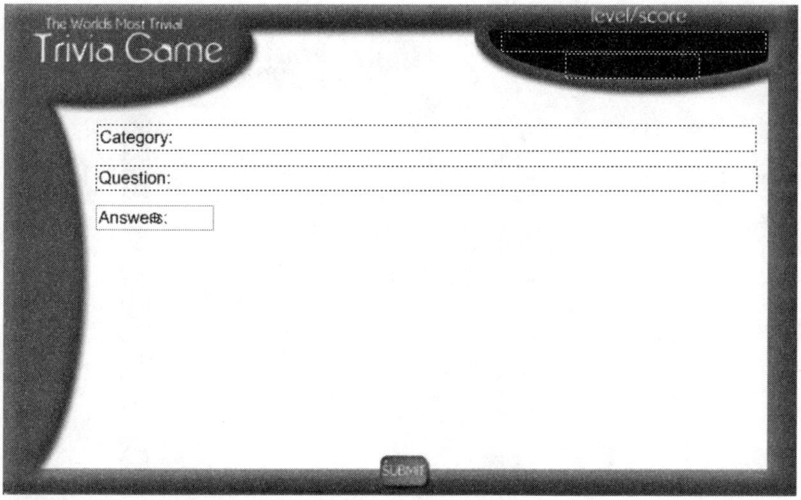

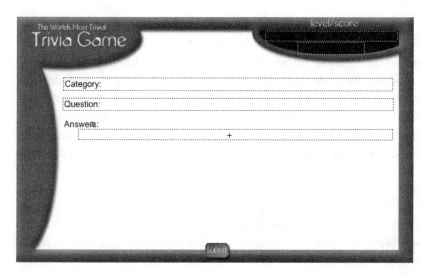

Figure 6-22. Answer title box placement

Figure 6-23. Answer textbox placement

Double-click the *answerClip0* clip to open it in edit mode. Add a new layer above the textbox. Choose the Oval tool from the Toolbox. Set the fill to a light gray and the outline color to black. Draw a circle on the Stage that is about 15-pixels across. This is going to be a radio button next to the answer, so it needs to be pretty small. Use Figure 6-24 as a guide to place the radio button where it needs to go and determine what size it should be. Adjust the size of your button if needed.

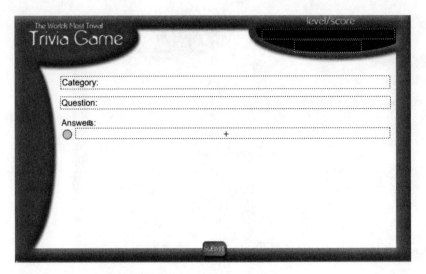

Figure 6-24. Radio button placement

Using the Arrow tool, double-click in the center of this new circle, selecting both the fill and outline. Press F8 (or choose Insert ➤ Convert to Symbol). Give it a name of *radioButton*, choose the Movie Clip option, and click OK. In the Properties Panel, give the clip an instance name of *radioButton*. Double-click the clip to move into edit mode for it. Create a new layer above the current layer. Using the Oval tool again, draw a new circle in the new layer in the center of the radio button that has a Fill Color of black and no outline color (white with a red line through it in the color palette). This will be the center of the radio button, so leave a little space between its edges and the outer edge of the first circle you drew. Use Figure 6-25 as a guide.

Using the Arrow tool, double-click in the center of this new circle to select it. Press F8 (or choose Insert ➤ Convert to Symbol). Give it a name of *radioButtonDot*, choose the Movie Clip option, and click OK. In the Properties Panel, give the clip an instance name of *dot*.

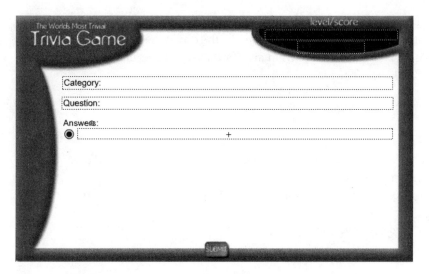

Figure 6-25. Radio button center placement

There should now be two layers in this clip: the radio button itself in one and the center dot in the other. Create a new layer *between* these two layers. Choose the Rectangle tool from the Toolbox and draw a box that would just cover the radio button and answer text with any Fill Color and no outline color. Use the Arrow tool and click this new shape to select it. Press F8 (or choose Insert ➤ Convert to Symbol). Give it a name of *invisiButton*, choose the Button option, and click OK. Double-click this new button to move into edit mode. In the button's Timeline, there are four frames representing the button's four states: Up, Over, Down, and Hit. The only state with a keyframe at this point is the Up state. Click and drag that keyframe to the Hit frame. This will make this button invisible on the Stage but still clickable. You use this method when you want to make any object clickable, such as the radio button. Using the "bread crumb" location list (directly above the Stage in the authoring environment), click the *radioButton* clip name to move back to editing it. Click Frame 1 of the bottom layer and use the Actions Panel to enter the code in Listing 6-36 for that frame.

Listing 6-36. Actions for radioButton Clip

```
stop();
dot._visible = false;
```

Select invisiButton and enter the code from Listing 6-37 into the Actions Panel for the button. This is the code that will make the dot of the *radioButton* for this answer visible, tell the interface what answer the user chose, and then fire off the script to check that answer.

Listing 6-37. Answer Button

```
on(release) {
 //make dots for all other answers invisible in case something was already selected
  for(i=1;i<=_root.numAnswers;i++) {
    setProperty(["_root.answerClip"+i+".radioButton.dot"],_visible,False);
}
  //make this dot visible
  dot._visible = True;
  //set answer id for this answer
  _root.chosenAnswer = _parent.answerID;
}
```

Creating Game Play Objects

That is the question and answers display. You are going to add some elements now for telling users if they were right or wrong. Move all the way back to the main Timeline. Click the redLight layer in Frame 60, press Control+R (or choose File ➤ Import), and browse to the image redLight.png in the files you downloaded. With the new image selected, use the Properties Panel to enter *322* for its X position and *53* for its Y position.

Press Control+R (or choose File ➤ Import) and browse to the image green-Light.png in the files you downloaded. Select that image on the Stage and delete it. This will remove it from the Stage but leave it in the library for you to use later.

Select the redLight image again, press F8 (or choose Insert ➤ Convert to Symbol), give it a name of *redLight,* choose the Movie Clip option, and click OK. In the Properties Panel, give this clip an instance name of *redLight*. Double-click this new clip to move into edit mode. Click and drag the only keyframe in the Timeline of this clip to Frame 2. Now click Frame 13 and press F5 (or choose Insert ➤ Frame).

Create two new layers above this layer. In the layer directly above this one, click Frame 2 and press F7 (or choose Insert ➤ Blank Keyframe). Use the Text tool from the Toolbox to set the options in the Properties Panel; set the type to Static Text, the font to Arial, the size to 15 points, and the color to red. Next, click the Stage and type *WRONG*. Choose the Arrow tool again and drag the text to be centered and directly underneath the redLight image. Use Figure 6-26 as a guide.

Figure 6-26. WRONG answer text placement

In the layer above the *WRONG* text, do the following:

1. Click Frame 2 and press F7 (or choose Insert ➤ Blank Keyframe).

2. Choose the Oval tool from the Toolbox. You are going to create a gradient fill for this oval to fake a glow around this red light.

3. In the Color Mixer Panel, click the drop-down list and select Radial.

4. The wide color bar in this palette should have two rectangles directly under it with little triangle (arrow) tops pointing to a position on the color bar. Each of those rectangles represents a key point in the gradient. Click the rectangle on the far left.

5. Using the color selector in the upper-left corner of the Color Mixer Panel, click and choose red from the drop-down palette.

6. Click the right rectangle below the color bar and also choose red for it.

7. With this one still selected, use the alpha slider in the Color Mixer Panel to set this one's alpha to zero.

8. Move to the Stage and draw a circle that is slightly larger than the redLight image. It should make the redLight look like it is glowing.

9. Adjust the size of your "glow" to look like Figure 6-27.

Figure 6-27. Red light glow placement

10. In the layer for this red glow, click Frame 8 and press F6 (or choose Insert ➤ Keyframe).

11. In this same layer, click Frame 5 and press F7 (or choose Insert ➤ Blank Keyframe).

12. Also, in this layer, click Frame 11 and press F7 (or choose Insert ➤ Blank Keyframe).

13. Finally, click Frame 13 of this layer and press F7 (or choose Insert ➤ Blank Keyframe).

14. Click Frame 1 of this layer and in the Actions Panel enter *stop();*.

15. Click Frame 13 of this layer and in the Actions Panel enter *gotoAndPlay(2);*.

16. Now the glow will flash on and off when this clip plays, making the red light look as though it is blinking.

You are now going to create this same effect but with a green light for the correct answers:

1. Open the Library Panel by pressing F11 (or choose Window ➤ Library).

2. Find the MovieClip named *redLight*. Make sure it is the MovieClip and not the image itself.

3. Right-click the clip name and choose Duplicate from the pop-up menu.

4. A dialog box will pop up asking for the name of the new clip. Name it *greenLight* and click OK.

5. Double-click the greenLight clip in the Library Panel to open that clip in edit mode.

6. Select the red glow object in Frame 2.

7. Using the Color Mixer Panel, edit the gradient by changing the colors to green and the alpha settings to the same: 100% on the left and 0% on the right.

8. When you are finished editing the colors, click Frame 2 of that layer and press Control+Alt+C (or choose Edit ➤ Copy Frames).

9. Click Frame 8 of that layer and press Control+Alt+V (or choose Edit ➤ Paste Frames).

10. Now lock that layer to avoid accidentally selecting it while working on the layers below it.

11. Move to the bottom layer with the redLight image in it. Click the redLight image to select it.

12. In the Properties Panel is a SWAP button. Press that and choose green-Light.png from the pop-up list.

13. Click OK. This swaps out the redLight image for the greenLight image.

14. Lock this layer.

15. In the only layer left unlocked, double-click the WRONG text and change it to *CORRECT*.

16. With that text selected, change its color to green.

17. Move back to the main Timeline.

18. Click Frame 60 of the greenLight layer.

19. Click and drag the greenLight MovieClip from the Library Panel onto the Stage. You will not be able to see the green light on the Stage because the light itself is not visible until later in the MovieClip. You will see a white dot (with a plus in it if it is selected) where the clip is on the Stage.

20. Using the Properties Panel, set the instance name of this clip to *greenLight*, enter *322* for its X position, and enter *53* for its Y position.

Those are all the elements for the answer station. Now for the code—click Frame 60 of the control layer. In the Actions Panel, enter the code from Listing 6-38 into that frame.

Listing 6-38. question2 Station Code

```
//set some properties for the text display
_root.categoryTxt.autoSize = true;
_root.questionTxt.autoSize = true;
_root.answerTxt.autoSize = true;

_root.categoryTxt.text = "Category: " + _root.Category;

//set level text to level color passed to it
_root.levelTxt.textColor = "0x" + _root.LevelColor;
_root.levelTxt.text = "LEVEL: " + _root.Level;

//set score text to white
_root.scoreTxt.textColor = "0xFFFFFF";
_root.scoreTxt.text = "SCORE: " + _root.Score;

_root.questionTxt.text = "Question: " + _root.Question;

//set vertical position of answerTitle based on height of question text
_root.answerTitle._y = 150.7 + _root.questionTxt._height;
//set vertical position of 1st answer clip based on answerTitle position
_root.AnswerClip0._y = _root.answerTitle._y + 18;

//create answerClips for each answer
for (i=1;i<=_root.numAnswers;i++) {
```

```
  duplicateMovieClip(_root.AnswerClip0,"AnswerClip"+i, i+1000);
  if (i>1) {
    //set vertical position of answer clip
    setProperty(["_root.AnswerClip"+i],_y,eval(["_root.AnswerClip"+(i-1)+"._y"]) +↩
    eval(["_root.AnswerClip"+(i-1)+".answerTxt._height"]) + 4);
  }
  //set variables for answer clip
  set(["_root.AnswerClip"+i+".answerID"],eval(["_root.Answer"+i+"ID"]));
  set(["_root.AnswerClip"+i+".strAnswer"],eval(["_root.Answer"+i+"Text"]));
}

//set vertical position of submit button based on last answer clip
_root.submitButton._y = eval(["_root.AnswerClip"+(i-1)+"._y"]) + ↩
 eval(["_root.AnswerClip"+(i-1)+".answerTxt._height"]) + 20;

//make the original answer clip used to copy all other
//answer clips to invisible to hide it
_root.answerClip0._visible=false;
```

On the content2 layer, click Frame 70 and press F7 (or choose Insert ➤ Blank
Keyframe). Do the same thing for the content1 layer in Frame 70. In Frame 70 of
the content1 layer, use the Text tool from the Toolbox to set the type to Dynamic
Text, the font to Arial, the size to 15 points, the color to black, and the border to on.
Type *PROCESSING...* on the Stage. Center the text you just typed both horizontally
and vertically using the Align Panel. With the textbox selected, press F8 (or choose
Insert ➤ Convert to Symbol). Give it a name of *submittingAnswerClip,* choose the
Movie Clip option, and click OK. Using the Actions Panel, enter the code from
Listing 6-39 for that MovieClip.

Listing 6-39. Answer Clip Code

```
onClipEvent(load) {
  _root.done = 0;
  //send answer to ASP and wait for return data
  _root.loadVariables("Answer.aspx?Answers="+_root.chosenAnswer);
  startTime = getTimer();
}

onClipEvent(enterFrame) {
  //timeout check
  if ((getTimer() - startTime)/1000 < _root.TimeoutLength) {
    if (_root.done=="1") {
      if (_root.error != "") {
```

```
      _root.strReturn = "question";
      _root.gotoAndStop("error");
    } else {
      _root.gotoAndStop("continue");
    }
  }
} else {
  _root.error = "The server timed out while trying to retrieve the next↩
question. Please press OK below to try again.";
  _root.strReturn = "question";
  _root.gotoAndStop("error");
}
}
```

Click Frame 80 of the content1 layer and press F7 (or choose Insert ➤ Blank Keyframe). While still in that frame, press Control+R (or choose File ➤ Import). Browse to the continueButton.png image in the files you downloaded and choose it. Select the newly imported image and press F8 (or choose Insert ➤ Convert to Symbol). Give it a name of *buttonContinue*, choose Button, and click OK. Use the Actions Panel and enter the code from Listing 6-40 into the button.

Listing 6-40. Continue Button

```
on(release) {
  //remove all answer clips to prepare for new ones
  for (i=1;i<=_root.numAnswers;i++) {
    removeMovieClip(["_root.AnswerClip"+i]);
  }
  //reset all global vars relating to questions and answers
  _root.Question = "";
  _root.numAnswers = "";
  _root.Category = "";
  _root.Level = "";
  _root.LevelColor = "";
  _root.chosenAnswer = "";
  _root.gotoAndStop("question");
}
```

With the continue button selected, press F8 (or choose Insert ➤ Convert to Symbol). Give it a name of *continueButtonClip,* choose the Movie Clip option, and click OK. Give this clip an instance name of *continueButtonClip* using the Properties Panel, enter *296* for its X position, and enter *315* for its Y position.

Click Frame 80 of the control layer and use the Actions Panel to enter the code from Listing 6-41 for this frame.

Listing 6-41. Continue Code

```
_root.continueButton._y = eval(["_root.AnswerClip"+(i-1)+"._y"]) + ↵
eval(["_root.AnswerClip"+(i-1)+".answerTxt._height"]) + 20;
if (_root.Feedback == "1") {
  _root.greenLight.gotoAndPlay(2);
} else {
  _root.redLight.gotoAndPlay(2);
}
```

Click Frame 90 on the *control* layer and use the Actions Panel to enter the *stop();* command.

Click Frame 90 on the content1 layer and press F7 (or choose Insert ➤ Blank Keyframe). Do the same thing in Frame 90 of the cat/quest/answ, redLight, and greenLight layers. Click Frame 90 of the content1 layer again, choose the Text tool from the Toolbox, and set its properties using the Properties Panel. Set the type to Static Text, the font to Arial, the size to 15 points, and the color to black. Type *GAME OVER*. Use the Properties Panel to enter *267* for its X position and enter *41* for its Y position. Now press F8 (or choose Insert ➤ Convert to Symbol). Give it a name of *gameOverClip*, choose the Movie Clip option, and click OK. Use the Actions Panel to enter the code from Listing 6-42 for this clip.

Listing 6-42. Game Summary Code

```
onClipEvent(load) {
  _root.done = 0;
  _root.error = "";
  //send query to ASP and wait for return data
  _root.loadVariables("gameOver.aspx");
  startTime = getTimer();
}

onClipEvent(enterFrame) {
//timeout check
  if ((getTimer() - startTime)/1000 < _root.TimeoutLength) {
    if (_root.done=="1") {
      if (_root.error != "") {
          _root.strReturn = "gameover";
        _root.gotoAndStop("error");
      } else {
```

```
            _root.gotoAndStop(_root._currentframe + 1);
         }
      }
   } else {
_root.error = "The server timed out while trying to retrieve the game summary. ⤸
Please press OK below to try again.";
      _root.strReturn = "gameover";
      _root.gotoAndStop("error");
   }
}
```

Next, do the following:

1. Click Frame 90 of the content2 layer.

2. Select the Text tool from the Toolbox and use the Properties Panel to set the type to Static Text, the font to Arial, the size to 13 points, and the color to black.

3. Type the text *RETRIEVING GAME SUMMARY....*

4. Center that text horizontally and vertically using the Align Panel.

5. Click Frame 91 of the content2 layer and press F7 (or choose Insert ➤ Blank Keyframe).

6. Do the same in Frame 91 of the content1 layer.

7. In Frame 91 on the content1 layer, select the Text tool from the Toolbox and set the type to Static Text, the font to Arial, the size to 15 points, and the color to black.

8. Type *GAME OVER* on the Stage.

9. Use the Properties Panel to set its X position to 267 and its Y position to 41.

10. Choose the Text tool from the Toolbox again and set its type to Static Text, its font to Arial, its size to 13 points, and its color to black.

11. Type the text *GAME SUMMARY:* on the Stage. Leave that text close to the *GAME OVER* text for now.

12. Choose the Text tool from the Toolbox again and set its type to Dynamic Text, its font to Arial, its size to 15 points, and its color to black. Also, make its borders visible and set the Display the Text As HTML option. The Display Text As HTML option is a new settings that you have not used previously. It allows the textbox to accept some basic HTML tags, such as <b></b>, <u></u>, and <br>, which you will use to format the *GAME SUMMARY* text.

13. Use Figure 6-28 as a guide to draw a large textbox on the Stage in Frame 91 of the content2 layer and to move the *GAME SUMMARY* text just above the new large textbox.

14. Use the Properties Panel to give the new dynamic textbox an instance name of *summaryTxt* and a variable name of *strSummary*.

Figure 6-28. Game summary placement

Next, you are going to use a new technique in Flash MX called *components*. Open the Components Panel. It should look something like Figure 6-29. Click and drag the ScrollBar icon to the Stage and drop it directly on the large dynamic textbox that you named *summaryTxt*. The component will attach itself automatically to this textbox and resize itself to match, so that it will be a working scrollbar for that textbox. If the text you put into that box runs past the bottom of what that box will hold, the scrollbar will allow the text to be scrolled up and down and viewed that way. How easy was that?

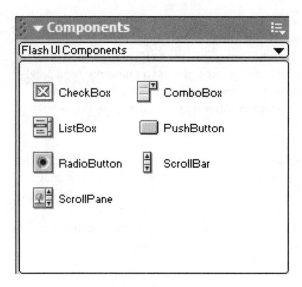

Figure 6-29. Components Panel

Next, do the following:

1. Click Frame 100 of the content1 layer and press F7 (or choose Insert ➤ Blank Keyframe).

2. Click Frame 100 of the content2 layer and press F7 (or choose Insert ➤ Blank Keyframe).

3. While still on the content2 layer, press Control+R (or choose File ➤ Import).

4. Browse to the directory where you saved the files you downloaded from the Web site and find the OKButton.png image. Select this image on the Stage after it is imported and press F8 (or choose Insert ➤ Convert to Symbol).

5. Give it a name of *buttonOK* and choose the Button option.

6. Using the Properties Panel, enter *332* for its X position and *317* for its Y position.

7. In Frame 100 of the content1 layer, use the Text tool to set the type to Static Text, the font to Arial, the size to 15 points, and the color to red. Then, type *ERROR* on the Stage.

8. Use the Properties Panel to move the text to an X position of 177 and a Y position of 97.

9. Also, in this same frame, use the Text tool to set the type to Dynamic Text, the font to Arial, the size to 15 points, the color to red, and the mode to Multiline. Draw the textbox from just below the *ERROR* text label to just above the OK button. Use Figure 6-30 as a guide for the size.

10. Use the Properties Panel to enter an instance name of *errorTxt* and a variable of *error* for this textbox.

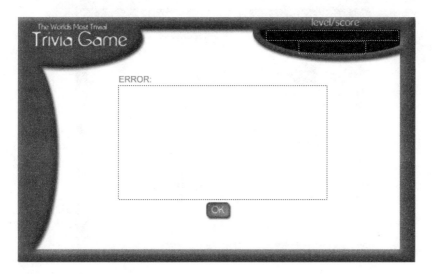

Figure 6-30. Error text placement

On the control layer in Frame 100, use the Actions Panel to enter the code from Listing 6-43 into that frame.

Listing 6-43. Error Code

```
stop();
//remove all answer clips
for (i=1;i<=_root.numAnswers;i++) {
  removeMovieClip(["_root.AnswerClip"+i]);
}
```

One last thing . . . select the interface object in the interface layer and set its alpha back to 0% now that you are finished using it as reference in placing objects.

That's it! You have completed the trivia game interface. Just publish the Flash movie and try it out.

Playing the Game

Finally, you are ready to try out the trivia game and see all the parts working together. Start the game; the first screen of course is the registration page. Figure 6-31 shows the page.

Figure 6-31. The registration screen

Register as a new player and then click the Register button. That will take you right into the game playing process. You see all of the elements of the game coming together on the screen. For instance, you'll see the question and four answers, the current level of the question, and the current score. Let's answer with the correct answer (American President in case you weren't sure). When you answer the question correctly, the bright flashing green light goes off. Figure 6-32 shows the screen at this Stage.

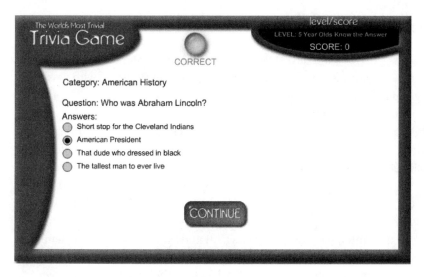

Figure 6-32. You got the answer right!

Now go through the various questions until you reach the final screen when the questions and score are recapped. This shows your questions and responses and your final score. Figure 6-33 shows the screen.

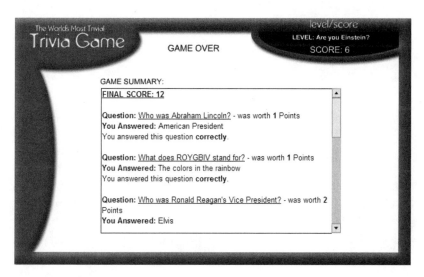

Figure 6-33. Your final score

Summary

In this chapter, you took the next step in building a highly interactive and complex database-driven gaming process and in enabling the user interface with Flash. You can easily expand this example into a full-fledged question and answer tool for conducting tests, games, and so on.

In the Flash interface, you used duplicated MovieClips to display information, used imported images as buttons, used dynamic and static textboxes to display data and labels, used the HTML capabilities of the dynamic textbox, and used Flash MX components to utilize a drag-and-drop scrollbar. You even dynamically placed your data elements on the screen based on the length of the element just above it so things would appear evenly spaced on the interface.

In the next chapter, you will shift gears a bit and build a cool event calendar tool. As complex as this example got in the database and coding end of things, the next chapter will get complicated on the Flash side of the equation.

CHAPTER 7

Building Calendars in a Flash

AN INTERACTIVE CALENDAR is great way to demonstrate the true power of Flash combined with dynamic data. In this chapter you will build a database-driven calendar that displays events. The example demonstrates some the most complicated techniques yet, both on the Flash side and on the server side.

This example uses Active Server Pages (ASP) and SQL Server for implementation. The database in this case is fairly simple. However, the logic for managing and manipulating dates and times gets much more complicated. You will also throw in a few bells and whistles to make this a useful application right out of the box.

Creating the Calendar Business Rules

The business rules for this calendar are fairly straightforward. You want to allow an administrator to set up events that will appear on the calendar. Events will have starting and ending dates and times. For example, an event could go from September 1, 2003 to November 1, 2003, or from 8 A.M. on September 10, 2003, to 9 A.M. September 10, 2003.

In addition, users will be able to classify events into types of events. This will allow the user to filter the events they want to see on the calendar. Example event types are meetings, holidays, seminars, reminders, and so on.

From a user perspective, the calendar will function like any other computer-based calendar. The user will be able to move through months and years and pick days to see events. You will add a few bells and whistles, including the ability to filter the list of events to see only events by type.

When the user finds an event they are interested in, they click it, and the event detail pops up for them to review. You will also build dynamic map links to show the location of events. That link will show up in the event detail.

TIP *If you are going to deploy a calendar targeted at business users, consider adding support for the vCalendar (.vcs) file format. The user can then add that event directly to their organizer (such as Outlook) calendar. You can find more information about the format and how to support it at* `http://msdn.microsoft.com/library/default.asp?url=/library/en-us/ dnvbpj00/html/appointments.asp.`

For the administrative side, you will build basic functionality to add, edit, and delete events and event types. We have not included any security for the administrative functions. See Chapter 5, "Building a Flashy Online Poll Engine," for an excellent example of how to implement administrative security if you want to ensure that only certain users can access the administrative functions.

The example built in this chapter is for basic calendar functionality. There are a multitude of options for taking advantage of the power of Flash to build eye-popping calendars with rich functionality. We will show you the basic techniques, and you can extend the calendar as you like.

Building the ASP and SQL Server Foundation

This chapter utilizes Microsoft SQL Server and ASP to build the data-driven foundation of the calendar. You can use either Windows 2000 or Windows XP with Internet Information Services (IIS) 5.0 or 6.0. The programming language is VBScript.

This chapter utilizes Microsoft's SQL Server Enterprise Manager to create the database. If you are running the Microsoft SQL Server Desktop Engine (MSDE) version of SQL Server and using Visual Studio .NET, refer to the instructions for setting up a database in Chapter 2, "Setting Up the Web Server and Database Environment." If you are not running MSDE, then you will need to have access to the SQL Server Enterprise Manager tools to set up the database.

NOTE *You can use also Microsoft Access for this solution. The primary change required is that you need to set up the connection string to the database to point to the .mdb file. See Chapter 2, "Setting Up the Web Server and Database Environment," for an example.*

Designing the Database

The calendar database is pretty simple and consists of only two tables that define the event and event type data that will support the business requirements as outlined in the previous section. Figure 7-1 shows the two tables and their relationship to each other.

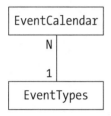

Figure 7-1. The calendar tables

Events will be assigned to one type And event types can relate to any number of events. Like we said, it is pretty simple. But, do not let that fool you; in this case, the data structure is simple, but the coding gets somewhat complicated, as you will see shortly.

Let's now look at each table starting with EventCalendar. Table 7-1 defines the fields for the table.

Table 7-1. EventCalendar Table Definition

FIELD NAME	DATA TYPE	DESCRIPTION
intEventID	int/identity	The primary key of the table and auto increments. Be sure and set the field to be an identity column.
intType	int	A foreign key to the EventTypes table that designates the type of event.
dteEventStart	datetime	The event start date.
dteEventEnd	datetime	The event end date.
strTitle	varchar (100)	The title of the event.
strLocation	varchar (500)	The location of the event.
blnMap	bit	Flag indicating if the location is formatted to build a map link.
strDescription	text	The description of the event.

Events will have types, starting dates and time, ending dates and times, titles, locations, and a description. Note that the date fields will store both the day and time. Listing 7-1 shows the SQL script to create the table.

Listing 7-1. EventCalendar Table SQL Create Script

```
if exists
    (select * from dbo.sysobjects where id = object_id(N'[dbo].[eventCalendar]')
    and OBJECTPROPERTY(id, N'IsUserTable') = 1)
drop table [dbo].[eventCalendar]
GO


if not exists (select * from dbo.sysobjects where id =
object_id(N'[dbo].[eventCalendar]')
  and OBJECTPROPERTY(id, N'IsUserTable') = 1)
 BEGIN
CREATE TABLE [dbo].[eventCalendar] (
    [intEventID] [int] IDENTITY (1, 1) NOT NULL ,
    [intType] [int] NULL ,
    [dteEventStart] [datetime] NULL ,
    [dteEventEnd] [datetime] NULL ,
    [strTitle] [varchar] (100) COLLATE SQL_Latin1_General_CP1_CI_AS NULL ,
    [strLocation] [varchar] (500) COLLATE SQL_Latin1_General_CP1_CI_AS NULL ,
    [blnMap] [bit] NULL ,
    [strDescription] [text] COLLATE SQL_Latin1_General_CP1_CI_AS NULL
) ON [PRIMARY] TEXTIMAGE_ON [PRIMARY]
END
GO
```

Table 7-2 defines the fields for the EventTypes table. As mentioned, each event will be classified under one type.

Table 7-2. EventTypes Table Definition

FIELD NAME	DATA TYPE	DESCRIPTION
intTypeID	int/identity	The primary key of the table and auto increments. Be sure and set the field to be an identity column.
strType	varchar (50)	The name of the event type.
strDescription	varchar (255)	The description of the event type.

Types are pretty simple with only a name and a description. Listing 7-2 shows the script for creating the table.

Listing 7-2. EventTypes Table SQL Create Script

```
if exists (select * from dbo.sysobjects where id = object_id(N'[dbo].[eventTypes]')
    and OBJECTPROPERTY(id, N'IsUserTable') = 1)
drop table [dbo].[eventTypes]
GO
if not exists (select * from dbo.sysobjects where id =
object_id(N'[dbo].[eventTypes]')
and OBJECTPROPERTY(id, N'IsUserTable') = 1)
 BEGIN
CREATE TABLE [dbo].[eventTypes] (
   [intTypeID] [int] IDENTITY (1, 1) NOT NULL ,
   [strType] [varchar] (50) COLLATE SQL_Latin1_General_CP1_CI_AS NULL ,
   [strDescription] [varchar] (255) COLLATE SQL_Latin1_General_CP1_CI_AS NULL
) ON [PRIMARY]
END
GO
```

To set up the database, follow the steps outlined in Chapter 2, "Setting Up the Web Server and Database Environment," for ASP and SQL Server. Name the database *Calendar*. Ensure you have the proper permissions to access the database from your project and set them appropriately in the SQL connection string. That does it for the database. Now you are ready to dive into setting up the project.

Developing the Calendar Administrator

The calendar administrator provides the tools required to manage events and event types. All of the administration pages are written in ASP with VBScript, and they interface with the database created in the previous section.

Before development begins, you need to create the Calendar directory structure. On your development Web server, create a new folder called *Calendar*. Create the Visual Studio project in that folder. Within the Calendar folder, create an Admin folder, which is where the administrative pages will live. Within the Calendar folder, also create a folder called *include*, which will be used for creating common elements across all of the pages. Finally, create an *images* folder for storing images used on all of the pages.

Before getting into the guts of the administrative pages, you need to put a few items in place. First, you need to define your connection to the database. You will do this in an include file that is used on all of the data-driven calendar pages. Create a new .asp file in the include directory and save it as *dbOpen.asp*. Listing 7-3 shows the code for the page.

Listing 7-3. dbOpen.asp

```
' OPEN DB CONNECTION
DIM oConn
Dim sConn

'  Build the connection string
sConn = "driver={SQL Server};" & _
    "server=myserver;uid=username;pwd=password;database=calendar"

'  Open the connection
set oConn = server.CreateObject("ADODB.Connection")

oConn.Open(sConn)
```

In the include file, you define the connection string where you want to open the database. Be sure to change this to the appropriate settings for your SQL Server. This then opens the connection to the database for use on the page where the file is included. Also, you need to build an include file for closing the database, as shown in Listing 7-4.

Listing 7-4. dbClose.asp

```
' CLOSE DB CONNECTION
oConn.Close
set oConn = nothing
```

By adding this at the bottom of every page where the database is opened, you ensure that the database connections are all closed.

You are going to need a simple navigation format for the administrative pages. Listing 7-5 and Listing 7-6 define navigation links for the event and event type pages.

Listing 7-5. AdminTypeNav.asp

```
   
<a href="ListTypes.asp">View Current</a>
<STRONG>:</STRONG>
<a href="ManageType.asp?f=add">Add New</a>
<STRONG>:</STRONG> <a href="ListEvents.asp">Manage Events</a>
<br><br>
```

Listing 7-6. AdminEventNav.asp

```
   
<a href="ListEvents.asp">View Current</a>
<STRONG>:</STRONG>
<a href="ManageEvent.asp?f=add">Add New</a>
<STRONG>:</STRONG> <a href="ListTypes.asp">Manage Event Types</a>
<br><br>
```

Each navigation bar provides three options. The View Current link goes to the listing page to show all of the current events and event types. The Add New link takes the user to the management page for each and indicates that a new event/type will be entered. The last navigation link, Manage Event Types, switches between managing events and types.

Throughout the administrator pages, you will also use a style sheet for the look-and-feel formatting of the pages as well as several graphics. We have provided the images in the Downloads section of the Apress Web site (http://www.apress.com). (You can also download the style sheet.) Table 7-3 defines some of the key styles.

Table 7-3. Key Styles

STYLE NAME	DESCRIPTION
Body	Defines the font style to be used for all text in the body of the document.
Head	Defines the style for page heading text.
Button	Formats button such as Submit and Cancel.
Fineprint, fineprintBK, fineprintW, fineprintBKthin, fineprintBold	These are a series of styles for displaying nonstandard body text.
A.Link, A.Visited, A.Active, A.Visited, A.Hover	Defines the link style for all links.

In addition, we have built a calendar function that formats dates and times for different display styles. There is also a function for building safe SQL text. You can find these in Functions.inc in the include directory. Finally, we have built a page for specifically formatting addresses to be used with Expedia.com's mapping service (http://www.expedia.com/pub/agent.dll?qscr=mrfn). This will allow the user of the calendar to easily find an event's location.

TIP *If you have not worked extensively with date formatting, you might want to take a minute and review the VBScript date functions* (http://msdn.microsoft.com)*. You will use them extensively in this chapter.*

Building the Events Listing Page

To get started, the first page you will build is a listing of events in the database. This page will find all events in a date range and display them in a formatted table. You will create options for working with each event including editing and deleting. Create a new .asp file called *ListEvents.asp* and save it in the Admin folder.

NOTE *Because the .asp pages in this chapter are rather long, we will present each section of the page and then make comments. These pages will be marked as* Continued.

The page includes the navigation for events, two input textboxes for setting the date range for events to be listed, and a table showing all of the events. Figure 7-2 shows a sample of the page.

Listing 7-7 shows the first section of the page. It includes the page setup and JavaScript functions. The page is set up with three files being included. The first is dbOpen.asp, which opens the database connection. The second is Functions.inc, which provides the date and SQL text formatting functions. Finally, it includes the style.css style sheet, which formats the Hypertext Markup Language (HTML) in the page.

This page has one JavaScript function, deleteItem, which is called when the user chooses to delete an event. If the user indicates Yes, then the JavaScript sends the user *back* to this page. The page sets two query string parameters. The first, f (for *function*), indicates that a delete should be performed. The second is the ID of the event to be deleted. That ID value is passed to the deleteItem function.

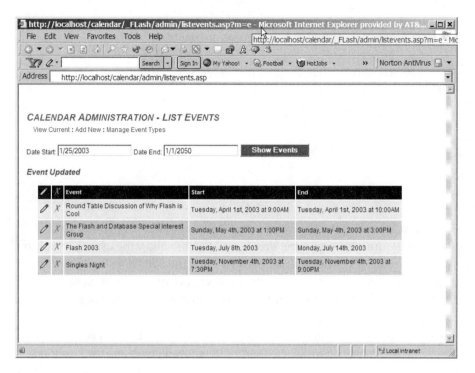

Figure 7-2. The events listing page

Listing 7-7. ListEvents.asp

```
<%@ Language=VBScript %>
<%Option Explicit%>

<HTML>
<HEAD>
<!--#include file="../include/dbOpen.asp"-->
<!--#include file="../include/functions.inc"-->
<link rel="stylesheet" type="text/css" href="../style.css">

<script language="javascript">
<!--

// Confirm the delete of the event
function deleteItem(id,title) {
    msg = 'Are you sure your want to delete '
    msg = msg + title + '?\nThis item CANNOT be recovered once deleted.';
    if (!confirm(msg)){
        return false;
```

```
        } else {
            //  Send the user back to this page and indicate a delete will
            //  be performed
            location.href = 'ListEvents.asp?f=delete&id=' + id;
        }
    }


//-->
</script>
</head>
<body>
```

The next section of the page begins the VBScript processing, as shown in Listing 7-8. If there are a large number events, you want to allow the user to be able to look at events for a given date range. The first thing the code does is check to see if the user has selected a date range for the events to be shown. If not, then the dates default to today and far out in the future so that all current and future events are listed.

Next, the code determines if the page is supposed to delete an event. If the f query string variable is set to delete, then a query is built to delete the specified event.

Listing 7-8. ListEvents.asp, Continued

```
<%
Dim rs, strBGColor, sSQL
Dim dtStart, dtEnd

'  Get the start and end dates to show the events
dtStart = trim(request.Form("dtStart"))
dtEnd = trim(request.Form("dtEnd"))

'  Check to see if there is no start date
if len(dtStart) = 0 then
    '  Default to for the start date
    dtStart = datepart("m", now) & "/" & _
            datepart("d", now) & "/" & _
            datepart("yyyy", now)
end if

'  See if there is no end date
if len(dtEnd) = 0 then
    '  Default to far out in the future to show all events
```

```
      dtEnd = "1/1/2050"
end if


'  Check to see if a delete should be performed
if request.QueryString("f") = "delete" then
        '  Execute the delete
        oConn.Execute("Delete from eventCalendar where intEventID = " & _
            Request.QueryString("id"))
end if


%>
```

After these initial tasks, the code builds the display of the page, as shown in Listing 7-9. The first thing that is shown is the navigation bar for the event-related pages. It includes the AdminEventNav.asp file. Note that the navigation bar has an option for adding a new event and links to the ManageEvent.asp page with a query string parameter that indicates that an add/insert should be performed.

Next, the code builds a form to allow the user to enter start and end dates for displaying listed events. The current starting and ending date variables are set as the values of the two input boxes. Finally, the code determines if additional query string parameters are set. These parameters are set whenever the user has completed an add, update, or delete. A visual cue displays on the page to indicate to the user that the action was successful.

Listing 7-9. ListEvents.asp, Continued

```
<!--  Start the table to display the events -->
<table width="750" cellspacing="5" cellpadding="0" border="0" valign="top">
    <tr>
        <td valign="top">
            <br><br>
            <span class="head">Calendar Administration - List Events</span><br>
        </td>
    </tr>
    <tr>
        <td valign=top>
            <!-- Nav for the event pages -->
            <!-- #include file="../include/admineventnav.asp" -->

            <!-- Form to allow the user to filer events by date range -->
            <form method="post" action="listevents.asp">
            Date Start:
                <input type="text" value="<%=dtStart%>" name="dtStart">
```

```
                    Date End:
                        <input type="text" value="<%=dtEnd%>" name="dtEnd">

                    <input class="button" type="submit" name="Submit"
                                value="Show Events">
                    <br><br>
                    </form>
        <%

        '  If an event was added, updated or deleted then indicate it to the user
        if Request.QueryString("m") = "a" then
            Response.Write("<span class=alert>New Event Added</span><br><br>")
        elseif Request.QueryString("f") = "delete" then
            Response.Write("<span class=alert>Event Deleted</span><br><br>")
        elseif Request.QueryString("m") = "e" then
            Response.Write("<span class=alert>Event Updated</span><br><br>")
        end if
```

Next, the code creates a query to retrieve the events for the given date range, as shown in Listing 7-10. All events that fall inside that date range are returned from the query. If nothing is returned, you indicate that to the user. Following that, the code builds the table for displaying the list of events with the appropriate header rows.

Listing 7-10. ListEvents.asp, Continued

```
'  Build the query to retrieve the events
sSQL = "select * from eventCalendar where dteEventStart >= '" & _
    dtStart & "' and dteEventEnd <= '" & dtEnd & _
    "' order by dteEventStart"

'  Execute the query
set rs = oConn.Execute(sSQL)

'  If no events are found then indicate so
if rs.EOF then
    Response.Write("No Calendar Items To Show")
else %>
    <!-- Build the event display table -->
    <table width=700 cellspacing=2 cellpadding=3 border=0 align=center>
        <!-- Table Header -->
        <tr bgcolor=black>
         <td class=fineprintW>
```

```
        <img src="../images/edit.gif" width=16 height=16 border=0>
    </td>

    <td class=fineprintW>
     <img src="../images/delete.gif" width=16 height=16 border=0>
    </td>

    <td class=fineprintW>Event</td>
    <td class=fineprintW>Start</td>
    <td class=fineprintW>End</td>
</tr>
```

Finally, the actual event data displays, as shown in Listing 7-11. Each row of the listing will alternate colors. Icons for updating and deleting the event display before the event name. For editing an event, the user is sent to the ManageEvent.asp page with an appropriate query string parameter that indicates an edit/update is to be performed. Note that the event date is formatted using the formatdate function from the Functions.inc file. In this case, the date and time appear in a friendly format (for example *Tuesday, April 1st, 2003 at 10:00AM*).

Listing 7-11. ListEvents.asp, Continued

```
<%
'  The row colors for the events will be rotated for easy viewing
strBGColor = "#cccccc"
while not rs.EOF
    if strBGColor = "#cccccc" then
        strBGColor = "#eeeeee"
    else
        strBGColor = "#cccccc"
    end if %>
<!-- Build the row with the right row color -->
<tr bgcolor="<%=strBGColor%>">
    <!-- Show the edit icon. When clicked on the user is sent to
         the manage event page with an indication the event should
         be deleted -->
    <td><a href="manageevent.asp?f=edit&id=<%=rs("intEventID")%>">
        <img src="../images/edit.gif"
           width=16 height=16 border=0>
        </a>
    </td>
    <!-- Show the delete icon. When clicked on the user is
         sent to this page with an indication the event should
          be deleted -->
```

```
                        <td>
                            <img src="../images/delete.gif" width=16 height=16 border=0
                                onClick="deleteItem('<%=rs("intEventID")%>','
                                <%=replace(rs("strTitle"),"'","\'")%>');"
                                style="cursor:hand;">
                        </td>

                        <!--  Show the event title -->
                        <td><%=rs("strTitle")%></td>
                        <td>
                    <!--  Show the formated date with or with out time -->
                    <%     if hour(rs("dteEventStart")) > 0 then
                                Response.write(formatDate(rs("dteEventStart"), _
                                        "%A, %B %d%O, %Y at %h:%N%P"))
                            else
                                Response.write(formatDate(rs("dteEventStart"), _
                                        "%A, %B %d%O, %Y"))
                            end if %>
                        </td>
                        <td>

                    <!--  Show the formated date with or with out time -->
                    <%     if hour(rs("dteEventEnd")) > 0 then
                                Response.write(formatDate(rs("dteEventEnd"), _
                                        "%A, %B %d%O, %Y at %h:%N%P"))
                            else
                                Response.write(formatDate(rs("dteEventEnd"), _
                                        "%A, %B %d%O, %Y"))
                            end if %>
                        </td>
                    </tr>
                <%
                    rs.MoveNext
                    wend
                %>
                </table>
            <%    end if
                set rs = nothing
            %>
                </td>
            </tr>
        </table>

<!--#include file="../include/dbClose.asp"-->
</body>
</HTML>
```

The page then closes out with a loop to show each event, the closing table tags, and the include to close the database connection.

Creating the Add and Update Events Pages

The next page handles adding events and updating existing events. This is where you have oh-so much fun working with dates and times (not really). Figure 7-3 shows a sample page with all of the appropriate form fields. Note that you create the date and time entry with a series of drop-down boxes.

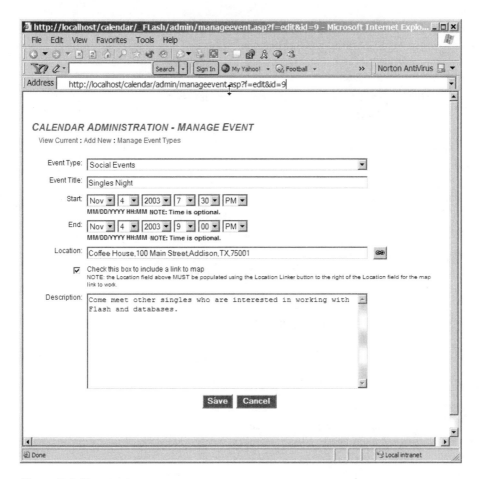

Figure 7-3. Event setup page

Create a new file called *ManageEvent.asp* and save it in the Admin folder.
Listing 7-12 shows the code for ManageEvent.asp. It starts out with the same three
files included. There is also a JavaScript script that is used for validating the fields
entered on the form. The only field that is not required is the checkbox that indicates if a link to the map for the location should be shown to the user.

Listing 7-12. ManageEvent.asp

```
<%@ Language=VBScript %>
<%Option Explicit%>
<HTML>
<HEAD>
<!--#include file="../include/dbOpen.asp"-->
<!--#include file="../include/functions.inc"-->
<link rel="stylesheet" type="text/css" href="../style.css">

<!-- Script language to validate the user's input -->
<script language="javascript">
<!--
// Check to see if something was entered
function notFilled(input) {
    var myreg = /\S+/;
    return(input.search(myreg) == -1)
}

function validateForm(){
    // If nothing was entered or no type was selected
    if(notFilled(document.add.intType.value) | _
        document.add.intType.value == "0") {
            document.add.intType.focus();
            alert('Event Type is required');
            return false;
    }
    // If no start month was entered
    if(notFilled(document.add.dteStartMonth.value) |
        document.add.dteStartMonth.value == "") {
            document.add.dteStartMonth.focus();
            alert('Start Date/Time is required');
            return false;
    }
    // If no start date was entered
    if(notFilled(document.add.dteStartDay.value)) {
        document.add.dteStartDay.focus();
```

```
        alert('Start Date/Time is required');
        return false;
    }
    //  If no start year was entered
    if(notFilled(document.add.dteStartYear.value)) {
        document.add.dteStartYear.focus();
        alert('Start Date/Time is required');
        return false;
    }
    //  If no end month was entered
    if(notFilled(document.add.dteEndMonth.value)) {
        document.add.dteEndMonth.focus();
        alert('End Date/Time is required');
        return false;
    }
    //  If no end date was entered
    if(notFilled(document.add.dteEndDay.value)) {
        document.add.dteEndDay.focus();
        alert('End Date/Time is required');
        return false;
    }
    //  If no end year was entered
    if(notFilled(document.add.dteEndYear.value)) {
        document.add.dteEndYear.focus();
        alert('End Date/Time is required');
        return false;
    }
    //  If no title was entered
    if(notFilled(document.add.strTitle.value)) {
        document.add.strTitle.focus();
        alert('Event Title is required');
        return false;
    }
    //  If no location was entered
    if(notFilled(document.add.strLocation.value)) {
        document.add.strLocation.focus();
        alert('Event Location is required');
        return false;
    }
    //  If no description was entered
    if(notFilled(document.add.strDescription.value)) {
        document.add.strDescription.focus();
        alert('Event Description is required');
```

```
            return false;
        }
        return true;
}


//-->
</script>
</head>
<body>
```

The first thing that has to happen on the page is to determine what action is being performed by the page. It is either an add or an edit. When the page is first called, the code sets the query string parameter, indicating the appropriate action. As you will see later in the page, it sets a hidden variable to store the action; that way, when the form is posted, you can determine if the data should be inserted or updated. So, initially both the query string and form fields determine the target action of the page.

Next, in Listing 7-13 the code reads the dates and times from the form in order to validate that they are valid (in the next section). It is important to ensure that the user set the drop-down boxes properly. For example, if the user entered *01/01/2003 09* and didn't set the minutes or A.M./P.M., then you do not have a valid date/time entry for the database.

Listing 7-13. ManageEvent.asp, Continued

```
<%
Dim rs, strBGColor,rs2, sSQL
Dim ErrorMsg
Dim ProcessFunc
Dim intType
Dim strTitle
Dim dteStartDateTime
Dim dteStartDate
dim dteStartTime
Dim dteEndDate
dim dteEndDateTime
Dim strLocation
Dim blnMap
Dim strDescription
Dim dteStartMonth, dteStartDay, dteStartYear
Dim dteStartHour, dteStartMinute, dteStartAMPM
Dim dteEndMonth, dteEndDay, dteEndYear, dteEndHour
Dim dteEndMinute, dteEndAMPM
Dim iCNT
```

```
'  Find out what action is being taken
if request.QueryString("f") = "edit" then processfunc = "edit"
if request.QueryString("f") = "add" then processfunc = "add"
if request.form("process") = "edit" then processfunc = "edit"
if request.form("process") = "add" then processfunc = "add"

'  Build the start date from the drop down boxes
dteStartDate = request.Form("dteStartMonth") & "/" & _
            request.Form("dteStartDay") & "/" & _
            request.Form("dteStartYear") & " " & _
            request.Form("dteStartHour") & ":" & _
            request.Form("dteStartMinute") & " " & _
            request.Form("dteStartAMPM")

'  Build the end date from the drop-down boxes
dteEndDate = request.Form("dteEndMonth") & "/" & _
            request.Form("dteEndDay") & "/" & _
            request.Form("dteEndYear") & " " & _
            request.Form("dteEndHour") & ":" & _
            request.Form("dteEndMinute") & " " & _
            request.Form("dteEndAMPM")

'  If no times were entered then remove the spaces and : left
'  from the date build
dteStartDate = replace(dteStartDate, " : " , "")
dteEndDate = replace(dteEndDate, " : " , "")
```

The next check determines if this is a postback to the page from the user after having worked with the event data, as shown in Listing 7-14. You can determine this by checking the process hidden variable. Because it is a form variable, you can set it only once the page is posted.

The next set of checks ensure that the dates and times entered are valid dates, that a start date previous to the current day was not entered, and that the end date is not before the start date. The last check happens with the VBScript DateDiff function, which determines the amount of time between two dates. The check determines the number of seconds between the start and end date. If it is a negative value, then the end date must be before the start date.

Listing 7-14. ManageEvent.asp, Continued

```
' Post Back
if Request.Form("process") = "add" or Request.Form("process") = "edit" then

    ' Check to ensure a valid date was entered
    if not isdate(dteStartDate) then
        ErrorMsg = "You did not enter a valid start date.<BR>"
    end if


    ' Check to ensure a valid date was entered
    if not isdate(dteEndDate) then
        ErrorMsg = ErrorMsg & "You did not enter a valid end date.<BR>"
    end if


    ' Ensure a start date in the past was not entered
    if isDate(dteStartDate) then
            if cdate(dteStartDate) < now then
                ErrorMsg = ErrorMsg & "You can not enter a date in the past.<BR>"
            end if
    end if


    ' See if everything is OK so far so that the DateDiff doesn't fail on
    ' on a non date
    if ErrorMsg = "" then
        ' Get the difference between the dates and see if a negative
        ' is returned which means the end date is before the
        ' start date
        if datediff("s", dteStartDate, dteEndDate) < 0 then
                ErrorMsg = ErrorMsg & "You can not enter an end date " & _
                "that is prior to the start date.<BR>"
        end if
    end if
```

If there is no error, then the code can perform the add or insert to store the data in the database, as shown in Listing 7-15. Note that for edits, the ID of the event that is being worked is initially passed as a query string parameter and is then stored in a hidden variable on the form that can be read when the page is posted.

NOTE *You can find the* SafeSQL *function in Functions.inc on the Apress Web site. The function basically doubles up any single quotes (') to ensure that SQL will insert the data properly and not cause an error.*

Listing 7-15. ManageEvent.asp, Continued

```
'  If there is no error message
if ErrorMsg = "" then

    '  Check for an add
    if request.Form("process") = "add" then

        '  Build the insert query
        sSQL = "INSERT INTO eventCalendar(intType, dteEventStart, "
        sSQL = sSQL & "dteEventEnd, strTitle, strLocation, blnMap, "
        sSQL = sSQL & "strDescription) VALUES ("
        sSQL = sSQL & Request.Form("intType") & ","
        sSQL = sSQL & "'" & dteStartDate & "',"
        sSQL = sSQL & "'" & dteEndDate & "',"
        sSQL = sSQL & "'" & safeSQL(Request.Form("strTitle")) & "',"
        sSQL = sSQL & "'" & safeSQL(Request.Form("strLocation")) & "',"
        '  Build the query with a 1 or 0 depending on what was entered
        if Request.Form("blnMap") = 1 then
            sSQL = sSQL & "1,"
        else
            sSQL = sSQL & "0,"
        end if
        sSQL = sSQL & "'" & safeSQL(Request.Form("strDescription")) & "')"

        '  Execute the query
        oConn.Execute(sSQL)

        '  Send the user to the event listing and indicate an add
        '  was done
        Response.Redirect("ListEvents.asp?m=a")

    end if

    '  Check for an edit
    if request.Form("process") = "edit" then
```

```
'  Build the update query
sSQL = "UPDATE eventCalendar SET "
sSQL = sSQL & "intType=" & Request.Form("intType") & ","
sSQL = sSQL & "dteEventStart = '" & dteStartDate & "', "
sSQL = sSQL & "dteEventEnd = '" & dteEndDate & "',"

'  Make sure the data is processed for a successful insert
sSQL = sSQL & "strTitle = '" & _
        safeSQL(Request.Form("strTitle")) & "',"

'  Make sure the data is processed for a successful insert
sSQL = sSQL & "strLocation = '" & _
        safeSQL(Request.Form("strLocation")) & "',"

if Request.Form("blnMap") = 1 then
      sSQL = sSQL & "blnMap=1,"
else
      sSQL = sSQL & "blnMap=0,"
end if
sSQL = sSQL & "strDescription='" & _
        safeSQL(Request.Form("strDescription")) & "' "

'  Indicate the event to be updated
sSQL = sSQL & "where intEventID=" & Request.Form("intEventID")

'  Execute the query
oConn.Execute(sSQL)

'  Send the user back to the event listing and indicate the
'  edit was successful
Response.Redirect("listevents.asp?m=e")

end if
```

The next section of the page handles retrieving the form data if there *is* an error in the dates and times entered, as shown in Listing 7-16. For the start and end hour and minute values, if nothing was entered on the form, then the values are set at -1. This ensures that nothing is set in the hour and minute select boxes.

Listing 7-16. ManageEvent.asp, Continued

```
else

    '  Show the error message
    ErrorMsg = "<font color=""red"">" & ErrorMsg & "</font>"

    '  Get the event data entered from the form
    intType = request.Form("intType")
    strTitle = request.Form("strTitle")

    '  Get the start date selections
    dteStartMonth = request.Form("dteStartMonth")
    dteStartDay = request.Form("dteStartDay")
    dteStartYear = request.Form("dteStartYear")
    dteStartHour = request.Form("dteStartHour")

    '  If no hour was entered then default hour to -1
    '  so nothing is shown as selected
    if len(dteStartHour) = 0 then
        dteStartHour = -1
    end if

    ' Get the start minute
    dteStartMinute = request.Form("dteStartMinute")

    '  If there is no minute then default the minute to
    '  -1 so nothing is shown as selected
    if len(dteStartMinute) = 0 then
        dteStartMinute = -1
    end if

    '  Get the AM/PM selection
    dteStartAMPM = request.Form("dteStartAMPM")

    '  Get the end date selections
    dteEndMonth = request.Form("dteEndMonth")
    dteEndDay = request.Form("dteEndDay")
    dteEndYear = request.Form("dteEndYear")
    dteEndHour = request.Form("dteEndHour")

    if len(dteEndHour) = 0 then
        dteEndHour = -1
    end if
```

```
        dteEndMinute = request.Form("dteEndMinute")

        if len(dteEndMinute) = 0 then
            dteEndMinute = -1
        end if

        dteEndAMPM = request.Form("dteEndAMPM")

        strLocation = request.Form("strLocation")
        blnMap = request.Form("blnMap")
        strDescription = request.Form("strDescription")
    end if
```

If the page is being called for the first time and is not a postback, then you
check to see if an edit is to be performed and the data for the event is retrieved
from the database, as shown in Listing 7-17. The heavy date and time lifting for the
administrative tools is in this page section. The SQL dteEventStart and dteEventEnd
fields store both the date and time values for the event. You have to break up this
data into the various components and default them in the select boxes. To compli-
cate things a bit more, the time component is stored in military time, but the
drop-down boxes show standard time because it is more commonly used.

The first thing that happens is that the date returned from SQL is broken up
into its parts. Then the code checks to see if there was a time retrieved. If so, then it
is broken up into its parts. Next, it checks to see if the time is greater than 12
(remember, it is returned in military time). If so, then 12 is subtracted from the
hours and the P.M. flag is set. Note you do *not* want to subtract 12 from 12 to get 0,
which isn't a proper hour in nonmilitary time. Then you retrieve the minutes. If
there is no time for the start date, then the times default to -1. The same logic follows for the end date and time.

Listing 7-17. ManageEvent.asp, Continued

```
' Not a postback
else


        ' See if an edit is being performed
    if request.QueryString("f") = "edit" then

                ' Get event from DB
                sSQL = "SELECT * FROM eventCalendar WHERE intEventID=" & _
                    Request.QueryString("id")
```

```
'  Execute the query
set rs = oConn.Execute(sSQL)

'  Get event from the the database
intType = rs("intType")
strTitle = rs("strTitle")

'  Get the start date
dteStartDateTime = rs("dteEventStart")

'  Break it up
dteStartMonth = datepart("m", dteStartDateTime)
dteStartDay = datepart("d", dteStartDateTime)
dteStartYear = datepart("yyyy", dteStartDateTime)

'  See if there is a time included
if len(trim(dteStartDateTime)) > 8 then

     '  Get the hour which returns in military time
     dteStartHour = datepart("h", dteStartDateTime)

     '  See if it is greater than or equal to 12 (pm)
     if cint(dteStartHour) >= 12 then

       '  If greater than 12 then subtract 12 to get non-military
       if dteStartHour > 12 then dtestartHour  = dtestarthour - 12

       '  Indicate PM
       dteStartAMPM = "PM"

     else

       '  If 1 to 11
     If (cint(dteStartHour) >= 0) and (cint(dteStartHour) < 12) then
         '  Indicate AM
         dteStartAMPM = "AM"

       '  If 0 then set to 12
       if dteStartHour = 0 then dteStartHour = 12
     end if

     end if
```

```
        '  Get the minute
         dteStartMinute = datepart("n", dteStartDateTime)


        '  Set to minus 1 if there is no value
        if dteStartAMPM = "" then
            dteStartMinute = "-1"
        end if

    else

        '  Don't show anything selected in the times
        dteStartHour = "-1"
        dteStartMinute = "-1"
        dteStartAMPM = ""

    end if

    '  Follow the same logic for the end date/time
    dteEndDateTime = rs("dteEventEnd")

    dteEndMonth = datepart("m", dteEndDateTime)
    dteEndDay = datepart("d", dteEndDateTime)
    dteEndYear = datepart("yyyy", dteEndDateTime)

    if len(trim(dteEndDateTime)) > 8 then

        dteEndHour = datepart("h", dteEndDateTime)

        if cint(dteEndHour) >= 12 then
            if dteEndHour > 12 then dteEndHour  = dteEndHour - 12
            dteEndAMPM = "PM"
        else

            If cint(dteEndHour) >= 0 and cint(dteEndHour) < 12 then
                dteEndAMPM = "AM"
                if dteEndHour = 0 then dteEndHour = 12
            end if

        end if

        dteEndMinute = datepart("n", dteEndDateTime)

        if dteEndAMPM = "" then
```

```
                    dteEndMinute = "-1"

            end if


    else


        dteEndHour = "-1"
        dteEndMinute = "-1"
        dteEndAMPM = ""


    end if

    strLocation = rs("strLocation")
    blnMap = rs("blnMap")
    strDescription = rs("strDescription")
```

If an add (versus an edit) is being performed, then the time fields default to -1 so that nothing is initially selected, as shown in Listing 7-18. After that, the form for displaying the event data starts, including the standard navigation bar for the event pages.

Listing 7-18. ManageEvent.asp, Continued

```
    else

        '  Default to minus 1 for a new event so that nothing
        '   is selected in the drop downs
        dteEndHour = "-1"
        dteEndMinute = "-1"
        dteEndAMPM = ""

        dteStartHour = "-1"
        dteStartMinute = "-1"
        dteStartAMPM = ""

    end if

end if

%>
<table width="750" cellspacing="5" cellpadding="0" border="0" valign="top">
    <tr>
        <td valign="top">
            <br><br>
```

```
                    <span class="head">Calendar Administration - Manage Event</span><br>
            </td>
        </tr>
        <tr>
            <td valign=top>

            <!-- #Include File="../include/admineventnav.asp" -->

            <%
                    '   Show any errors
                    response.Write ErrorMsg & ""
            %>
            <form name=add id=add method=post onsubmit="return validateForm()">
```

As mentioned earlier, you set up hidden fields (`process` and `intEventID`) for tracking what action (add or edit) is being performed by the page and, if an edit, what event record is being edited, as shown in Listing 7-19. Next, the code creates a select box for showing the list of event types. A check determines if the current event type (if editing an event) matches the current event type record, and, if so, then that event type is selected to show the current value.

Listing 7-19. ManageEvent.asp, Continued

```
<!-- Store in a hidden variable if we are adding or editing.
     This tells the page what to do when the page is posted -->
<% if processfunc = "add" then %>
<input type=hidden name=process value=add>
<%else%>
<input type=hidden name=process value=edit>
<!-- Store the ID of the event being edited -->
<input type=hidden name=intEventID value=<%=request.QueryString("id")%>>
<%end if%>

<table width=700 cellspacing=2 cellpadding=3 border=0 align=center>
    <tr>
        <td align=right valign=top>Event Type: </td>
        <td><select name=intType style="width:500px">
            <option value=0 selected>Select an Event Type</option>
        <%

            '  Get the event types
            sSQL = "SELECT * FROM eventTypes ORDER BY strType ASC"
```

```
              set rs2 = oConn.Execute(sSQL)

              '  Loop through the types
              while not rs2.EOF

                      '  Check to see if the event type matches the previously
                      '  selected event type
                      if cint(intType) = cint(rs2("intTypeID")) then
                          '  Show selected
                          Response.Write("<option selected value=" & _
                                  rs2("intTypeID") & ">" & _
                                  rs2("strType") & _
                                  "</option>")
                      else
                          '  No selection
                          Response.Write("<option value=" & _
                                  rs2("intTypeID") & _
                                  ">" & rs2("strType") & _
                                  "</option>")
                      end if
                      rs2.MoveNext
              wend
              set rs2=nothing %>
              </select></td>
    </tr>
    <tr>
        <td align=right valign=top>Event Title: </td>
        <td>
          <input value="<%=strTitle%>" type=text name=strTitle
          style="width:500px" maxlength=255>
        </td>
    </tr>
```

To display the date and times, you build a series of select boxes for month, date, year, hour, minute, and A.M./P.M., as shown in Listing 7-20. For each, a check determines what the current value is and ensures that option is selected. The logic is the same for both the start and end dates and times.

The code builds the months with the month abbreviation displayed and a numeric value for each month. The days are generated in a loop. Next, the days are generated with 31 days listed. It is up to the user to ensure they do not select an invalid end day for a month with fewer than 31 days. Finally, the years display. In each case the current value for the data is checked for a match, and the matching item is selected.

TIP *The years could be autogenerated for several years by taking the current year and adding a year to it and then looping for the number of years you want to display.*

Listing 7-20. ManageEvent.asp, Continued

```
<tr>
    <td align=right valign=top>Start: </td>
    <td>
<!-- Start month - default to previous value -->
<select name="dteStartMonth">
    <option></option>
    <option value="1" <%if dteStartMonth=1 then _
            response.Write("selected")%>>Jan</option>
    <option value="2" <%if dteStartMonth=2 then _
            response.Write("selected")%>>Feb</option>
    <option value="3" <%if dteStartMonth=3 then _
            response.Write("selected")%>>Mar</option>
    <option value="4" <%if dteStartMonth=4 then _
            response.Write("selected")%>>Apr</option>
    <option value="5" <%if dteStartMonth=5 then _
            response.Write("selected")%>>May</option>
    <option value="6" <%if dteStartMonth=6 then _
            response.Write("selected")%>>Jun</option>
    <option value="7" <%if dteStartMonth=7 then _
                response.Write("selected")%>>Jul</option>
    <option value="8" <%if dteStartMonth=8 then _
                response.Write("selected")%>>Aug</option>
    <option value="9" <%if dteStartMonth=9 then _
                response.Write("selected")%>>Sep</option>
    <option value="10" <%if dteStartMonth=10 then _
                response.Write("selected")%>>Oct</option>
    <option value="11" <%if dteStartMonth=11 then _
                response.Write("selected")%>>Nov</option>
    <option value="12" <%if dteStartMonth=12 then _
                response.Write("selected")%>>Dec</option>
</select>

<!-- Start Dat - default to previous value -->
<select name="dteStartDay" ID="Select1">
    <option></option>
```

```
<% for iCNT = 1 to 31 %>
<option value="<%=iCnt%>" <%if cint(dteStartDay)=iCNT then _
        response.Write("selected")%>><%=iCNT%></option>
<% next %>
</select>


<!--  Start year - default to previous value -->
<select name="dteStartYear" ID="Select2">
    <option></option>
    <option value="2003" <%if dteStartYear=2003 then _
            response.Write("selected")%>>2003</option>
    <option value="2004" <%if dteStartYear=2004 then _
            response.Write("selected")%>>2004</option>
    <option value="2005" <%if dteStartYear=2005 then _
            response.Write("selected")%>>2005</option>
</select>
```

Next, the time select boxes appear, as shown in Listing 7-21. The hours display one through 12 for both A.M. and P.M. The code builds the minutes zero through 60 in a loop. And, it builds a select box for A.M. and P.M. For each, the current start date values for the event values are defaulted.

Listing 7-21. ManageEvent.asp, Continued

```
<!--  Start hour - default to previous value -->
<select name="dteStartHour" ID="Select3">
    <option value=""></option>
    <option value="1" <%if cint(dteStartHour)=1 then _
        response.Write("selected")%>>1</option>
    <option value="2" <%if cint(dteStartHour)=2 then _
        response.Write("selected")%>>2</option>
    <option value="3" <%if dteStartHour=3 then _
        response.Write("selected")%>>3</option>
    <option value="4" <%if dteStartHour=4 then _
        response.Write("selected")%>>4</option>
    <option value="5" <%if cint(dteStartHour)=5 then _
        response.Write("selected")%>>5</option>
    <option value="6" <%if dteStartHour=6 then _
        response.Write("selected")%>>6</option>
    <option value="7" <%if dteStartHour=7 then _
        response.Write("selected")%>>7</option>
    <option value="8" <%if dteStartHour=8 then _
        response.Write("selected")%>>8</option>
```

```
    <option value="9" <%if dteStartHour=9 then _
            response.Write("selected")%>>9</option>
    <option value="10" <%if dteStartHour=10 then _
            response.Write("selected")%>>10</option>
    <option value="11" <%if dteStartHour=11 then _
            response.Write("selected")%>>11</option>
    <option value="12" <%if dteStartHour=12 then _
            response.Write("selected")%>>12</option>
</select>

<!--  Start minute - default to previous value -->
<select name="dteStartMinute" ID="Select4">
    <option value=""></option>
    <% for iCNT = 0 to 60 %>
    <option value="<%=right("0" & iCnt, 2)%>" <%if _
        cint(dteStartMinute)=iCNT then _
        response.Write("selected")%>><%=right("0" & iCNT, _
        2)%></option>
    <% next %>
</select>

<!--  Start AM/PM - default to previous value -->
<select name="dteStartAMPM" ID="Select5">
    <option value=""></option>
    <option value="AM" <%if dteStartAMPM="AM" then _
        response.Write("selected")%>>AM</option>
    <option value="PM" <%if dteStartAMPM="PM" then _
        response.Write("selected")%>>PM</option>
</select>
    <br>
    <span class=fineprintBK>MM/DD/YYYY HH:MM
      NOTE: Time is optional.</span>

    </td>
</tr>
```

The logic for displaying the end date and time is the same as the start date and time, as shown in Listing 7-22.

Listing 7-22. ManageEvent.asp, Continued

```
<!--  End date/time follows the same logic -->
<tr>
```

```
        <td align=right valign=top>End: </td>
        <td>

<select name="dteEndMonth" ID="Select6">
    <option></option>
    <option value="1" <%if dteEndMonth=1 then _
        response.Write("selected")%>>Jan</option>
    <option value="2" <%if dteEndMonth=2 then _
        response.Write("selected")%>>Feb</option>
    <option value="3" <%if dteEndMonth=3 then _
        response.Write("selected")%>>Mar</option>
    <option value="4" <%if dteEndMonth=4 then _
        response.Write("selected")%>>Apr</option>
    <option value="5" <%if dteEndMonth=5 then _
        response.Write("selected")%>>May</option>
    <option value="6" <%if dteEndMonth=6 then _
        response.Write("selected")%>>Jun</option>
    <option value="7" <%if dteEndMonth=7 then _
        response.Write("selected")%>>Jul</option>
    <option value="8" <%if dteEndMonth=8 then _
        response.Write("selected")%>>Aug</option>
    <option value="9" <%if dteEndMonth=9 then _
        response.Write("selected")%>>Sep</option>
    <option value="10" <%if dteEndMonth=10 then _
        response.Write("selected")%>>Oct</option>
    <option value="11" <%if dteEndMonth=11 then _
        response.Write("selected")%>>Nov</option>
    <option value="12" <%if dteEndMonth=12 then _
        response.Write("selected")%>>Dec</option>
</select>

<select name="dteEndDay" ID="Select7">
    <option></option>
    <% for iCNT = 1 to 31 %>
    <option value="<%=iCnt%>" <%if cint(dteEndDay)=iCNT then _
        response.Write("selected")%>><%=iCNT%></option>
    <% next %>
</select>

<select name="dteEndYear" ID="Select8">
    <option></option>
    <option value="2003" <%if dteEndYear=2003 then _
        response.Write("selected")%>>2003</option>
```

```
        <option value="2004" <%if dteEndYear=2004 then _
                response.Write("selected")%>>2004</option>
        <option value="2005" <%if dteEndYear=2005 then _
                response.Write("selected")%>>2005</option>
</select>

<select name="dteEndHour" ID="Select9">
    <option value=""></option>
    <option value="1" <%if cint(dteEndHour)=1 then _
            response.Write("selected")%>>1</option>
    <option value="2" <%if cint(dteEndHour)=2 then _
            response.Write("selected")%>>2</option>
    <option value="3" <%if dteEndHour=3 then _
            response.Write("selected")%>>3</option>
    <option value="4" <%if dteEndHour=4 then _
            response.Write("selected")%>>4</option>
    <option value="5" <%if cint(dteEndHour)=5 then _
            response.Write("selected")%>>5</option>
    <option value="6" <%if dteEndHour=6 then _
            response.Write("selected")%>>6</option>
    <option value="7" <%if dteEndHour=7 then _
            response.Write("selected")%>>7</option>
    <option value="8" <%if dteEndHour=8 then _
            response.Write("selected")%>>8</option>
    <option value="9" <%if dteEndHour=9 then _
            response.Write("selected")%>>9</option>
    <option value="10" <%if dteEndHour=10 then _
            response.Write("selected")%>>10</option>
    <option value="11" <%if dteEndHour=11 then _
            response.Write("selected")%>>11</option>
    <option value="12" <%if dteEndHour=12 then _
            response.Write("selected")%>>12</option>

</select>

<select name="dteEndMinute" ID="Select10">
    <option value=""></option>
    <% for iCNT = 0 to 60 %>
    <option value="<%=right("0" & iCnt, 2)%>"
            <%if cint(dteEndMinute)=iCNT then _
            response.Write("selected")%>>
            <%=right("0" & iCNT, 2)%></option>
    <% next %>
```

```
</select>

<select name="dteEndAMPM" ID="Select11">
    <option value=""></option>
    <option value="AM" <%if dteEndAMPM="AM" then _
        response.Write("selected")%>>AM</option>
    <option value="PM" <%if dteEndAMPM="PM" then _
        response.Write("selected")%>>PM</option>
</select>

    <br>
    <span class=fineprintBK>MM/DD/YYYY HH:MM
        NOTE: Time is optional.</span>

    </td>
</tr>
```

After the dates and times display, you build fields for entering the location, indicating if a map link should be shown, and for displaying an event description, as shown in Listing 7-23. For the location, you build a pop-up link to the Location-Linker.asp page. This page builds the location information in a format that will then be used to automatically build the link to the Expedia.com map. The LocationLinker.asp page pops up as a modal dialog Web page that always stays on top of the parent browser.

Listing 7-23. ManageEvent.asp, Continued

```
<tr>
    <td align=right valign=top>Location: </td>
    <td>
      <input value="<%=strLocation%>" type=text name=strLocation
        style="width:500px" maxlength=500>
       
      <!-- Show the button to offer to build the map link for
        the location -->
      <button TITLE="Create a Map Link"
        style="BORDER-STYLE:outset; background-image:
          WIDTH:22px; HEIGHT:22px;"
        id="linker" name="linker" hidefocus="true"
        unselectable="true"
        onclick="strLocation.value =
          window.showModalDialog('locationLinker.asp',
          strLocation.value,'dialogHeight: 400px;
```

```
                                dialogWidth: 465px; center: Yes; help: No;
                                  resizable: No; status: No;');">
                              <img src="../images/link.gif" width=16 height=16 border=0>
                              </button>
                        </td>
                  </tr>
                  <tr>
                        <td align=right valign=top>
                          <input <% if blnMap = True then response.Write("checked")%>
                              type=checkbox name=blnMap value=1>
                        </td>
                        <td>Check this box to include a link to map<br>
                        <span class=fineprint>NOTE: the Location field above MUST be
                        populated using the Location Linker button to the right of
                        the Location field for the map link to work.</span></td>
                  </tr>
                  <tr>
                        <td align=right valign=top>Description: </td>
                        <td>
                         <textarea name=strDescription rows=10
                            style="width:500px"><%=strDescription%></textarea> 
                        </td>
                  </tr>
                  <tr>
                        <td colspan=2 align=center>
                          <input type=submit value=Save class=button>
                           
                          <button name=cancel class=button
                              onClick="javascript:history.back(1);">Cancel</button>
                        </td>
                  </tr>
                  </table>
                  </form>

            </td>
      </tr>
</table><br><br>
<!--#include file="../include/dbClose.asp"-->
</body>
</HTML>
```

Finally, you close the page with Save and Cancel buttons and then close the database. And that is it for managing event data. The most complicated aspect of the page is getting the date and time formatting to work properly.

> **NOTE** *We chose to build select boxes for entering the dates and times, but you can take alternative approaches. For example, you could use a pop-up calendar for selecting the dates. The user could enter the time values into input boxes with one for hours and minutes, and then you could perform some simple validation.*

Creating the Type Management Pages

The type management pages are a little simpler and work in a similar fashion. The type listing page shows the name and the description of existing types. Figure 7-4 shows the layout of the page.

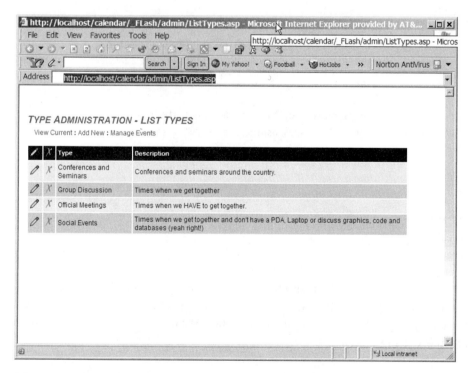

Figure 7-4. The type listing page

Add a new page to the project and save it in the Admin folder as *ListTypes.asp*. Listing 7-24 shows the code for the page. The page starts in a similar fashion to the event pages. You set the includes for the database connection, the general functions, and the formatting style sheet. A JavaScript function follows next that is used for validating the user who wants to delete the event type.

Listing 7-24. ListTypes.asp

```
<%@ Language=VBScript %>
<%Option Explicit%>
<HTML>
<HEAD>
<!--#include file="../include/dbOpen.asp"-->
<!--#include file="../include/functions.inc"-->
<link rel="stylesheet" type="text/css" href="../style.css">

<script language="javascript">
<!--
//  Validate the request to delete the type
function deleteItem(id,title) {
    msg = 'Are you sure your want to delete ' +
            title + '?\nThis item CANNOT be recovered once deleted.';
    if (!confirm(msg)){
        return false;
    } else {
        //  Send the user back to this page and indicate a delete
        location.href = 'ListTypes.asp?f=delete&id=' + id;
    }
}

//-->
</script>
</head>
<body>
```

The next section of the page checks to see if the type should be deleted, as shown in Listing 7-25. If the f query string variable is set to delete, then the code builds a query to delete the specified type. The ID of the type to delete is passed on the query string as well.

Following that, you create the header for the type listing. It includes the beginning table structure for the page as well as the menu bar for the type pages. Following the header, a check determines if the user just completed an add, edit, or delete. If so, then a message appears to the user confirming their action.

Listing 7-25. ListTypes.asp, Continued

```asp
<%
Dim rs, strBGColor,rs2, sSQL
Dim dtStart, dtEnd


' Check for the delete
if request.QueryString("f") = "delete" then
    ' Execute the delete query
    oConn.Execute("delete from eventTypes where intTypeID = " & _
                    Request.QueryString("id"))
end if


%>
<table width="750" cellspacing="5" cellpadding="0" border="0" valign="top">
    <tr>
        <td valign="top">
            <br><br>
                    <span class="head">Type Administration - List Types</span><br>
        </td>
    </tr>
    <tr>
        <td valign=top>
            <!-- #include file="../include/admintypenav.asp" -->
                <%
        ' Indicate success for an add, edit or delete
        if Request.QueryString("m") = "a" then
            Response.Write("<span class=alert>New Type Added</span><br><br>")
        elseif Request.QueryString("f") = "delete" then
            Response.Write("<span class=alert>Type Deleted</span><br><br>")
        elseif Request.QueryString("m") = "e" then
            Response.Write("<span class=alert>Type Updated</span><br><br>")
        end if
```

Next, the list of types appears, as shown in Listing 7-26. You retrieve the current types in the database using a select query. The results are ordered by the name of the type. If there are no types in the database, then you indicate that to the user. The user can still click Add New on the menu bar to add a new type. You then create the header for the type listing table.

Listing 7-26. ListTypes.asp, Continued

```
'  Get the list of types
sSQL = "select * from eventTypes order by strType"

'  Execute the query
set rs = oConn.Execute(sSQL)

'  Indicate no event types
if rs.EOF then
    Response.Write("No Event Types To Show")
else %>
    <table width="700" cellspacing=2 cellpadding=3
                border=0 align=left>
      <tr bgcolor=black>
       <td class=fineprintW>
                <img src="../images/edit.gif" width=16 height=16 border=0>
       </td>
       <td class=fineprintW>
                <img src="../images/delete.gif" width=16 height=16 border=0>
       </td>
       <td class=fineprintW>Type</td>
       <td class=fineprintW>Description</td>
      </tr>
```

The row colors for the type listing are going to alternate colors for easy readability, as shown in Listing 7-27. For each type, an edit and delete graphic appear to the left of the type name and description. The edit button links to the ManageType.asp page and indicates on the query string that an edit is to be performed and what the ID of the type is. The delete image links back to the page ListTypes.asp, indicates a delete is to be performed, and passes the ID of the type to be deleted.

Finally, you close the page and the database. That is it for listing types.

Listing 7-27. ListTypes.asp, Continued

```
                    <%
                ' Rotate the row color
                strBGColor = "#cccccc"
                while not rs.EOF
                    if strBGColor = "#cccccc" then
                        strBGColor = "#eeeeee"
                    else
                        strBGColor = "#cccccc"
                    end if %>
                    <!-- Show the edit button which when clicked on sends the user
                              to the manage types page -->
                <tr bgcolor="<%=strBGColor%>">
                    <td>
                        <a href="managetype.asp?f=edit&id=<%=rs("intTypeID")%>">
                    <img src="../images/edit.gif" width=16 height=16 border=0>
                        </a>
                    </td>

        <!-- Show the delete button which when clicked on sends the user
             back to this page -->
          <td>
            <img src="../images/delete.gif" width=16
                            height=16 border=0
                             onClick="deleteItem('<%=rs("intTypeID")%>','
                              <%=replace(rs("strType"),"'","\'")%>');"
                              style="cursor:hand;">
          </td>
            <!-- Show the type and description -->
            <td><%=rs("strType")%></td>
            <td><%=rs("strDescription")%></td>
          </tr>
        <% rs.MoveNext
          wend %>
        </table>
    <%    end if
        set rs = nothing
    %>
        </td>
    </tr>
</table>
<!--#include file="../include/dbClose.asp"-->
</body>
</HTML>
```

Creating the Adding/Editing Type Data Page

You use the final page in the administrator for adding and editing type data. Add a new file to the project called *ManageType.asp* and save it in the Admin folder. Listing 7-28 shows the page.

The page starts with the standard includes. A validation JavaScript follows next for ensuring that the user enters a type name and description.

Listing 7-28. ManageType.asp

```
<%@ Language=VBScript %>
<%Option Explicit%>
<HTML>
<HEAD>
<!--#include file="../include/dbOpen.asp"-->
<!--#include file="../include/functions.inc"-->
<link rel-"stylesheet" type="text/css" href="../style.css">

<script language="javascript">
<!--
//  Check to ensure something was entered
function notFilled(input) {
    var myreg = /\S+/;
    return(input.search(myreg) == -1)
}

//  Validate that a name and description were put in
function validateForm(){

    if(notFilled(document.add.strType.value)) {
        document.add.strType.focus();
        alert('Type Name is required');
        return false;
    }
    if(notFilled(document.add.strDescription.value)) {
        document.add.strDescription.focus();
        alert('Event Description is required');
        return false;
    }
    return true;
}

//-->
```

```
</script>
</head>
<body>
```

Following next is the logic to determine if the page is going to add a new type or edit an existing type, as shown in Listing 7-29. The logic for using the query string and hidden form variables is the same as on the ManageEvent.asp page. If it is an add, then the code builds the SQL query to insert the new type. If it is an edit, then the code builds a SQL query to update the existing data. Note that the ID of the type to be updated was initially passed on the query string to the page. It is then stored as a hidden variable on the form so it can be retrieved when the data is updated.

Listing 7-29. ManageType.asp, Continued

```
<%
Dim rs, strBGColor,rs2, SQL
Dim ErrorMsg
Dim ProcessFunc
Dim strType
Dim strDescription

'  Find out what action is to be taken
if request.QueryString("f") = "edit" then processfunc = "edit"
if request.QueryString("f") = "add" then processfunc = "add"
if request.form("process") = "edit" then processfunc = "edit"
if request.form("process") = "add" then processfunc = "add"

'  Post Back
if Request.Form("process") = "add" or Request.Form("process") = "edit" then

    '  Check for an add
    if request.Form("process") = "add" then

        '  Build the SQL insert statement
            SQL = "insert into eventTypes(strType, strDescription) values('" & _
          safeSQL(request.Form("strType")) & "', '" & _
          safeSQL(request.Form("strDescription")) & "')"

        '  Execute
        oConn.Execute(SQL)
```

```
        ' Send the user back to the type listing and indicate a successful add
        Response.Redirect("ListTypes.asp?m=a")

    end if

    ' Check for an edit
    if request.Form("process") = "edit" then

        ' Build the SQL udpate statement
        SQL = "update eventTypes set " & _
            "strType = '" & safeSQL(request.Form("strTYpe")) & "', " & _
                    "strDescription = '" & _
                    safeSQL(request.Form("strDescription")) & _
        "' " & _
            "where intTypeID = " & Request.Form("intTypeID")

        ' Execute
        oConn.Execute(SQL)

        ' Send the user back to the type listing page
        Response.Redirect("listTypes.asp?m=e")

    end if
```

The first time the page is displayed and an edit of an existing type is being performed, the data is retrieved from the database for the type ID passed on the query string, as shown in Listing 7-30. Note that the processing logic is pretty simple compared to ManageEvent.asp because you do not have to deal with all of that messy date and time data.

Listing 7-30. ManageType.asp, Continued

```
' Not a postback
else

    ' Check for an initial edit
    if request.QueryString("f") = "edit" then

        ' Get the type from DB
                SQL = "select * from eventtypes where intTypeID = " & _
            Request.QueryString("id")

        ' Execute the query
```

```
            set rs = oConn.Execute(SQL)


            '  Get type data from the the database
            strType = rs("strType")
            strDescription = rs("strDescription")
        end if
    end if


%>
<table width="750" cellspacing="5" cellpadding="0" border="0" valign="top">
    <tr>
        <td valign="top">
        <br><br>
                <span class="head">Calendar Administration - Manage Type</span><br>
        </td>
    </tr>
    <tr>
        <td valign=top>

        <!-- #Include File="../include/admintypenav.asp" -->

        <form name=add id=add method=post onsubmit="return validateForm()">
```

Next, you set up hidden variables (processfunc and intTypeID) for indicating if
an insert of a new type or an update of an existing type is happening in the form,
as shown in Listing 7-31. Also, the value of the type ID is stored in a hidden variable when an edit of an existing type is being performed.

Listing 7-31. ManageType.asp, Continued

```
        <!--  Indicate what type of action is being taken so the right
            things happens on the form post -->
        <% if processfunc = "add" then %>
        <input type=hidden name=process value=add>
        <%else%>
        <input type=hidden name=process value=edit>
        <input type=hidden name=intTypeID value=<%=request.QueryString("id")%>>
        <%end if%>

        <table width=700 cellspacing=2 cellpadding=3 border=0 align=center>
            <tr>
                <td align=right valign=top>Type Name: </td>
                <td>
```

```
                              <input value="<%=strType%>"
                                   type=text name=strType
                                   style="width:500px" maxlength=255></td>
              </tr>
              <tr>
                  <td align=right valign=top>Description: </td>
                  <td>
                              <textarea name=strDescription rows=10
                                 style="width:500px"><%=strDescription%>
                                 </textarea> </td>
              </tr>
              <tr>
                  <td colspan=2 align=center>
                              <input type=submit value=Save
                              class=button> 
                              <button name=cancel class=button
                                onClick="javascript:history.back(1);">Cancel
                              </button>
                              </td>
              </tr>
              </table>
              </form>

        </td>
    </tr>
</table><br><br>
<!--#include file="../include/dbClose.asp"-->
</body>
</HTML>
```

That is it for building the administrative functions of the calendar. We took a pretty basic approach to managing the event data. There certainly are alternative approaches you can take. For example, it is feasible to repurpose the Flash user front end for viewing the calendar and use it for editing existing events and adding new events. One of the benefits of *not* doing that is that you can see all events in one list versus having to page through the graphical interface.

Utilizing the Calendar Administrator

Now it is time to see the calendar administration in action. First, load the ListTypes.asp page. Click the Add New menu item to add a new type. The screen shows fields for entering the type name and description fields, as shown in Figure 7-5.

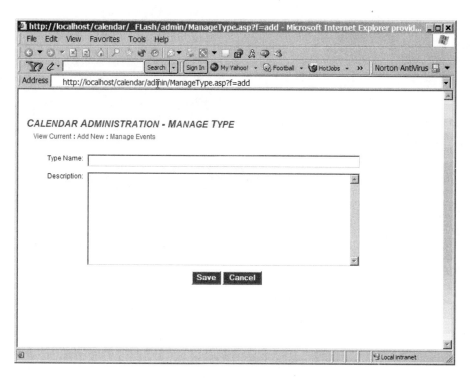

Figure 7-5. Entering the type name and description

Next, enter your event type data and save it. You will be taken back to the type listing page. Now click the edit icon for the newly added event type to edit it. The current data displays and can be edited. Make some changes and then save. Figure 7-6 shows the type listing screen with the message *Type Updated*, which indicates the update took place.

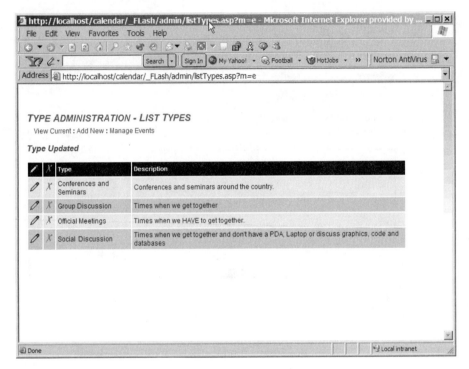

Figure 7-6. The type has been updated.

Next, click the Manage Events menu option to go to the event listing page. In the example data shown in Figure 7-6, several events appear with various dates. If the data range for display is changed to show only April events, only one event appears, as shown in Figure 7-7. Note the dates entered.

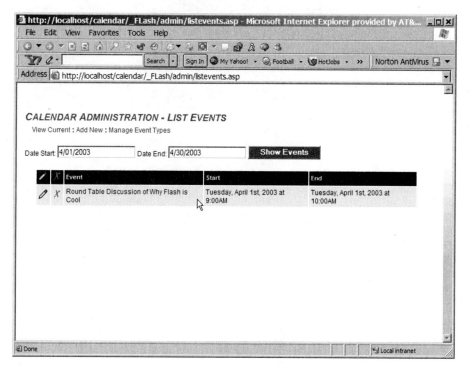

Figure 7-7. The events in April

Click Add New on the menu bar to add an event. Figure 7-8 shows the screen.

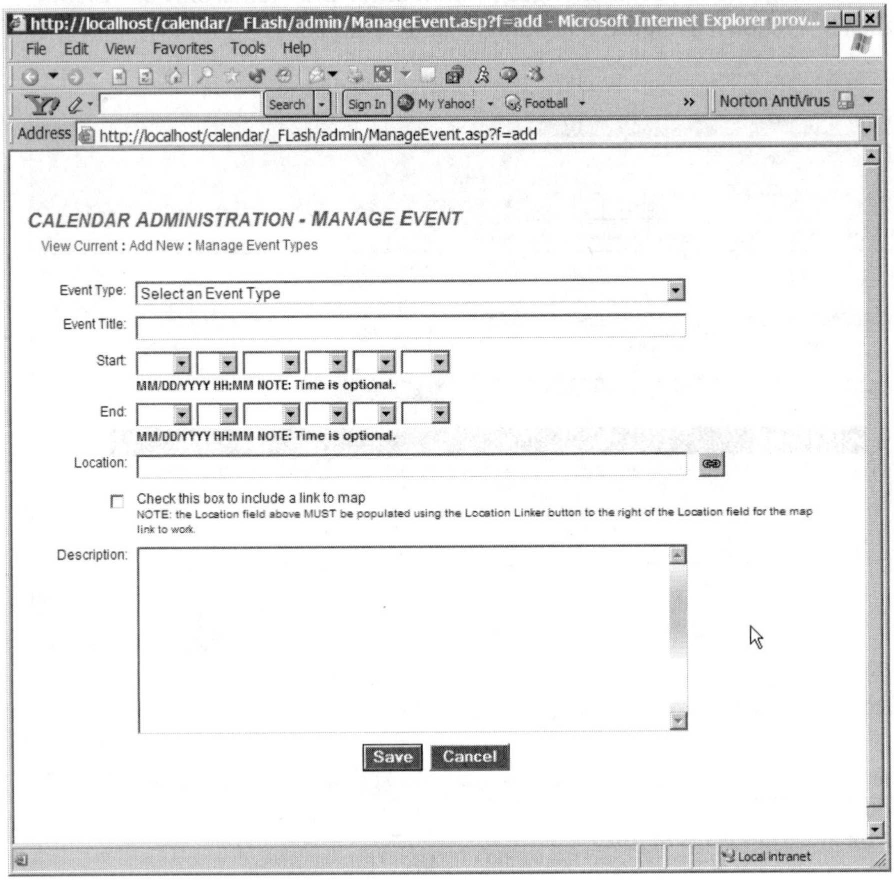

Figure 7-8. Adding an event

Now fill in all of the information as appropriate for the event. But, enter a start date that is in the past and enter an end date with only the Hour field filled out. When you submit the data to be saved, you will get two error messages, as shown in Figure 7-9.

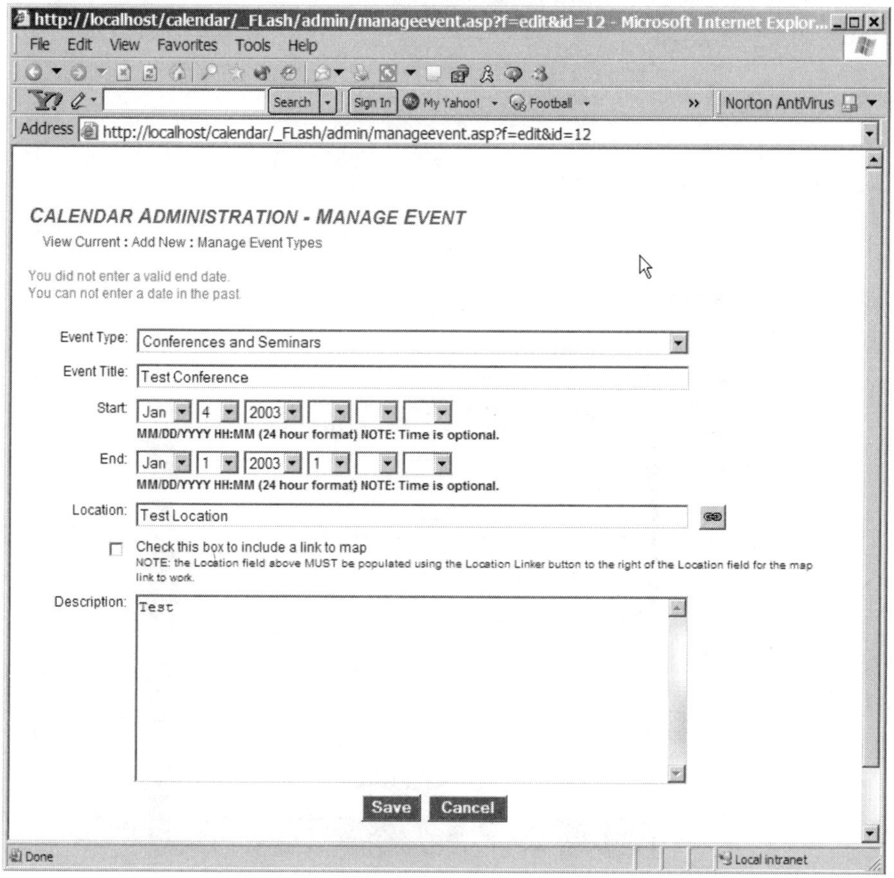

Figure 7-9. The error messages

Now enter the dates and times properly and save the event. Even after going through all of the date manipulation logic, the dates and times display properly. Figure 7-10 shows an event being edited. It also shows the location linker displayed.

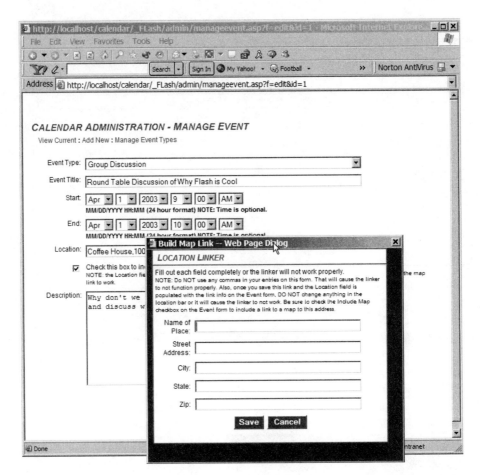

Figure 7-10. Editing an event

Finally, try to delete an event from the event listing page. A JavaScript alert box will pop up asking you to confirm that the event should be deleted. Figure 7-11 shows the alert box.

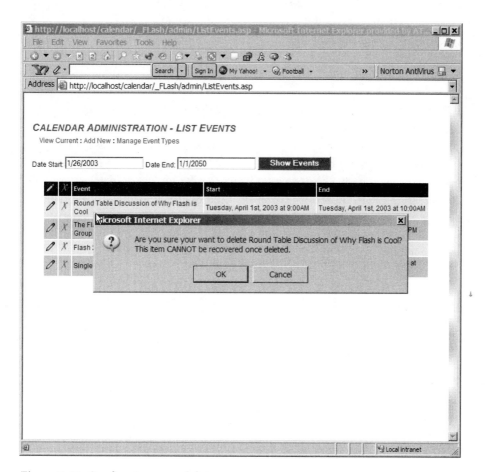

Figure 7-11. Confirming your delete

That is it for the administrative tools. Now you are ready to see how the Flash calendar interface displays and handles all of this event data.

Building the Flash Calendar Interface

To build your calendar interface while sticking with the methods used in the previous projects in this book, you must first determine what this calendar is going to do, how it will do it, and what it is going to look like while it does it.

What It Should Do

The Flash calendar must be able to take a collection of variables containing information about dates and events and dynamically generate a calendar with this information formatted and visible on it. It is not as daunting a task as it sounds. The key is organizing your information.

You know you need to create a graphical calendar for any date necessary. You know you are going to show one month at a time. So, the information you need to pass to Flash so it knows how to format and display that month is as follows:

- Month

- Year

- How many days in the month

- Weekday of the first day of the month

You also know that there will be next and previous buttons. One set will move the calendar one month forward or backward, and the other set will move the calendar one year forward or backward. So, you also need to tell the Flash calendar the following:

- Next month

- Previous month

- Next year (one for moving forward one month and one for moving forward one year)

- Previous year (one for moving back one month and one for moving back one year)

- Today's date

- Current month (number)

- Current month (in text format for display purposes)

- Current year

That is enough information to be able to format the calendar and navigate from month to month or from year to year. The other vital bits are the events to display on the calendar. You will use the date of the event to generate dynamic variable names to make it easy to determine to which day the information belongs. There are two variables for each day on the calendar:

- event# (the # is the number of the day. For example, June 15 would be event15)

- eventPop# (the # is the same as the event's)

The event variable will hold the title of the event that will display on the calendar itself. The eventPop will be used in a rollover pop-up box on the calendar that will show the same title but also the date and time (if available).

That is what the calendar should do, and this shows the variables and information needed to make it do it. Now let's move on to how it should work.

How It Should Work

You will first create the ASP script that will generate the information in the format determined previously. You are going to utilize the same methods you have used previously in this book and create a script that returns a QueryString type of output for Flash to read and parse. So you will create a blank .asp page in the Calendar directory and call it *calendar.asp*. Listing 7-32 is the script that goes into the page.

Listing 7-32. calendar.asp

```
'include the database opening code and functions
<!-- #include file="include/dbOpen.asp" -->
<!-- #include file="include/functions.inc" -->

<%
'Pull events from database and
'output data in plain text to a Flash calendar application
```

```
    if len(Request.QueryString("toMonth")) > 0
       and len(Request.QueryString("toYear")) > 0 then
    ' if QueryString contains a month and year to display, use it
       strCurrentDate = Request.QueryString("toMonth") & ↵
          "/1/" & Request.QueryString("toYear")
    else
    'else use current date
       strCurrentDate = date
    end if
'set up values for current date
    intToDay = day(date)
    intThisMonth = month(date)
    intThisYear = year(date)
'format for output to Flash
    strThisYear = "&intThisYear=" & intThisYear
    strThisMonth = "&intThisMonth=" & intThisMonth
    strToday = "&intToDay=" & intToDay
'set up values for requested date
    intDay = day(strCurrentDate)
    intMonth = month(strCurrentDate)
    intYear = year(strCurrentDate)
    intFirstDayOfMonth = intMonth & "/1/" & intYear
'format for output to Flash
    strMonthText = "&monthtext=" & monthname(intMonth)
    strToMonth = "&tomonth=" & intMonth
    strToYear = "&toyear=" & intYear
    strBdow = "&bdow=" & weekday(intFirstDayofMonth)
'find last day of month
    for x = 28 to 31
       if isdate(intMonth & "/" & x & "/" & intYear) then
          intLastDay = x
          intLastDayOfMonth = intMonth & "/" & x & "/" & intYear
          strLastDay = "&lastday=" & x
       end if
    next
'set up calendar date navigation vars
'all vars are based on requested date
    strNMonth = "&nmonth=" & month(dateadd("m",1,strCurrentDate))
    strNMonthYear = "&nmonthyear=" & year(dateadd("m",1,strCurrentDate))
    strPMonth = "&pmonth=" & month(dateadd("m",-1,strCurrentDate))
    strPMonthYear = "&pmonthyear=" & year(dateadd("m",-1,strCurrentDate))
    strNYear = "&nyear=" & year(dateadd("yyyy",1,strCurrentDate))
    strPYear = "&pyear=" & year(dateadd("yyyy",-1,strCurrentDate))
```

```
'stick everything so far into one string
    strVarText = strLastDay & strMonthText & strToMonth & strToYear & ↵
strBdow & strNMonth & strPMonth & strPMonthYear & strNMonthYear & ↵
strNYear & strPYear & strToDay & strThisMonth & strThisYear
'pull each days events from database and put into vars
    for y = 1 to intLastDay
    'each date has two vars here incremented with a number on the end
    'ex. strEvents1=xxx&strEventsPop1=xxx&strEvents2=xxx&strEventsPop2=xxx
    'the number is the date
        strEvents = strEvents & "&event" & y & "="
        strEventsPop = strEventsPop & "&eventsPop" & y & "=" & chr(10)
    'for adding filter for different event types
        select case Request.QueryString("f")
        case "Meetings"
            intFilter = 1
        case "Events"
            intFilter = 2
        case else
            intFilter = 0
        end select
    'pull events from database
    strSQL = "SELECT * FROM eventCalendar WHERE " & _
    "convert(datetime,convert(varchar,DatePart(yyyy, dteEventStart)) + '-' + " & _
    "convert(varchar,DatePart(mm, dteEventStart)) + '-' + " & _
    "convert(varchar,DatePart(dd,dteEventStart))) <= " & _
    "'" & intYear & "-" & intMonth & "-" & y & "'" & " AND " & _
    "convert(datetime,convert(varchar,DatePart(yyyy, dteEventEnd)) + '-' + " & _
    "convert(varchar,DatePart(mm, dteEventEnd)) + '-' + " & _
    "convert(varchar,DatePart(dd,dteEventEnd))) >= " & _
    "'" & intYear & "-" & intMonth & "-" & y & "'" & _
    "ORDER BY dteEventStart, dteEventEnd"
    Set rs = oConn.Execute(strSQL)
        do while not rs.EOF
            strEvents = strEvents & Server.URLEncode(rs("strTitle") & chr(10))
            if hour(rs("dteEventStart")) > 0 then
            'if hour of date is > 0 then display time
            strEventsPop = strEventsPop & Server.URLEncode(rs("strTitle") & chr(10) & _
            formatDate(rs("dteEventStart"),"%A, %B %d%O, %Y %h:%N%P") & _
                    chr(10) & chr(10))
            else
            'else don't
```

```
            strEventsPop = strEventsPop & Server.URLEncode(rs("strTitle") & chr(10) & _
            formatDate(rs("dteEventStart"),"%A, %B %d%O, %Y") & chr(10) & chr(10))
            end if
            rs.MoveNext
        loop
        set rs = nothing
    next

'stick all output vars into one string
    strVarText = strVarText & strEvents & strEventsPop

'output that string
    Response.Write("dummy=nothing" & strVarText & "&done=1")
'done=1 needs to be the LAST value sent
'it will tell the Flash app that it has received all the data

%>


<!-- #include file="include/dbClose.asp" -->
```

You need to build one more .asp page that will be called when someone clicks a day with events. We call it the "day-at-a-glance" script. It just pulls all the events for a particular date and displays them nicely in a pop-up page. Create another .asp page in the same directory and call it *calendarDayGlance.asp*. Listing 7-33 is the code that goes on that page.

Listing 7-33. Calendar Day at a Glance

```
<%@ Language=VBScript %>
<%option explicit%>
<html>
<head>
    <title>Day at a Glance</title>
    <link rel=stylesheet type="text/css" href="/style.css">

<SCRIPT LANGUAGE="JavaScript">
<!--
// Show the print dialogue
function printWindow() {
bV = parseInt(navigator.appVersion);
if (bV >= 4) window.print();
}
```

```
// -->
</script>

</head>
<body bgcolor="#333333">

<!--#include file="include/dbOpen.asp" -->

<table width=100% height=100%><tr><td>
<table width=400 cellspacing=0 cellpadding=0 border=0 align=center>
<tr>
    <td width=400 align=center valign=top align=center>
<a href="javascript:printWindow();"><span class=fineprintW>
Print this page</span></a><br>
<table width=380 cellspacing=0 cellpadding=0 border=1
 bordercolor="#737373" align=center bgcolor="#FFFFFF">
<tr>
    <td bgcolor="#ffffff"><table width=370 cellspacing=0
 cellpadding=4 border=0 align=center><tr><td class=subHead>
Event Calendar Day at a Glance -
<%=Request.QueryString("qdate")%></td></tr></table></td>
</tr>
<tr>
    <td>
    <table width=380 cellspacing=0 cellpadding=4 border=0 align=center>
<%

Dim strBGColor, strName, strAddress, strCity, strState, strZip, rs, arAddress, SQL
strBGColor = "#cccccc"

'  Get the event - note that we have to get the mm/dd/yy of the store date
'  to compare to the current day
SQL = "SELECT * FROM eventCalendar " & _
    "WHERE convert(datetime,convert(varchar,DatePart(yyyy, dteEventStart)) " & _
    "+ '-' + convert(varchar,DatePart(mm, dteEventStart)) " & _
    "+ '-' + convert(varchar,DatePart(dd,dteEventStart))) <= '" & _
    request.QueryString("qdate") & "' " & _
    "AND convert(datetime,convert(varchar,DatePart(yyyy, dteEventEnd)) " & _
    "+ '-' + convert(varchar,DatePart(mm, dteEventEnd)) " & _
    "+ '-' + convert(varchar,DatePart(dd,dteEventEnd))) >= '" & _
    request.QueryString("qdate") & "' " & _
    " ORDER BY dteEventStart, dteEventEnd"
```

```
' Get the data
Set rs = oConn.Execute(SQL)

' Loop through the events for the day
do while not rs.EOF

    ' Rotate the row colors
    if strBGColor = "#cccccc" then
        strBGColor = "#eeeeee"
    else
        strBGColor = "#cccccc"
    end if %>


<tr bgcolor="<%=strBGColor%>">
    <td>
    <b><%=rs("strTitle")%></b><BR>

    <!-- Build the date display based on the whether times should be shown -->
    <%  if rs("dteEventEnd") > rs("dteEventStart") then
        ' Check for times for both dates
        if hour(rs("dteEventStart")) > 0 and hour(rs("dteEventEnd")) > 0 then %>
            <span class=fineprintBKthin><b>
            <%=formatDate(rs("dteEventStart"),"%A, %B %d%O, %Y %h:%N%P")%>
             - 
            <%=formatDate(rs("dteEventEnd"),"%A, %B %d%O, %Y %h:%N%P")%>
            </b></span>
        <%  else %>
            <!-- No times shown -->
            <span class=fineprintBKthin><b>
            <%=formatDate(rs("dteEventStart"),"%A, %B %d%O, %Y")%>
             - 
            <%=formatDate(rs("dteEventEnd"),"%A, %B %d%O, %Y")%>
            </b></span>
        <%  end if
    else
        ' Only show the start date if for some reason the
        ' end date isn't defined
        if hour(rs("dteEventStart")) > 0 then %>
            <span class=fineprintBKthin><b>
            <%=formatDate(rs("dteEventStart"),"%A, %B %d%O, %Y at %h:%N%P")%>
            </b></span>
        <%  else %>
```

```
        <span class=fineprintBKthin><b>
        <%=formatDate(rs("dteEventStart"),"%A, %B %d%0, %Y")%>
        </b></span>
    <%   end if
    end if


    ' See if there is a location
    if rs("strLocation") <> "" then

        ' Split up values between commas
        arAddress = split(rs("strLocation"),",")

        ' Ensure there are all fields
        if ubound(arAddress) > 3 then
            strName = arAddress(0)
            strAddress = arAddress(1)
            strCity = arAddress(2)
            strState = arAddress(3)
            strZip = arAddress(4)

            ' Show the location
            Response.Write("<br><br><b>Location:</b><br>" & strName & _
                        "<br>" & strAddress & _
                        "<br>" & strCity & ", " & _
                            strState & " " & strZip)

            ' Build the map link
            if rs("blnMap") then
              Response.Write("<br><a
              href=""http://maps.expedia.com/default.asp?Street=" & _
              server.URLEncode(strAddress) & "&City=" & _
              server.URLEncode(strCity) & _
              "&State=" & server.URLEncode(strState) & "&ZIP=" & _
              server.URLEncode(strZip) & """ target=""_new"">Click For Map</a>")
            end if
        else
            Response.Write("<br><br><b>Location:</b><br>" & rs("strLocation"))
        end if
    end if
    Response.Write("<br><br><b>Details:</b><br>")
    Response.write(rs("strDescription"))
    %>
</td>
```

```
            </tr>
         <% rs.MoveNext
loop
set rs = nothing
%>

            </table>
            </td>
      </tr>
      </table>
         <a href="javascript:printWindow();"><span class=fineprintW> ⬠
            Print this page</span></a>
            </td>
      </tr>
      </table>
      <br>
            </td>
         </tr>
         </table>
         </td>
      </tr>
      </table>
   </td></tr></table>
   <!-- #include file="include/dbClose.asp" -->

   </body>
   </html>
   <!-- #include file="include/functions.inc" -->
```

That was easy enough; now let's move on to the Flash.

How It Should Look

This is also an easy issue. You want it to look like a calendar. It will display one
month at a time, just like a calendar on a wall. It will display events on the day
they happen. So it should look like a grid of sorts with numbers in each box. There
should be the month name at the top, with the days of the week above each of the
seven columns in the grid—just like a regular calendar. You want to highlight each
box that has an event in it, so you will change the background color of each box
that includes an event. You also want to know where today is on the calendar if
displaying the current month. So you will change the color of the date number if it
is today's date.

Now that you have all of the planning done, let's build it.

Designing the Flash Interface

You will set up the Timeline with all of the different sections, and then you will build the actual graphics that will drive the calendar. Finally, you will write the code that will control the entire thing.

Let's start by opening the Flash development environment and getting a fresh, blank movie on the screen. In the Properties Panel, click the Dimensions button; enter *700* for the width, *480* for the height, and *20* for a frame rate. You will leave the background white for this example.

NOTE *Feel free to customize the color scheme to fit your needs. For this example, we will specify colors in the step-by-step explanation, but those colors are not essential to the calendar—you can use any colors. It is also easy to go back after building the calendar and change the colors to achieve a new look.*

On the Timeline, rename the only existing layer to *control* and click Frame 1, selecting it. In the Actions Panel, type *stop();* and press Return. Click Frame 2 and press F6 (or select Insert ➤ Keyframe). With this frame still selected, use the Properties Panel to give the frame a label of *loadVars*. This will be where you load the data into the Flash calendar. Click Frame 10 and press F6 (or select Insert ➤ Keyframe). In the Actions Panel, type *stop();* and press Return. Also, give this frame a label of *initialize*. This is where you will wait for the data to load from the ASP script you called in the *loadVars* section. Click Frame 20 and press F6 (or select Insert ➤ Keyframe). In the Actions Panel, type *stop();* and press Return. Also, give this frame a label of *initialize2*. This is where you will parse the data received from the database. Click Frame 30 and press F6 (or select Insert ➤ Keyframe). Give this frame a label of *serverTimeout*. This will be an error screen if the script times out while trying to retrieve the data. Move all the way over to Frame 110 and click it to select it. Press F6 (or select Insert ➤ Keyframe). In the Actions Panel, type `gotoAndPlay("loadVars");`, which will tell the calendar to go back and try to load the data again.

That is all of the frames that the entire calendar will use. Now you will add the layers into which your objects and clips will go. Use the Add Layer button to add five new layers. Rename the layers from top to bottom as follows:

- eventPop

- initializer

- headings

- title header/buttons

- grid clips

The control layer should be on the bottom at this point. These are all the layers needed to build the calendar.

On the initializer layer, click Frame 1. Use the Text tool and type the words *Initializing Calendar* on the Stage. We used static, 24-point, black Verdana font for ours. Use something clean and easy to read. With this new text selected, press F8 (or select Insert ➤ Convert to Symbol). Give it a name of *initializeClip* and choose the Movie Clip option. Click OK. Using the Align Panel, center the clip vertically and horizontally so it is directly in the center of the Stage. This is going to be the preloader. This is simply a MovieClip that checks to see if the entire calendar has loaded into the user's browser, and when it has, it lets the calendar continue with what it needs to do. Using the Actions Panel, enter the code from Listing 7-34 into the MovieClip.

Listing 7-34. The Preloader

```
onClipEvent(enterFrame) {
    if (_root._framesLoaded >= _root._totalFrames) {
        _root.gotoAndPlay("loadVars");
    }
}
```

This code checks the _root, or main Timeline, to see if all the frames have loaded. When it returns true, it moves to the loadVars frame. That is the basic, simple preloader. The only problem with this is it is just static text on the screen while it waits to load. It is usually a good idea to add some sort of movement to let the user know that something is going on while they sit there. Sometimes developers add a progress indicator (bar) for larger downloads. The calendar is not a large download, so, most likely, it will not take long to load. A bar is not necessary in that case. Also, you will reuse this clip when loading the data, so the bar would not work in that instance either. You will, instead, add a slight bit of movement or change the text itself using keyframes.

Double-click the initializeClip to move into edit mode. On the Timeline of the MovieClip, click Frame 15 and press F6 (or select Insert ➤ Keyframe). Click Frame 30 and press F6 (or select Insert ➤ Keyframe). Click Frame 45 and press F5 (or select Insert ➤ Frame). Click Frame 1 again. Double-click the text on the Stage and add a period to the end of the text. Move to Frame 15, double-click the text on the Stage, and add a period, a space, and another period (. .) to the end of that text. Move to Frame 30, double-click the text on the Stage, and add a period, a space, a period, a space, and a period (. . .) to the end of the text. Now when the clip plays, it will add the three periods, one at a time, to the text over time. Then it will reset to one period and start over again. This will give a sense that the clip is doing something behind the scenes because of the change over time, comforting for users while waiting for things.

Move back to the main Timeline again and click Frame 2 of the initializer layer. Press F6 (or select Insert ➤ Keyframe). As mentioned, you will reuse this clip for the holding clip while the data loads from the database to the Flash. One thing you need to do is click the MovieClip in Frame 2, and in the Actions Panel, delete the code *only in the MovieClip instance found in Frame 2*. This code was for preloading, which you already did in Frame 1. You are only using the clip as a display in Frame 2, so you do not need that code here.

Click Frame 2 of the control layer and add the code from Listing 7-35.

Listing 7-35. loadVars

```
//tells Flash it hasn't received all the data yet
done=0;
//this is for calendar navigation
//if a next or prev button is pressed
//this resets all the color clips to white
//and then calls the calendar script again
//using the new requested date
if (qs > 0) {
    _root.grid = Number(_root.bdow);
    for (i=1; i<=Number(_root.lastday); i++) { // resetting calendar days
        set (["_root.event"+_root.grid],"");
        eval(["_root.grid"+_root.grid]).gotoAndStop(1);
        _root.grid++;
    }
    //Remove duplicated day clips and will be recreated on render
    for (i=1; i<43; i++) {
```

```
        removeMovieClip(["_root.grid"+i])
    }
}
//load data from database
if (qs == 1) {
loadVariables(["calendar.asp?f="+_root.f+"&toMonth="+tomonth+"&toYear="+pyear],"");
} else if (qs == 2) {
    loadVariables(["calendar.asp?f="+_root.f+"&toMonth="+pmonth+"&toYear=" ↵
+pmonthyear],"");
} else if (qs == 3) {
    loadVariables(["calendar.asp?f="+_root.f+"&toMonth="+nmonth+"&toYear=" ↵
+nmonthyear],"");
    lvcommand = "calendar.asp?f="+_root.f+"&toMonth="+nmonth+"&toYear="+nmonthyear;
} else if (qs == 4) {
    loadVariables(["calendar.asp?f="+_root.f+"&toMonth="+tomonth+"&toYear=" ↵
+nyear],"");
} else {
    loadVariables("calendar.asp?f="+_root.f,"");
}
//reset the nav flag
qs = 0;
```

Click Frame 10 of the initializer layer and press F6 (or select Insert ➤ Keyframe). This is the third and final use for the inializeClip because you use it to wait for the data to be completely received from the database. With the clip selected, use the Actions Panel to enter the code from Listing 7-36.

Listing 7-36. Receiving the Data

```
//this just tests for completion of data retrieval
//and keeps time so if it takes more than 15 seconds
//to retrieve the data, it errors out.
//once data retrieval is complete, move to next section

//set start time
onClipEvent(load) {
    startTime = getTimer();
}
onClipEvent(enterFrame) {
    //if data is received successfully, move on
    if (_root.done == "1") {
        _root.gotoAndStop("initialize2");
    }
```

```
    //if this has taken more than 15 seconds and
    //still is not done yet, send to error screen
    if ((getTimer() - startTime) > 15000) {
        _root.gotoAndPlay("serverTimeout");
    }
}
```

Click Frame 11 of the initializer layer and press F7 (or select Insert ➤ Blank Keyframe). Now click Frame 30 of the initializer layer and press F7 (or select Insert ➤Blank Keyframe). Using the Text tool and the same static, black, 24-point Verdana text, type the following onto the Stage: *The server timed out waiting for a response. Attempting to reconnect....*

Center this text vertically and horizontally on the Stage.

That is everything in the calendar except the calendar itself. You will now add a month name, weekday names, and buttons to move forward and backward in time. Also, you will build a MovieClip that will represent one day on the calendar. Then you will write some code that will duplicate and lay out that clip to make a calendar on the screen.

On the headings layer, click Frame 20 and press F7 (or select Insert ➤ Blank Keyframe). Using the Text tool in Static Text mode, create day-of-the-week headings similar to Figure 7-12. Be sure that each day of the week is a separate textbox so you can move them around and align them to their proper column on the calendar when it is built.

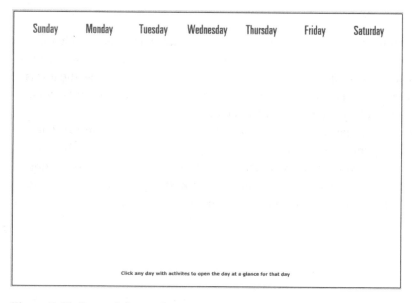

Figure 7-12. Days of the week

On the title header/buttons layer, click Frame 20 and press F7 (or select Insert
➤ Blank Keyframe). Using the Text tool in Dynamic Text mode, draw a textbox
similar to the one in Figure 7-13. In the Properties Panel, set the properties for that
textbox for the text to be centered. Choose the font and color you want. In the Var
property, give this textbox a variable name of *displayMonth*.

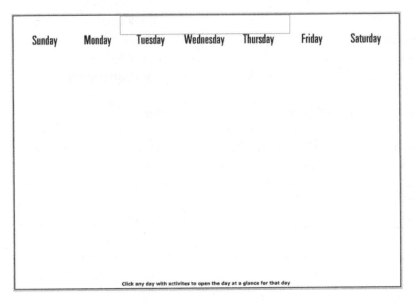

Figure 7-13. The month name textbox

You will build the actual little box that will be a day on the calendar. In this box
you will need to have the outline around it, the day number, the event text, a button to click for more detail for the events of that day, scrollbars in case the text is
longer than the day has room for, and a block to change the background color of
the day if there are any events found on that day.

On the gridClips layer, click Frame 20 and press F7 (or select Insert ➤ Blank
Keyframe). Using the Rectangle tool, set the properties to have no fill with a one-
pixel black outline. Now draw a rectangle somewhere on the Stage. The size does
not matter because you will resize it using the Properties Panel and manual entry.
Choose the Arrow tool from the toolbar and double-click the outline just drawn to

select it. Using the Properties Panel, enter a width of *97* and a height of *69*. Press F8 (or select Insert ➤ Convert to Symbol), enter *dayClip* for the name, choose the Movie Clip option, and click OK. With this clip selected, use the Properties Panel to enter an instance name of *grid0,* an X position of *13,* and a Y position of *56.*

Double-click the grid0 clip to open it in edit mode. Right now there is one layer with the outline you drew in it. Rename that layer *outline.* Now add six more layers. They should have the following names in the following order, so rename and rearrange them to match this:

- scrollers

- invisiButton

- outline

- textMask

- text

- color changer

- control

In Frame 1 of the control layer, use the Actions Panel to enter the code from Listing 7-37.

Listing 7-37. gridClip Control Frame 1

```
stop();
scrollers._visible = false;
```

This stops the day clip in Frame 1 and hides the scrollbars (which you will build a little later).

In Frame 1 of the text layer, use the Text tool in Dynamic Text mode and draw a textbox matching the size as closely as possible to Figure 7-14.

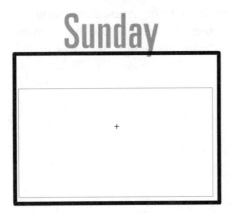

Figure 7-14. The day event textbox

We used 8-point Verdana text because Verdana is easy to read at small sizes, and the size needs to be small for the text to fit into the day clip. Use the Properties Panel and give this textbox a variable name of *event*. Also in Frame 1 of the text layer, use the Text tool in Dynamic Text mode again and draw another textbox that matches the size as closely as possible to Figure 7-15. Use the Properties Panel and give this textbox a variable name of *_parent.dayNum*.

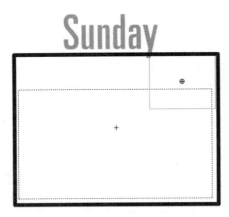

Figure 7-15. The day number textbox

This will be the day of the month text. We used 15-point Verdana text for it. Make sure it is right justified so it will always be in the top-right corner of the day clip. Use the Arrow tool, click the day number textbox to select it, and press F8 (or select Insert ➤ Convert to Symbol). Give it a name of *dayNum* and a type of Movie Clip and click OK. In the Properties Panel, give it an instance name of *dayNum*.

In the textMask layer, use the Rectangle tool with no outline and any fill color (it will not appear when the calendar runs) and draw a rectangle that fits inside the outline you drew earlier. Make sure it does not go outside the outline and that there is no white space between this rectangle and the outline. When you have your rectangle the correct size, right-click the textMask layer and choose Mask from the context menu. Your rectangle will disappear (actually it just becomes invisible), and the layers will look a little different. The rectangle you drew is now a mask layer, and the text layer will only show text that is within that rectangle you drew. This is a safety precaution to make sure text does not stray outside the day clip into another day.

You need to add a second frame to this clip, so click Frame 2 of the outline layer and press F5 (or select Insert ➤ Blank Keyframe). Do the same thing for the textMask and text layers. Now click Frame 2 of the scrollers layer and press F6 (or select Insert ➤ Keyframe). Do the same thing for the invisiButton, color changer, and control layers.

Click Frame 1 of the textMask layer and press Control+Alt+C (or select Edit ➤ Copy Frames). Click Frame 2 of the color changer layer and press Control+Alt+V (or select Edit ➤ Paste Frames). This is going to be the background color that this day will change to if there are events on that day. Change the color of the rectangle to something that fits your color scheme. If your text is a dark color, then make sure your background color changes to something light (and visa versa).

You will create something that we call the *invisiButton*. This is a button in Flash that is invisible but is still clickable. You will do this because you want the entire day to be clickable if there are events on that day. Because the rectangle frame you copied in the previous step should still be on the Clipboard, just click Frame 2 of the invisiButton layer and press Control+Alt+V (or select Edit ➤ Paste Frames). Make sure the rectangle is selected and press F8 (or select Insert ➤ Convert to Symbol). Give it a name of *invisiButton,* choose Button for the type, and click OK. Now you have a big colored button on the screen that covers everything in the day. Here is the trick to making that button invisible: Double-click the button to open it in edit mode. There is only one frame with a keyframe in it, and that is the Up state. Simply click the keyframe, drag it to the hit frame, and release it there. Now go back to the dayNum clip, and the button will look like a cyan color on the Stage but will be invisible when the calendar runs.

With the invisiButton selected, use the Actions Panel to enter the code from Listing 7-38 for the button.

Listing 7-38. Day Clip Button Code

```
on (press) {
getURL(["javascript:calPop('/calendarDayGlance.asp?qdate="+_root.tomonth+"/"+↵
dayNum+"/"+_root.toyear+"')"],"");
}


on (rollover) {
    // set the vars to display that days info
    _root.eventPop.event = eval(["_root.eventsPop"+ dayNum]);
    // decide whether popup will display left or right of mouse
    // based on which side of calendar the mouse is on
    _root.eventPop.gotoAndPlay(2);
}
on (rollout, dragout) {
    // clear the vars on close of popup
    _root.eventPop.event = "";
    _root.eventPop.gotoAndStop(1);
}
```

The rollover and rollout (and dragout) events are for the pop-up event information box that you will build a little later.

At this point you are going to build the scrollbars that will only be visible if the text goes longer than the day box will hold. Scrollbars might be a misleading term; scroll *buttons* might be better because there really is no bar.

NOTE *Flash MX has some built-in components to create things such as scrollbars, checkboxes, radio buttons, and a whole bunch of other things as well as components that you can find online. You can easily use these components by dragging and dropping them from the Components Panel onto your Stage or onto an object on your Stage. We are not using the built-in scrollbar component here because we don't really want scrollbars so much as just some buttons to scroll the text. Scrollbars would take up too much valuable real estate in the day boxes.*

Click Frame 2 of the scrollers layer. First, you need to build two buttons. You will use simple triangles for the up and down buttons. To do this, just use the Rectangle tool while holding the Shift key down, and it will constrain the tool to a perfect square (don't worry about size for now; you will resize it after you have the buttons built). Now select that square and rotate it 45 degrees. You can do this by using the Scale and Rotate method (Control+Alt+S or select Modify ➤ Transform ➤ Scale and Rotate), or you can use the Free Transform tool from the toolbar and hold the Shift key while rotating to constrain the rotation to 15-degree increments. Once the square is rotated around and looks like a diamond, use the Arrow tool and drag a selection box around the top half of the diamond. Make sure you select exactly half of the shape. Now delete the selected half. You should be left with a tri-angle pointing down. Set the color to something that matches the scheme and add an outline if desired. Now select the entire shape and copy and paste it into the same layer. With one of the triangles completely selected (only one of them), select Modify ➤ Transform ➤ Flip Vertical. Now one triangle should point up, and one should point down.

Select the up triangle and press F8 (or select Insert ➤ Convert to Symbol). Give it a name of *btnUpScroll* and a type of Button. Click OK. Do the same thing with the down triangle and give it a name of *btnDownScroll* and a type of Button. Scale and place them to look like Figure 7-16.

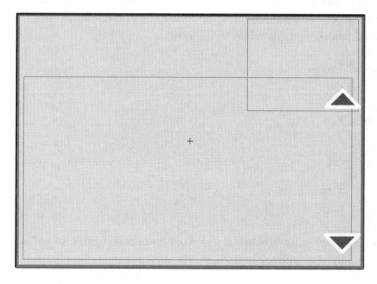

Figure 7-16. The up and down buttons

Select both buttons and press F8 (or select Insert ➤ Convert to Symbol). Give the symbol the name of *scrollers* and a type of Movie Clip. Use the Properties Panel and give the new clip an instance name of *scrollers*. Select the clip and use the Actions Panel to enter the code from Listing 7-39 for the clip.

Listing 7-39. Scollers Clip

```
onClipEvent (enterFrame) {
    if (_parent.event.maxscroll > 1 and this._Visible == false) {
        this._visible = true;
    }
    if (scrollerDirection == "up") {
        event.scroll++;
    } else if (scrollerDirection == "down") {
        event.scroll--;
    }
}
```

This simply checks the textbox for that day to see if there is more text than can be displayed at any one time. If the text is larger than the textbox, the scroll buttons will be visible; if not, they will be invisible. And it checks to see if one of the scroll buttons is click and, if so, scrolls the text in the proper direction.

Double-click the scrollers clip to open it in edit mode. Rename the layer in this clip to *buttons*. Click the triangle pointing up to select it and enter the code from Listing 7-40 into the Actions Panel for that button.

Listing 7-40. Up Scroll Button

```
on (press) {
    parent.scrollerDirection = "up";
}

on (release,dragOut) {
    parent.scrollerDirection = "stop";
}
```

Click the triangle pointing down to select it and enter the code from Listing 7-41 into the Actions Panel for that button.

Listing 7-41. Down Scroll Button

```
on (press) {
    parent.scrollerDirection = "down";
}

on (release,dragOut) {
    parent.scrollerDirection = "stop";
}
```

Move all the way back out to the main Timeline. This grid0 clip that you just created is going to be the master clip from which you will duplicate all the calendar days. At this point you will need to duplicate all the days and parse the data received from the database into the calendar. On the control layer, click Frame 20 and enter the code from Listing 7-42 into the Actions Panel for that frame.

Listing 7-42. Duplicating Day Clips

```
stop();

//This will be the incremented grid number
//during the duplication loop below
i=1;
//make the master grid clip invisible as
//it is only for duplication purposes and
//will not be used for an actual day
grid0._visible=false;

//duplicate 6 rows of 7 columns of day boxes
for (row=1;row<7;row++) {
   for (col=1;col<8;col++) {
      i++;
      duplicateMovieClip(grid0,"grid"+i,i+100);
      setProperty(["grid"+i],_x,grid0._x+(97*(col-1)));
      setProperty(["grid"+i],_y,grid0._y+(69*(row-1)));
   }
}


//*********************************************************
// process data received from db
//*********************************************************
//month and year displayed at top of calendar
_root.displayMonth = _root.monthtext + ", " + _root.toyear;

//what grid square will the first day be on
_root.grid = Number(_root.bdow);

//make all grids before the first day invisible
for (i=1; i<Number(_root.bdow); i++) {
   setProperty (["_root.grid"+i],_visible, false);
}

//set what grid squares are after the last day
```

```
//make them invisible
afterLast = Number(_root.bdow) + Number(_root.lastday);
for (i=afterLast; i<44; i++) {
   setProperty (["_root.grid"+i],_visible, false);
}


for (i=1; i<=Number(_root.lastday); i++) { // setting calendar days
   //display day number
   set (["_root.grid"+_root.grid+".dayNum"], i);
   //set event title
   set (["_root.grid"+_root.grid+".event"],eval(["event"+i]));

   //if there is an event that day
   if (length(eval(["_root.grid"+_root.grid+".event"])) > 0) {
      //moves the clip to frame 2 where color background
      //and clickable button are activated
      eval(["_root.grid"+_root.grid]).gotoAndStop(2);
   }

   // set today to different color
   if (int(intThisMonth) == int(tomonth) and int(toyear) == int(intThisYear)) {
      if (i == intToDay) {
         clrDayNum = new Color(["_root.grid"+_root.grid+".dayNum"]);
         clrDayNum.SetRGB(0x0054A6);
         }
   }

   //increment grid number
   _root.grid++;
}
```

Click Frame 21 of the headings layer and press F7 (or select Insert ➤ Blank Keyframe). Click Frame 21 of the title header/buttons layer and press F7 (or select Insert ➤ Blank Keyframe). Click Frame 21 of the gridClips layer and press F7 (or select Insert ➤ Blank Keyframe). Click Frame 21 of the eventPop layer and press F7 (or select Insert ➤ Blank Keyframe). This ensures that the grid, titles, and buttons only show for the frame that they are supposed to show for and not anything after (such as the error display frame).

You are so close to being done now! There are only two things left to build, the buttons to move forward and backward in time on the calendar and an event detail pop-up box.

Building the Navigation Buttons

You will build with the navigation buttons first. Click Frame 20 of the title header/buttons layer. Using the tools from the toolbar, build four buttons like those in Figure 7-17.

Figure 7-17. In order: Move one year back, move one month back, move one month forward, and move one year forward

Now place those shapes using Figure 7-18 as a reference.

Figure 7-18. Placing the navigation buttons

Select the "one year back" shape and press F8 (or select Insert ➤ Convert to Symbol). Give it a name of *buttonPrevYear,* select the Button type, and click OK. Use the Actions Panel to enter the code in Listing 7-43 for this button.

Listing 7-43. Previous Year Button

```
on (press) {
    qs = 1;
    _root.gotoAndPlay("loadVars")
}
```

Select the "one month back" shape and press F8 (or select Insert ➤ Convert to Symbol). Give it a name of *buttonMonthYear,* select the Button type, and click OK. Use the Actions Panel to enter the code in Listing 7-44 for this button.

Listing 7-44. Previous Month Button

```
on (press) {
    qs = 2;
    _root.gotoAndPlay("loadVars")
}
```

Select the "one month forward" shape and press F8 (or select Insert ➤ Convert to Symbol). Give it a name of *buttonNextMonth,* select the Button type, and click OK. Use the Actions Panel to enter the code in Listing 7-45 for this button.

Listing 7-45. Next Year Button

```
on (press) {
    qs = 3;
    _root.gotoAndPlay("loadVars")
}
```

Select the "one year forward" shape and press F8 (or select Insert ➤ Convert to Symbol). Give it a name of *buttonNextYear,* select the Button type, and click OK. Use the Actions Panel to enter the code in Listing 7-46 for this button.

Listing 7-46. Previous Year Button

```
on (press) {
    qs = 4;
    _root.gotoAndPlay("loadVars")
}
```

Open each button and give each an Over and Down state that looks different from the Up state. For example, change the colors and so on.

NOTE *This is an optional step and only for aesthetic purposes. You could also define a Hit state as a simple square that encompasses the entire button to make the "clickable" area of the button more consistent.*

Creating the Detail Pop-Up Box

The final element to the calendar is an optional element. It is a box that will pop up when someone puts their mouse over a day with events in it. This box displays for a few seconds and will have more detail, such as a short description and time. You can omit this element, and the calendar will function just fine without it.

Click Frame 20 of the eventPop layer and press F7 (or select Insert ➤ Blank Keyframe). Select the Rectangle tool from the toolbar. Below the toolbar should be a section called *Options*. With the Rectangle tool selected, click the button in the Options Panel. This will open a dialog box asking for a radius to make the corners rounded. Enter *16* and click OK. Now draw a rectangle onto the Stage. Use the Properties Panel to resize the rectangle to 190 pixels wide by 57 pixels high. Size is important here, so make sure it is the correct dimensions. Change the fill and outline colors to work with the color scheme. We used a light red fill and a black outline. The fill color needs to be light enough so the text can be easily seen (or dark if your text color is lighter).

Select the entire shape and press F8 (or select Insert ➤ Convert to Symbol). Give it a name of *eventPop*, choose the type of Movie Clip, and click OK. Use the Properties Panel to give it an instance name of *eventPop*. Double-click the clip to open it in edit mode. Select the rectangle and press Control+C (or select Edit ➤ Copy). Now press F8 (or select Insert ➤ Convert to Symbol). This time give it a name of *eventPopBG*, choose the type of Movie Clip, and click OK. Double-click this clip to open it in edit mode. Add a layer to this clip. Click Frame 22 of the new layer and press F7 (or select Insert ➤ Blank Keyframe). Click this new keyframe and enter the code from Listing 7-47 for that frame.

Listing 7-47. Event Box Background

```
if (_parent.event.scroll == _parent.event.maxScroll) {
    _parent.event.scroll=0;
} else {
    _parent.event.scroll++;
}
```

This code will automatically scroll the text in the pop-up box if it is longer than the box. It will scroll slowly so it can be read as it scrolls up. When it gets to the end, it starts over again.

Click Frame 22 of the layer with the rectangle in it and press F5 (or select Insert ➤ Frame). Move back out one clip to the eventPop clip. Add two new layers to it. Click the keyframe with the eventPopBG clip in it to select it. Now drag that frame to Frame 20 and drop it there. Select Frame 20 of the layer on the top of the order and press F7 (or select Insert ➤ Blank Keyframe). Now press Control+Shift+V (or select Edit ➤ Paste in Place). This should paste your rectangle into this frame. This will be your text mask.

There should be one layer left with nothing in it. Click Frame 20 of this layer and press F5 (or select Insert ➤ Blank Keyframe). Use the Text tool in Dynamic Text mode and draw a textbox that just fits inside the rectangle shape.

NOTE *You will have to hide the top layer to see the textbox underneath it for now.*

We used 8-point Verdana font. Make sure the Properties Panel is set to Multi-line for this textbox. Once you have your textbox placed properly, right-click the top layer and choose Mask from the context menu. Just like before, this will make sure no text wanders outside the boundaries of the space allotted.

Click Frame 1 of the eventPopBG layer. Enter the *stop()*;command in the Actions Panel for that frame. Now click Frame 20 of that same layer and enter the code from Listing 7-48 into the Actions Panel for that frame.

Listing 7-48. Event Clip Placement

```
if (_root._xmouse > 349) { xpos = _root._xmouse - (190.8/2); }
if (_root._xmouse < 350) { xpos = _root._xmouse + (190.8/2); }
setProperty (_root.eventPop,_x,xpos);
setProperty (_root.eventPop,_y,_root._ymouse - 15);
if (event.maxScroll-1 > 0) {
    event = "\n\n" + event + "\n\n";
}
stop();
```

This simply checks to see where on the calendar the cursor is positioned so the clip knows whether to pop up to the left or to the right of the cursor without running off the screen. Then it checks to see if there is any text overflow and adds some white space if there is. This is just to make the scroll cleaner looking.

Move all the way back out to the main Timeline and select the eventPop clip. Use the Actions Panel to enter to code from Listing 7-49 for this clip.

Listing 7-49. Swap Depths

```
onClipEvent(load) {
    this.swapDepths(_root.grid42);
}
```

This just swaps the Z-order of this clip with the last day clip on the grid so the pop-up box will be on top of all the day clips and not accidentally show up underneath any of the day clips.

 NOTE Z-order *is the depth or layer order that objects are in. In other words, it determines which objects are on top of each other and which are underneath. This is important when dealing with duplicated clips; no matter which layer you have the original clip on, the duplicated clips will always be on top of everything else based on the depth you gave the clip when duplicating it.*

The calendar interface is now complete. Publish your files, upload them, and watch it work, as shown in Figure 7-19.

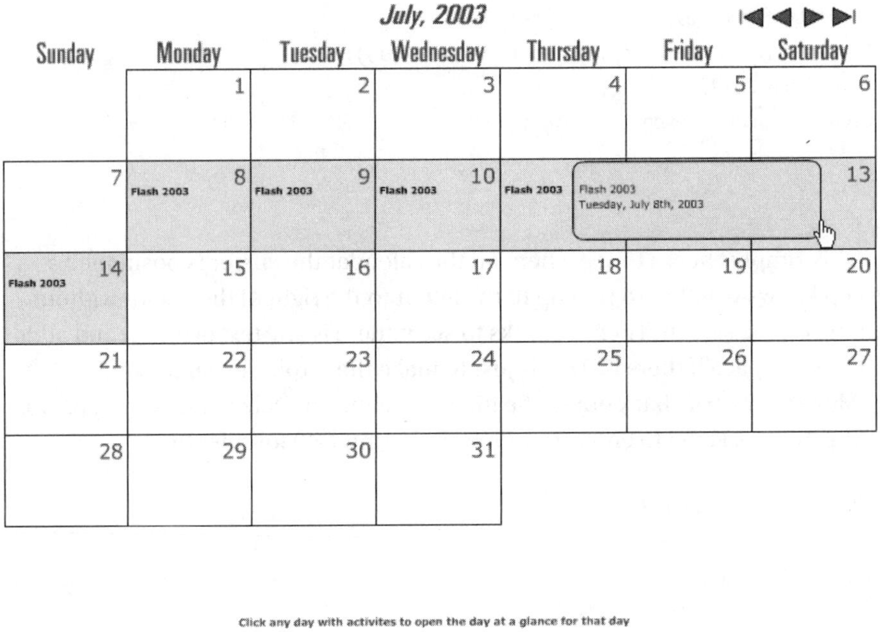

			July, 2003			◄◄ ◄ ► ►◄
Sunday	Monday	Tuesday	Wednesday	Thursday	Friday	Saturday
	1	2	3	4	5	6
7	8 Flash 2003	9 Flash 2003	10 Flash 2003	Flash 2003 Flash 2003 Tuesday, July 8th, 2003		13
14 Flash 2003	15	16	17	18	19	20
21	22	23	24	25	26	27
28	29	30	31			

Click any day with activites to open the day at a glance for that day

Figure 7-19. The event calendar

Summary

In this chapter you built a great foundation for creating snazzy dynamic calendars in Flash. You also were able to dig into some of the date and time functionality built into VBScript. In Flash you used the ever-handy invisiButton, dynamic color changing, more MovieClip duplication, variables, some scrolling text, and all the things you have learned up to now to build a calendar to interface with your event data.

In the next chapter you will shift gears and move into the arena of business reporting. Let's face it—building great-looking reports in HTML complete with dazzling graphical charts is not the easiest thing in the world. It usually takes some type of special ActiveX plug-in to do anything more than text reporting. We will show how Flash can come to the rescue and provide powerful ways to display business data.

CHAPTER 8

Building Graphical Reports

IN THIS FINAL CHAPTER, you are going to use the power of Flash to build data-driven graphical reports. Specifically, we will show you how to generate queries that create bar and pie charts.

This example uses ASP.NET and Microsoft Access for implementation. You will be working with the familiar concepts of e-business ordering data. The reports will be administrative in nature and show different types of activity for a sample e-commerce store.

Understanding the E-Commerce Database Requirements

The e-commerce database structure for this example is fairly intuitive. You will have orders, baskets, basket items, and shoppers. Shoppers will create baskets, add basket items, and then place their orders. For the purposes of this chapter, we will show a fairly simple model; e-commerce data structures can certainly get much more complicated.

The sample data for the database will be giant kids' toys such as giant wagons and giant yo-yos. The database is also populated with basket, shopper, and order data that you will be able to use in order to generate your Flash graphical reports.

Designing the Database

The database consists of five tables: Basket, BasketItem, Item, Order, and Shopper. The tables relate to each other to model the core e-commerce data. Figure 8-1 shows the relationships between the tables.

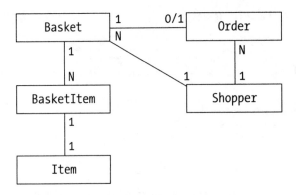

Figure 8-1. Orders database structure

Shoppers will come to the site and shop (of course). When they view items, they will add items to their basket. A shopper can then place an order based on a basket. Thus, shoppers can have any number of baskets and orders. But, a basket or order will relate to only one shopper.

Baskets can turn into orders, but they might not always. Thus, the relationship between baskets and orders is one basket to zero or one order. Baskets will contain items. A basket can have one or more items. Thus, the BasketItem table has a one-to-one relationship with the Item table. In other words, as you would expect, each item in the Basket table corresponds to an item in the Item table.

NOTE *In an actual e-commerce system, you might not want to explicitly define a relationship between the BasketItem and Item tables. Instead, the item data would actually be copied into the BasketItem table at the time the product is purchased. That way, the price, description, name, and so on of the item when the customer purchases the product will not change with subsequent updates to the data in the Item table. A good example of this is when the shopper adds an on-sale product to their basket. If the sale ends while they are still shopping, they will still have the sale price in their basket.*

Let's now dissect each table starting with Item. Table 8-1 defines the fields for the Item table.

Table 8-1. Item Table Definition

FIELD NAME	DATA TYPE	DESCRIPTION
ItemID	AutoNumber	The primary key of the table and auto increments
ItemName	Text (field size 50)	Stores the name of the item
ItemDesc	Memo	Stores the description of the item
ItemPrice	Currency	Store the price of the item

This table is pretty straightforward. The AutoNumber data type ensures you have unique values created for the primary key. The default for the data type is to increment. The other three fields are standard and define the item data.

The next table, Basket, defines the primary basket data. Table 8-2 defines the fields for the Basket table.

Table 8-2. Basket Table Definition

FIELD NAME	DATA TYPE	DESCRIPTION
BasketID	AutoNumber	The primary key of the table and auto increments
ShopperID	Number	Foreign key that relates the basket to the shopper
DateCreated	Date/Time	Date and time the basket was created
Total	Currency	Stores the total value of the order
Tax	Currency	Stores the tax amount for the order
Shipping	Currency	Stores the shipping amount for the order

The primary purpose of the Basket table is to store the core pricing components of the basket including tax, shipping, and total. Tax and shipping will be calculated for the order. The total is determined by adding the cost of all of the basket items, the tax, and the shipping.

The BasketItem table defines all of the items in the shopping basket. Table 8-3 defines the fields for the BasketItem table.

Table 8-3. BasketItem Table Definition

FIELD NAME	DATA TYPE	DESCRIPTION
BasketID	AutoNumber	The primary key of the table and auto increments
ItemID	Number	Foreign key that relates the basket item to the Item table
Quantity	Number	Number of each item purchased

The BasketItem table basically refers to the Item table and indicates how many of each item the shopper would like to purchase.

The Order table ties together the Shopper and Basket tables as well as stores the order date. Table 8-4 defines the fields for the table.

Table 8-4. Order Table Definition

FIELD NAME	DATA TYPE	DESCRIPTION
OrderID	AutoNumber	The primary key of the table and auto increments
BasketID	Number	Foreign key that points to the basket of items that was ordered
ShopperID	Number	Foreign key pointing to the shopper who placed the order
OrderDate	Date/Time	The date and time the order was placed

In a live e-commerce system, this is probably where the payment data (for example, credit card information, billing address, and so on) for the order would also reside.

Your final table is for the shopper data. Table 8-5 defines the fields for the Shopper table.

Table 8-5. Shopper Table Definition

FIELD NAME	DATA TYPE	DESCRIPTION
ShopperID	AutoNumber	The primary key of the table and auto increments
ShopperFirstName	Text (field size 50)	First name of the shopper
ShopperLastName	Text (field size 50)	Last name of the shopper
ShopperAreaCode	Text (field size 3)	Area code of the shopper
ShipperPhone	Text (Field Size 7)	Phone number of the shopper
ShopperStreet	Text (Field Size 50)	Street of the shopper
ShopperCity	Text (Field Size 20)	City of the shopper
ShopperState	Text (Field Size 2)	State of the shopper
ShipperZip	Long Integer	ZIP code of the shopper
DateRegistered	Date/Time	Date the shopper first registered their information

The Shopper table's data is pretty straightforward. It contains the basic name and address data to identify the shopper. Note that you do not have any foreign keys in this table because the ShopperID is stored in the Basket and Order tables.

That does it for the design of your database. Next, you will create Access queries that will return the data you want to chart in your application.

Building Access Queries

In the previous chapters, you created most of your SQL queries in Active Server Pages (ASP) or ASP.NET code. You then passed the query to the database for execution. In this chapter, you are going to do the same thing but with a twist. You are going to leverage Access querying capabilities to return the data you will need in your application.

Access queries act like regular tables to applications calling the Access database. As you will see, you can query the Access query just as you would a table. You will be able to utilize these queries from your ASP.NET pages to return the data for the various reports.

To get started, with the database open, click the Queries option on the Objects tab. You can create new queries with a number of methods, such as using a wizard, writing SQL, and using a graphical design interface. For these examples, you will build the queries using the graphical Design view.

To create your first query, click the Create Query in Design View option. Access opens the Design view, and a dialog box pops up asking for the tables you want to include in your query. Figure 8-2 displays the Show Table dialog box.

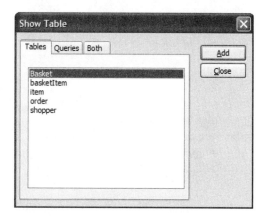

Figure 8-2. The Show Table dialog box

For your first query, you are going to calculate the number of abandoned baskets and their total value. Abandoned baskets are baskets that the shopper added items into but did not purchase. For the query, add the Basket table to the query. The Design view should now look like Figure 8-3.

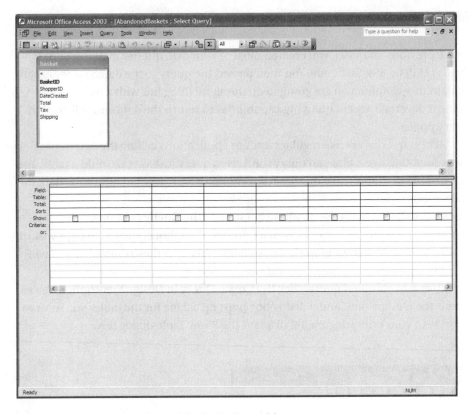

Figure 8-3. The Design view with the Basket table

Now you are ready to set up the return fields (columns) for the query. The first column will be a calculated value of the number of abandoned baskets. In the design grid, enter the Field name as *Abandoned Baskets*. In the Total row of the design grid, select Count. Ensure that the Table row is set to Basket and the Show checkbox is selected.

In the next column, you are going to add the value of the baskets. Double-click the Total column of the Basket table to add it to the design grid. In the Total row of the design grid, select Sum.

Your last column sets up the where clause for your query. In this case, you need to return all baskets that have not been turned into orders. Double-click the BasketID column of the Basket table to add it to the design grid. On the Total row, select Where to indicate this is a where clause option. Uncheck the Show checkbox so the BasketID does not show up in the returned results. Now you have to set the criteria for the where clause. In this case, you are going to use a subselect query and the Not In clause. The criteria statement is as follows:

```
Not In (select basketid from [order])
```

The subselect retrieves all of the BasketIDs from the Order table. This is effectively the list of all baskets that were ultimately placed as orders. The Not In clause then says, "Give me all of the BasketIDs from the Basket table that are not in the Order table."

The final Design view looks like Figure 8-4.

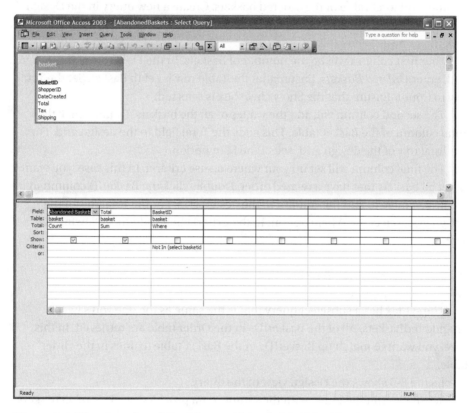

Figure 8-4. The query for adding the number of abandoned baskets

Now save the query as *AbandonedBaskets*. If you run the query, you will get the number of baskets and their total values. For the sample data, this is three baskets and $70,127 (those are expensive toys!). Listing 8-1 shows the SQL generated by the query.

Listing 8-1. AbandonedBaskets SQL Code

```
SELECT Count(basket.BasketID) AS [Abandoned Baskets],
    Sum(basket.Total) AS SumOfTotal
FROM basket
WHERE (((basket.BasketID) Not In (select basketid from [order])));
```

Your next query is the opposite of AbandonedBaskets; you want to get the number and total value of the ordered baskets. Create a new query in the Design view. From the Show Table dialog box, add the Basket table. (Your Design view will look the same as Figure 8-3.)

Your first column will be the number of baskets. In the Field row of the design grid, enter *Ordered Baskets*. Ensure that the Table row is set to Basket. Set the Total row to Count. Ensure that the Show checkbox is selected.

The second column will add the values of all the baskets. Double-click the Total column of the Basket table. This adds the Total field to the design grid. For the Total row of the design grid, select the Sum option.

The final column will set up your where clause criteria. In this case, you want to get all baskets that have a related order. Double-click the BasketID column in the Basket table to add the column to the design grid. For the Total row of the design grid, select the Where option. In the Criteria field, add the following SQL syntax:

```
In (select basketid from [order])
```

The syntax has a subselect query that is the same as the one you saw for AbandonedBaskets. All of the BasketIDs in the Order table are retrieved. In this case, you want to match up BasketIDs in the Basket table to ones in the Order table.

Figure 8-5 shows the Design view of the query.

When you run the query with the sample data provided, a count of 45 baskets is returned that totals $911,656. Listing 8-2 shows the SQL generated by the query.

Listing 8-2. OrderedBaskets SQL Code

```
SELECT Count(basket.BasketID) AS [Ordered Baskets], Sum(basket.Total) AS SumOfTotal
FROM basket
WHERE (((basket.BasketID) In (select basketid from [order])));
```

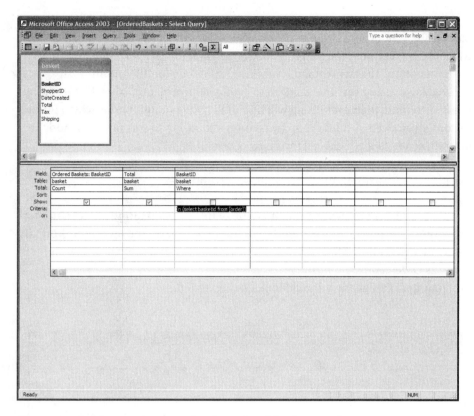

Figure 8-5. Setting up the query for the ordered baskets total

For your next query, you will want to return the order totals by month. As you will see, getting this data to return properly is a little tricky. Start a new query in the Design view. In the Show Table dialog box, add the Basket and Order tables.

You are going to return two display values in the query. The first will show the month and year. The second will show the order total. To set up the month and year display, copy the following code into the Field row of the first column in the design grid:

```
Month: Format$(order.OrderDate,'mmmm yyyy')
```

This statement basically takes the order date from the Order table and formats it. In this case, you are formatting it to display as *MONTH YEAR* by using the Format$ function of Access. The field will be named *Month* when returned to the user. Set the Total row in the design grid to the Group By option.

For the second returned column, you are going to return the total value of the baskets for that month. Double-click the Total column of the Basket table, which will add the column to the design grid. On the Total row in the design grid, select the Sum option. That will total the value of the baskets for that month.

You have to add the final column to get the appropriate sorting. If you sort by the first column, then everything will be sorted by the month name, which is not the order you need. A third group by column allows you to sort properly. Add the following code to the Field cell for a new column:

```
Year(order.OrderDate)*12+DatePart('m',order.OrderDate)-1
```

This statement basically adds the value of the year and month to get a numerical value that can be sorted properly. For the Total row, set the option to Group By. Set Sort to Ascending. Make sure the Show checkbox is not selected. Save the query as *OrderTotalsByMonth*.

Your final Design view should look like Figure 8-6.

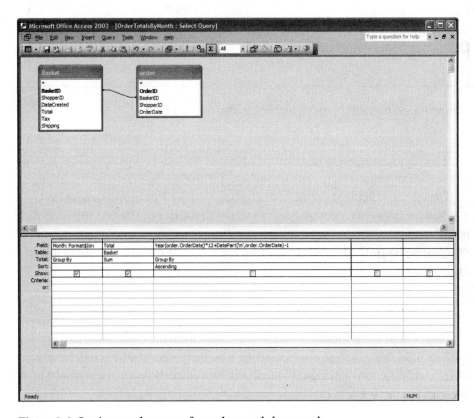

Figure 8-6. Setting up the query for order totals by month

When you run the query with the provided sample data, several months of 2002 sales appear with corresponding monthly totals. Listing 8-3 shows the SQL generated by the Design view.

Listing 8-3. OrderTotalsByMonth SQL Code

```
SELECT DISTINCTROW Format$(order.OrderDate,'mmmm yyyy') AS [Month],
Sum(Basket.Total) AS SumOfTotal
FROM Basket INNER JOIN [order] ON Basket.BasketID = order.BasketID
    GROUP BY Format$(order.OrderDate,'mmmm yyyy'),
            Year(order.OrderDate)*12+DatePart('m',order.OrderDate)-1
ORDER BY Year(order.OrderDate)*12+DatePart('m',order.OrderDate)-1;
```

This query shows the power of the Access query building capabilities. This somewhat complex SQL code is automatically generated for you.

Your next two queries will focus on analyzing the basket activity. The first will calculate the number of baskets created each month. The second will calculate the number of items added to baskets each month.

Create a new query in the Design view. To create the baskets by month query, add the Baskets table with the Show Table dialog box. The first field will return the month and year in the *MONTH YEAR* format like the previous query. Copy the following code to the Field row:

```
Month: Format$(Basket.DateCreated,'mmmm yyyy')
```

In this case, you are formatting the basket date versus the order date. Set the Total row to Group By.

The second column will count the number of items in the basket. Double-click the BasketID field of the Basket table to add it to the design grid. Set the name of the return field to Number of Baskets. The final field cell for the column should be as follows:

```
Number of Baskets: BasketID
```

For the Total row, set the value to the Count option. The final column will sort the months as in the previous query. Set the field cell to the following:

```
Year(Basket.DateCreated)*12+DatePart('m',Basket.DateCreated)-1
```

Set the Total row to the Group By option. Set the Sort row to Ascending to order the data. As with the previous query, you come up with a numerical value for the date, which allows you to sort them in the proper order. Save the query as *BasketsByMonth*.

Figure 8-7 shows the final Design view for the query.

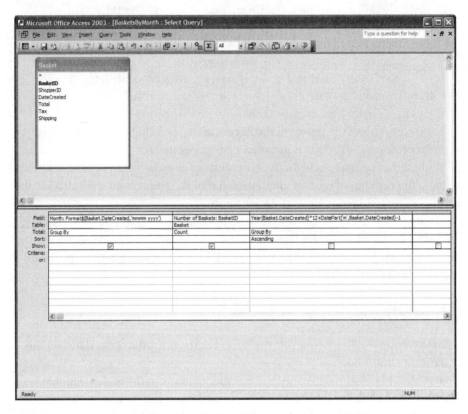

Figure 8-7. Calculating the number of baskets created each month

When the query runs, it lists the total number of orders for each month that orders are placed. Listing 8-4 shows the SQL generated by the Design view.

Listing 8-4. BasketsByMonth SQL Code

```
SELECT DISTINCTROW Format$(Basket.DateCreated,'mmmm yyyy') AS [Month],
Count(Basket.BasketID) AS [Number of Baskets]
FROM Basket
    GROUP BY Format$(Basket.DateCreated,'mmmm yyyy'),
                Year(Basket.DateCreated)*12+DatePart('m',Basket.DateCreated)-1
ORDER BY Year(Basket.DateCreated)*12+DatePart('m',Basket.DateCreated)-1;
```

Your final query will return the number of items placed in baskets by month. It will work similarly to the previous two queries. Start a new query in the Design view. From the Show Table dialog box, add the Basket and BasketItem tables.

The first field will show the basket date formatted as *MONTH YEAR* just like the previous query. Copy the following code to the Field cell for the column:

```
Month: Format$(Basket.DateCreated,'mmmm yyyy')
```

Set the Total row to the Group By option. The next column will return the number of items. Double-click the BasketID from the BasketItem table. Set the Total row to the Count option. Finally, your last column will once again sort the data by month for you. Add the following code to the cell:

```
Year(Basket.DateCreated)*12+DatePart('m',Basket.DateCreated)-1
```

Set the Total row for the field to the Group By option. Set the Sort option to Ascending, which will sort the data by month. Save the query as *BasketItemsByMonth*.

Figure 8-8 shows the final Design view for the query.

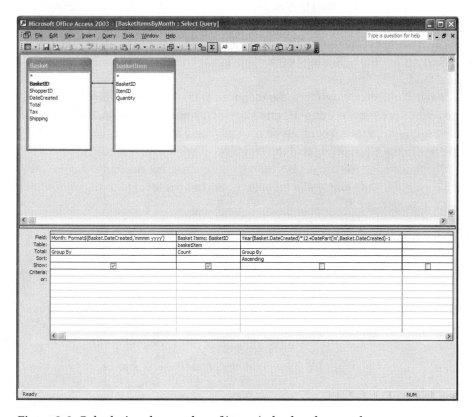

Figure 8-8. Calculating the number of items in baskets by month

When you run the query, the month-by-month dates are displayed for when items were placed in baskets. The second column shows the total numbers of items added to the baskets. Listing 8-5 shows the SQL generated by the Design view.

Listing 8-5. BasketItemsByMonth SQL Code

```
SELECT DISTINCTROW Format$(Basket.DateCreated,'mmmm yyyy') AS [Month],
Count(basketItem.BasketID) AS [Basket Items]
FROM Basket INNER JOIN basketItem ON Basket.BasketID = basketItem.BasketID
    GROUP BY Format$(Basket.DateCreated,'mmmm yyyy'),
        Year(Basket.DateCreated)*12+DatePart('m',Basket.DateCreated)-1
ORDER BY Year(Basket.DateCreated)*12+DatePart('m',Basket.DateCreated)-1;
```

That does it for the query building in Access. As mentioned earlier, you will utilize these queries in your ASP.NET application to retrieve the graph data.

Building the ASP.NET Interface

Now you are ready to work on the ASP.NET interface for your project. The primary goal of the interface is to give the user options to execute the report queries. Then the query data is sent to the Flash object.

To get started, create a new Visual Basic ASP.NET project in Visual Studio .NET. Save the project as *Charting*. If you need additional information, follow the steps outlined in Chapter 2, "Setting Up the Web Server and Database Environment," for Visual Studio .NET projects.

You will utilize one Web form for the project. The Web form will provide a series of buttons for executing the reports. When you click a button, the raw form data displays in DataGrid controls on the Web page. In addition, a window will pop up with the Flash object and the graphical chart.

The first step in the project is to add your database connection string to the Global.asax.vb file. Open the file for editing. Update the Session_Start subroutine as shown in Listing 8-6.

Listing 8-6. Global.asax Session_Start *Subroutine*

```
Sub Session_Start(ByVal sender As Object, ByVal e As EventArgs)
        ' Fires when the application is started    .

        ' Set the connection string to the local path to find the MDB
        Session("strConn") = "PROVIDER=Microsoft.Jet.OLEDB.4.0;" & _
                            "DATA SOURCE= " & _
                            Server.MapPath("database/ECommerce.mdb") & ";"

End Sub
```

You are setting up a session-level variable that is initialized when the user connects to the Web site. The connection strings utilizes OLE-DB to connect to the Access database. The data source essentially needs to point to the location of the Access .mdb file on the server. You utilize the `Server.MapPath` function to get the path to the current location. Then you reference the database subdirectory to point to the ECommerce.mdb file.

Next, you need to set up the Web form for your project. Delete the WebForm1.aspx and WebForm1.aspx.vb files that were added when you created the project. You can do this by right-clicking in the Solution Explorer on the WebForm1.aspx file and selecting Delete.

Now add a new Web form to the project by right-clicking the project name in the Solution Explorer and selecting Add ➤ Add Web Form. In the Add New Item dialog box that pops up, set the name to *reportsMenu.aspx*. This will add the Web form and the code-behind file to the project.

First, you will build the reporting interface. Follow these steps to add the appropriate items to the interface:

1. Select the Web Forms tab on the Toolbox.

2. Drag a Label control to the top of the page. Set the Text property of the control to *E-Commerce Reporting*.

3. Drag four Button controls below the Label control and stack them on top of each other.

4. Set the ID of the first Button control to *bsktsMonth*. Set the Text property for the control to *Baskets By Month*.

5. Set the ID of the second Button control to *bskItemsMonth*. Set the Text property for the control to *Items Added By Month*.

6. Set the ID of the third Button control to *bsktUtilization*. Set the Text property for the control to *Basket Utilization*.

7. Set the ID of the fourth Button control to *ordersMonth*. Set the Text property for the control to *Order Totals By Month*.

8. Add two DataGrid controls below the buttons and place them side by side.

9. Name the first grid *dgDataDisplay*.

10. Name the second grid *dgDataDisplay2*.

That does it for creating the design elements on the interface. Your reportsMenu.aspx layout should look like Figure 8-9.

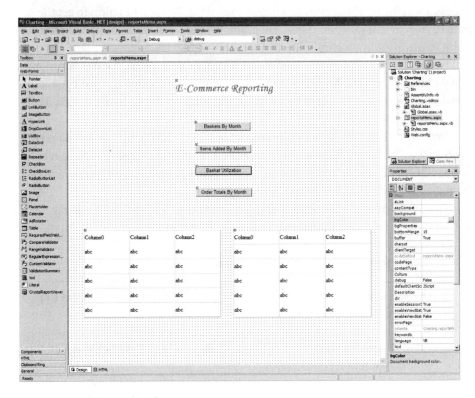

Figure 8-9. The interface layout

Now that you have the interface designed, you are ready to build the code in your Visual Basic code-behind pages. The easiest way to create the subroutines for the click events of each button is in the .aspx design interface by double-clicking each button. When you do so, you are taken to the code-behind page, and the click event subroutine is created.

Let's first start with the bsktsMonth report. When you click the button, you want the data from the BasketsByMonth query that you created in the Access database to display. Listing 8-7 shows the code for the subroutine.

Listing 8-7. bsktsMonth_Click *Subroutine*

```
Private Sub bsktsMonth_Click(ByVal sender As System.Object, _
            ByVal e As System.EventArgs) Handles bsktsMonth.Click

        Dim objCMD As New OleDb.OleDbCommand()
        Dim objConn As New OleDb.OleDbConnection()
        Dim strSQL As String
        Dim objDR As OleDb.OleDbDataReader

        ' Open the connection
        objConn.ConnectionString = Session("strConn")
        objConn.Open()

        ' Set the connection for the Command object
        objCMD.Connection = objConn

        ' Query against the Access query/view for the baskets by month
        strSQL = "select * from BasketsByMonth"

        ' Set the query
        objCMD.CommandText = strSQL

        ' Set the DataReader
        objDR = objCMD.ExecuteReader(CommandBehavior.CloseConnection)

        ' *** NOTE - additional Flash interface code will be added here
        dgDataDisplay.DataSource = objDR
        dgDataDisplay.DataBind()
        dgDataDisplay2.Visible = False

    End Sub
```

In the first section of the code, you create the necessary ADO.NET objects to interface with the database. First, you create an OLE-DB command, which sets up the command to be executed. Next, you create a Connection object to connect with the Access database. You also need a DataReader to read the data from the database.

NOTE *You will use these same objects in the rest of the button click events.*

After the variable declarations, the connection to the database opens. The session variable that you set up in Global.asax sets the connection. After the connection opens, the Command object is set up with the connection. The query will execute against the connection.

Next, you create your SQL query. As mentioned earlier, the Access query acts like a table in that you can query against it and return results. In this case, you want to query for the basket orders by month from BasketsByMonth. A SQL select query will return the data.

Next, you set the DataReader to the returned data from the Command object. Note that for the Command object, the ExecuteReader method executes. This returns the data as a forward, read-only set of data, which is all you need for your reporting purposes (you have no need to read backward in the set of data).

Finally, you set the DataReader as the data source for your DataGrid. Then the data is bound and displayed in the DataGrid by calling the DataBind method. That does it for retrieving the data for the baskets by month and displaying it on the Web page. Also note that the second DataGrid is set to not display by setting the Visible property to *False*.

Next, you will set up the click event for the Items by Month button. Listing 8-8 shows the bsktsItemsMonth_Click subroutine.

Listing 8-8. bsktsItemsMonth_Click *Subroutine*

```
Private Sub bsktItemsMonth_Click(ByVal sender As System.Object, _
            ByVal e As System.EventArgs) Handles bskItemsMonth.Click

    Dim objCMD As New OleDb.OleDbCommand()
    Dim objConn As New OleDb.OleDbConnection()
    Dim strSQL As String
    Dim objDR As OleDb.OleDbDataReader

    ' Open the connection
    objConn.ConnectionString = Session("strConn")
    objConn.Open()

    ' Set the connection for the command
    objCMD.Connection = objConn
```

```
' Build the query to retrieve the number of baskets for each month
strSQL = "select * from BasketsItemByMonth"

' Set the command query
objCMD.CommandText = strSQL

' Set the DataReader
objDR = objCMD.ExecuteReader(CommandBehavior.CloseConnection)

' *** NOTE - additional Flash interface code will be added here
dgDataDisplay.DataSource = objDR
dgDataDisplay.DataBind()
dgDataDisplay2.Visible = False

End Sub
```

As with the previous click event, this subroutine starts by creating your database objects, as shown in Listing 8-9. The connection then opens using the same session variable.

The SQL query in this case makes the select statement against the BasketItemsByMonth query that you set up in Access. This will return the number of baskets items created by month.

Once the query is created, the Command object is set up. The DataReader is then set up with the returned data from the ExecuteReader method of the Command object. Finally, the data is bound to the DataGrid and displayed.

The next click event is for the Basket Utilization button. The subroutine starts with the same variable declarations and sets up the database Connection and Command objects.

Listing 8-9. reportsMenu.aspx

```
Private Sub bsktUtilization_Click(ByVal sender As System.Object, ByVal e As _
System.EventArgs) Handles bsktUtilization.Click

    Dim objCMD As New OleDb.OleDbCommand()
    Dim objConn As New OleDb.OleDbConnection()
    Dim strSQL As String
    Dim objDR As OleDb.OleDbDataReader

    ' Open the connection
    objConn.ConnectionString = Session("strConn")
    objConn.Open()
```

```
' Set the command connection
objCMD.Connection = objConn

' Build the query to return the number of abandoned baskets
strSQL = "select * from AbandonedBaskets"

' Set the command query
objCMD.CommandText = strSQL

' Set the DataReader
objDR = objCMD.ExecuteReader(CommandBehavior.CloseConnection)

' *** NOTE - additional Flash interface code will be added here
dgDataDisplay.DataSource = objDR
dgDataDisplay.DataBind()

' Close the reader for reuse
objDR.Close()

' Reopen the connection
objConn.Open()

' Get the number of ordered baskets
strSQL = "select * from OrderedBaskets"

' Set the command query
objCMD.CommandText = strSQL

' Set the DataReader
objDR = objCMD.ExecuteReader(CommandBehavior.CloseConnection)

' *** NOTE - additional Flash interface code will be added here
dgDataDisplay2.Visible = True
dgDataDisplay2.DataSource = objDR
dgDataDisplay2.DataBind()

End Sub
```

You have to execute two queries in this click event to return the abandoned and ordered baskets, as shown in Listing 8-10. You set the first query to retrieve the abandoned baskets. You set up the Command object and DataReader as you did previously and then bind the data to the first DataGrid.

Before the second query can execute, you need to close and then open your connection for reuse. Note that you also create a second connection.

Once the connection reopens, you set up the query for the ordered baskets. Then you set the Command and Reader objects. Finally, the data displays in the second DataGrid. Note that you have to set the Visible property to *True* for the DataGrid to display.

Your last click event is for the orders by month report. It follows the same template as the previous three click event subroutines. The first section of the code sets up the variables, the database Connection object, and the Command object.

Listing 8-10. reportsMenu.aspx (Continued)

```
Private Sub ordersMonth_Click(ByVal sender As System.Object, ByVal e As _
System.EventArgs) Handles ordersMonth.Click

    Dim objCMD As New OleDb.OleDbCommand()
    Dim objConn As New OleDb.OleDbConnection()
    Dim strSQL As String
    Dim objDR As OleDb.OleDbDataReader

    '  Open the database connection
    objConn.ConnectionString = Session("strConn")
    objConn.Open()

    '  Set the connection for the command
    objCMD.Connection = objConn

    '  Build the query to return the order totals from the Access query/view
    strSQL = "select * from OrderTotalsByMonth"

    '  Set the query for the Command object
    objCMD.CommandText = strSQL

    '  Set the DataReader
    objDR = objCMD.ExecuteReader(CommandBehavior.CloseConnection)

    ' *** NOTE - additional Flash interface code will be added here
    dgDataDisplay.DataSource = objDR
    dgDataDisplay.DataBind()
    dgDataDisplay2.Visible = False

End Sub
```

For this subroutine, you query the OrdersTotalsByMonth Access query to return the report data. The `ExecuteReader` method of the `Command` object executes to retrieve the data and pass it to the DataReader. Finally, the DataGrid is bound to the data, and the data displays.

Be sure to compile the project/solution to make it ready for execution. Select Build ➤ Build Solution. That will build the .NET assemblies.

That does it for building the ASP.NET and database part of the equation.

Utilizing the ASP.NET Interface

To get started, open the reportsMenu.aspx page (for example, `http://localhost/Charting/reportsMenu.aspx`) in your browser. When the page comes up, it should look like Figure 8-10.

Figure 8-10. The reports menu

Now click the Baskets by Month button to see the monthly basket data. Figure 8-11 shows the page with the DataGrid.

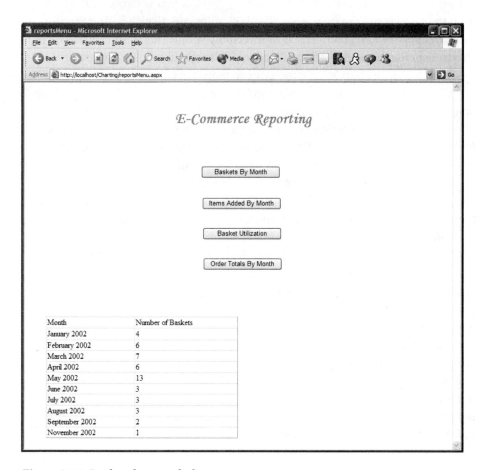

Figure 8-11. Baskets by month data

Note the sorting of the months and the formatting of the date data. This is all performed in your Access query, which demonstrates the benefits of using queries within the database.

In the next section, you will build the graphical charts based on this data.

Charting the Data in a Flash

You are going to build generic charts within Flash MX that will receive the data from the queries you created earlier in this chapter and display it. Your amazement will begin when you realize how incredibly simple this is. You will create pie charts, bar charts, and line graphs. But the part that makes it so simple is that you are going to utilize Flash MX components to build the charts for you.

We briefly touched on Flash MX components in Chapter 7. They are prebuilt objects that you can easily place on the Stage using drag-and-drop functionality. Then, with a tiny bit of scripting (some require no scripting at all), they will perform duties that would take a Flash programmer hours, days, and maybe even weeks to build from scratch. Flash MX has a few components built in, such as scrollbars, checkboxes, radio buttons, and a few more. But there are no charting components that come with Flash MX. That gives us a chance to introduce you to the Macromedia Exchange. The Exchange is a place where developers can build components for Flash and all of the other Macromedia products (Dreamweaver, ColdFusion, and so on) and then upload them for others to use. Macromedia also places official components within the Exchange. Many components are freeware, and some are commercial. You can visit the Macromedia Flash MX Exchange by pointing your browser to `http://www.macromedia.com/cfusion/exchange/` and clicking Visit Flash Exchange on that page.

Macromedia has an official charting component that contains the charts you are going to use. You can download this component for free from the Exchange. Use the Exchange search tool and search for *Charting Components*. It helps filter the results if you search only the Flash Exchange (use the drop-down list to select the Flash Exchange only). The title of the component is simply *Charting Components 1.0*. Download the component.

To load this into Flash MX, you need to have the Extension Manager installed for Flash. This is a free program that you can download from Macromedia (`http://www.macromedia.com/exchange/em_download/`). Follow the instructions on the page to install the Extension Manager.

> **NOTE** *You will probably have to sign up for a Macromedia membership to download the Extension Manager as well as the extension (if you do not already have a membership). This membership is free.*

Once you have the Extension Manager installed, open Flash MX and select Help ➤ Manage Extensions. This will open the Extension Manager (see Figure 8-12).

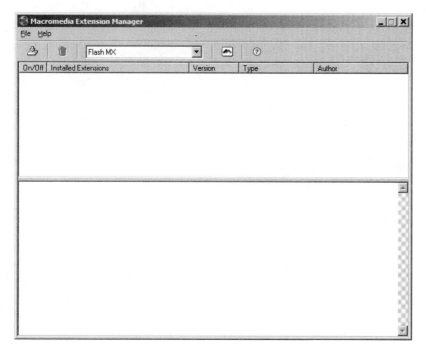

Figure 8-12. Extension Manager

In the Extension Manager, choose File ➤ Install Extension (see Figure 8-13). A file dialog box will open. Browse to where you saved the component you downloaded a little earlier, find the file, click it to select it, and click the Install button.

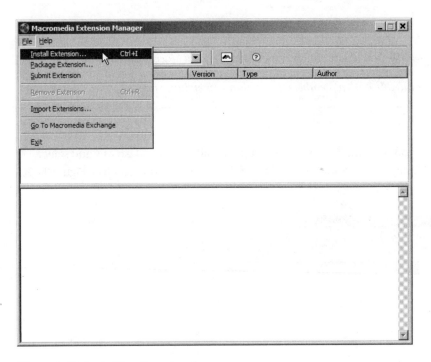

Figure 8-13. Installing the extension

This will install the component into Flash MX (see Figure 8-14). You should see a usage agreement that you must accept, and then you should see a window pop up that says it is installed (see Figure 8-15).

When Flash MX is open again, look at the Components Panel. By default you should see Flash UI Components (see Figure 8-16).

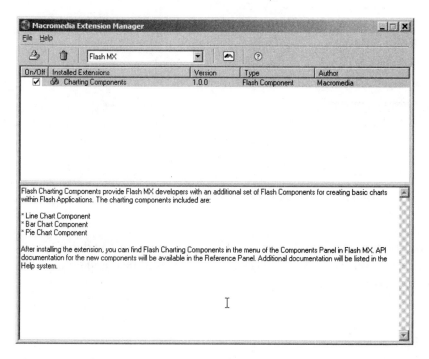

Figure 8-14. The Charting Components extension in the Extension Manager

Figure 8-15. A successful install

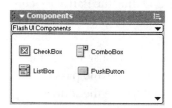

Figure 8-16. Components Panel

Click the drop-down list at the top of the panel, and you should also see the Flash Charting Components option (see Figure 8-17)—click it to select it.

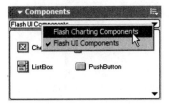

Figure 8-17. Choosing the Flash Charting Components option

You will see three icons of charts named *BarChart, LineChart,* and *PieChart* (see Figure 8-18). You can click and drag any of them to the Stage, and they will be ready for data. Try it . . . it is so easy.

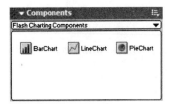

Figure 8-18. The charting icons

Now let's build your first chart. Start a new Flash movie (press Control+N or select File ➤ New). Use the Properties Panel to resize the movie to 400-pixels wide by 300-pixels high. Leave the background color as white. From the Components Panel, make sure you have the charting icons showing and drag the BarChart icon to the Stage. With the chart selected, use the Properties Panel to give this chart an instance name of *myChart*. Center the chart on the Stage.

You are going to use another Flash MX method you have not used yet to fill your chart with data. You will create a DataSet using ActionScript and pass the data into the Flash movie from an ASP script. This DataSet will be the source of data that the chart will display. Listing 8-11 contains all the code necessary to do this. Enter this code as frame actions into the Actions Panel for Frame 1.

Listing 8-11. Creating the DataSet

```
arrLabels = strLabels.split(",");
arrData = strData.split(",");

dataSet = new DataProviderClass();
for(var i=0; i< arrLabels.length; i++){
   dataSet.addItem({label:arrLabels[i], value: arrData[i]});
}

myChart.setXAxisTitle(XAxis);
myChart.setYAxisTitle(YAxis);
myChart.setChartTitle(ChartTitle);
myChart.setDataProvider(dataSet);
```

That is the entire bar chart Flash movie. Really, that is it. Save the file as *BarChart.fla* and publish the .swf file.

Now let's build your next chart. Start a new Flash movie (press Control+N or select File ➤ New). Use the Properties Panel to resize the movie to 400-pixels wide by 300-pixels high. Leave the background color as white. From the Components Panel, make sure you have the charting icons showing and drag the PieChart icon to the Stage. With the chart selected, use the Properties Panel to give this chart an instance name of *myChart*. Center the chart on the Stage.

Enter the code from Listing 8-12 as frame actions into the Actions Panel for Frame 1.

Listing 8-12. Frame Actions for the Pie Chart

```
arrLabels = strLabels.split(",");
arrData = strData.split(",");

dataSet = new DataProviderClass();
for(var i=0; i< arrLabels.length; i++){
   dataSet.addItem({label:arrLabels[i], value: arrData[i]});
}

myChart.setXAxisTitle(XAxis);
myChart.setYAxisTitle(YAxis);
myChart.setChartTitle(ChartTitle);
myChart.setDataProvider(dataSet);
```

Save the file as *PieChart.fla* and publish the .swf file.

Finally, let's build the line graph. Start a new Flash movie (press Control+N or select File ➤ New). Use the Properties Panel to resize the movie to 400-pixels wide by 300-pixels high. Leave the background color as white. From the Components Panel, make sure you have the charting icons showing and drag the LineChart icon to the Stage. With the chart selected, use the Properties Panel to give this chart an instance name of *myChart*. Center the chart on the Stage.

Enter the code from Listing 8-13 as frame actions into the Actions Panel for Frame 1.

Listing 8-13. Frame Actions for the Line Chart

```
arrLabels = strLabels.split(",");
arrData = strData.split(",");

dataSet = new DataProviderClass();
for(var i=0; i< arrLabels.length; i++){
    dataSet.addItem({label:arrLabels[i], value: arrData[i]});
}

myChart.setXAxisTitle(XAxis);
myChart.setYAxisTitle(YAxis);
myChart.setChartTitle(ChartTitle);
myChart.setDataProvider(dataSet);
```

Save the file as *LineChart.fla* and publish the .swf file.

That is it for the Flash charts. You will need to go back and modify your ASP.NET pages slightly to get them to work with your charts, however.

Open the reportsMenu.aspx page. Below where the dgDataDisplay DataGrid is and just above the </form> tag, add the code from Listing 8-14 and save it. This will add your Flash movies to the page.

 NOTE *Be sure to upload all three .swf files (BarChar.swf, PieChart.swf, and LineChart.swf) to the directory where this .aspx page resides.*

Listing 8-14. Adding the Flash Movies

```
<div style="Z-INDEX: 108; LEFT: 46px; POSITION: absolute; TOP: 472px">
<OBJECT classid="clsid:D27CDB6E-AE6D-11cf-96B8-444553540000" ⏎
codebase="http://download.macromedia.com/pub/shockwave/cabs/flash/swflash.cab# ⏎
version=6,0,0,0" WIDTH="400" HEIGHT="300" id="barChart" ALIGN="" VIEWASTEXT>
```

```
<PARAM NAME=movie VALUE="BarChart.swf?<%=strOutput%>">
<PARAM NAME=loop VALUE=false>
<PARAM NAME=menu VALUE=false>
<PARAM NAME=quality VALUE=high>
<PARAM NAME=bgcolor VALUE=#FFFFFF>
<EMBED src="BarChart.swf?<%=strOutput%>" loop=false menu=false
quality=high bgcolor=#FFFFFF  WIDTH="400" HEIGHT="300" NAME="barChart"
ALIGN="" TYPE="application/x-shockwave-flash" ↵
 PLUGINSPAGE="http://www.macromedia.com/go/getflashplayer">
</EMBED>
</OBJECT>
<OBJECT classid="clsid:D27CDB6E-AE6D-11cf-96B8-444553540000" ↵
codebase="http://download.macromedia.com/pub/shockwave/cabs/flash/swflash.cab# ↵
version=6,0,0,0" WIDTH="400" HEIGHT="300" id="pieChart" ALIGN="" VIEWASTEXT>
<PARAM NAME=movie VALUE="PieChart.swf?<%=strOutput%>">
<PARAM NAME=loop VALUE=false>
<PARAM NAME=menu VALUE=false>
<PARAM NAME=quality VALUE=high>
<PARAM NAME=bgcolor VALUE=#FFFFFF>
<EMBED src="PieChart.swf?<%=strOutput%>" loop=false menu=false
quality=high bgcolor=#FFFFFF  WIDTH="400" HEIGHT="300" NAME="pieChart"
ALIGN="" TYPE="application/x-shockwave-flash" ↵
PLUGINSPAGE="http://www.macromedia.com/go/getflashplayer">
</EMBED>
</OBJECT>
<OBJECT classid="clsid:D27CDB6E-AE6D-11cf-96B8-444553540000" ↵
codebase="http://download.macromedia.com/pub/shockwave/cabs/flash/swflash.cab# ↵
version=6,0,0,0" WIDTH="400" HEIGHT="300" id="lineChart" ALIGN="" VIEWASTEXT>
<PARAM NAME=movie VALUE="LineChart.swf?<%=strOutput%>">
<PARAM NAME=loop VALUE=false>
<PARAM NAME=menu VALUE=false>
<PARAM NAME=quality VALUE=high>
<PARAM NAME=bgcolor VALUE=#FFFFFF>
<EMBED src="LineChartChart.swf?<%=strOutput%>" loop=false menu=false
quality=high bgcolor=#FFFFFF  WIDTH="400" HEIGHT="300" NAME="lineChart"
ALIGN="" TYPE="application/x-shockwave-flash" ↵
 PLUGINSPAGE="http://www.macromedia.com/go/getflashplayer">
</EMBED>
</OBJECT>
</div>
```

Now you can delete the `dgDataDisplay` DataGrid just above where you put the Flash calls.

If you are a curious sort of person, you should be wondering what the `<%=strOutput%>` is in each of those Flash movie object calls. We are glad you asked! The script you used in each of your Flash charts looks for a simple set of variables passed through the QueryString (just like your other applications have done). This particular script is not going to require a separate .asp page to create the data because the .aspx page you have already created does that for you. You will simply compile all the data from the database for a particular report and put it in a publicly declared variable called *strOutput,* and that is what is passing to the Flash charts.

So, open the code-behind file for your reportsMenu.aspx page. At the top of the code are several declarations of the controls found on that page. Add the following declaration to that list:

```
Public strOutput As String
```

This is a public declaration of the variable you will be passing to the Flash charts. You are going to modify the code for each of the button clicks you created earlier in this chapter. Instead of binding the data to a DataGrid, you are going to loop through the DataReader and create the output string that you can pass to your Flash charts.

Make the necessary changes to the bsktsMonth_click subroutine to match Listing 8-15.

Listing 8-15. The bsktsMonth_click *Subroutine*

```
Private Sub bsktsMonth_Click(ByVal sender As System.Object, ByVal e As ↵
System.EventArgs) Handles bsktsMonth.Click

    Dim objCMD As New OleDb.OleDbCommand()
    Dim objConn As New OleDb.OleDbConnection()
    Dim strSQL As String
    Dim objDR As OleDb.OleDbDataReader

    Dim strLabels As String
    Dim strData As String

    ' Open the connection
    objConn.ConnectionString = Session("strConn")
    objConn.Open()

    ' Set the connection for the Command object
    objCMD.Connection = objConn
```

```
' Query against the Access query/view for the baskets by month
strSQL = "select * from BasketsByMonth"

' Set the query
objCMD.CommandText = strSQL

' Set the DataReader
objDR = objCMD.ExecuteReader(CommandBehavior.CloseConnection)

'loop through DataReader and create output for Flash
If objDR.Read Then
    strLabels = objDR("Month")
    strData = objDR("Number of Baskets")
    Do
        strLabels = strLabels & "," & objDR("Month")
        strData = strData & "," & objDR("Number of Baskets")
    Loop While objDR.Read
End If
objDR.Close()
strOutput = "dummy=1&ChartTitle=Baskets+Per+Month&XAxis=Month&YAxis= ↵
Number+of+Baskets&strLabels=" & strLabels & "&strData=" & strData

End Sub
```

As you can see, you simply created text strings containing comma-separated values of your data, which the ActionScript you wrote in your Flash charts will put into a DataSet and display on the charts.

Likewise, make the necessary changes to the bsktUtilization_Click subroutine to match Listing 8-16.

Listing 8-16. The bsktUtilization_Click *Subroutine*

```
Private Sub bsktUtilization_Click(ByVal sender As System.Object, ByVal e As ↵
System.EventArgs) Handles bsktUtilization.Click

    Dim objCMD As New OleDb.OleDbCommand()
    Dim objConn As New OleDb.OleDbConnection()
    Dim strSQL As String
    Dim objDR As OleDb.OleDbDataReader

    Dim strLabels As String
    Dim strData As String
```

```
'  Open the connection
objConn.ConnectionString = Session("strConn")
objConn.Open()


'  Set the command connection
objCMD.Connection = objConn


'  Build the query to return the number of abandoned baskets
strSQL = "select * from AbandonedBaskets"


'  Set the command query
objCMD.CommandText = strSQL


'  Set the DataReader
objDR = objCMD.ExecuteReader(CommandBehavior.CloseConnection)


'loop through DataReader and create output for Flash
If objDR.Read Then
    strLabels = "Abandoned - " & objDR("Abandoned Baskets")
    strData = objDR("SumOfTotal")
End If


'  Close the reader for reuse
objDR.Close()


'  Reopen the connection
objConn.Open()


'  Get the number of ordered baskets
strSQL = "select * from OrderedBaskets"


'  Set the command query
objCMD.CommandText = strSQL


'  Set the DataReader
objDR = objCMD.ExecuteReader(CommandBehavior.CloseConnection)


'loop through DataReader and create output for Flash
If objDR.Read Then
    strLabels = strLabels & ",Ordered - " & objDR("Ordered Baskets")
    strData = strData & "," & objDR("SumOfTotal")
End If
objDR.Close()
```

```
        strOutput = "dummy=1&ChartTitle=Basket+Utilization&XAxis= ↵
Baskets&YAxis=Total&strLabels=" & _
        strLabels & "&strData=" & strData
End Sub
```

This code is slightly different from the rest in that you used two separate queries that you compiled into your output data as comparison data. Basically, you manually built the DataSet pulling data from two different queries.

Now, make the necessary changes to the ordersMonth_Click subroutine to match Listing 8-17.

Listing 8-17. The ordersMonth_Click *Subroutine*

```
Private Sub ordersMonth_Click(ByVal sender As System.Object, ByVal e As ↵
 System.EventArgs) Handles ordersMonth.Click

    Dim objCMD As New OleDb.OleDbCommand()
    Dim objConn As New OleDb.OleDbConnection()
    Dim strSQL As String
    Dim objDR As OleDb.OleDbDataReader

    Dim strLabels As String
    Dim strData As String

    ' Open the database connection
    objConn.ConnectionString = Session("strConn")
    objConn.Open()

    ' Set the connection for the command
    objCMD.Connection = objConn

    ' Build the query to return the order totals from the Access query/view
    strSQL = "select * from OrderTotalsByMonth"

    ' Set the query for the Command object
    objCMD.CommandText = strSQL

    ' Set the DataReader
    objDR = objCMD.ExecuteReader(CommandBehavior.CloseConnection)

    'loop through DataReader and create output for Flash
    If objDR.Read Then
```

```
            strLabels = objDR("Month")
            strData = objDR("SumOfTotal")
            Do
                strLabels = strLabels & "," & objDR("Month")
                strData = strData & "," & objDR("SumOfTotal")
            Loop While objDR.Read
        End If
        objDR.Close()
        strOutput = "dummy=1&ChartTitle=Orders+Per+Month&XAxis=Month&YAxis=↩
Number+of+Baskets&strLabels=" & strLabels & "&strData=" & strData


End Sub
```

This code is the same as the first except it just loops through the DataReader and creates the output string from the data.

Finally, make the necessary changes to the ordersMonth_Click subroutine to match Listing 8-18.

Listing 8-18. The ordersMonth_Click *Subroutine*

```
Private Sub bsktItemsMonth_Click(ByVal sender As System.Object, ByVal e As ↩
 System.EventArgs) Handles bsktItemsMonth.Click

    Dim objCMD As New OleDb.OleDbCommand()
    Dim objConn As New OleDb.OleDbConnection()
    Dim strSQL As String
    Dim objDR As OleDb.OleDbDataReader

    Dim strLabels As String
    Dim strData As String

    ' Open the connection
    objConn.ConnectionString = Session("strConn")
    objConn.Open()

    ' Set the connection for the commad
    objCMD.Connection = objConn

    ' Build the query to retrieve the number of baskets for each month
    strSQL = "select * from BasketItemsByMonth"

    ' Set the command query
    objCMD.CommandText = strSQL
```

```
'  Set the DataReader
'objDR = objCMD.ExecuteReader(CommandBehavior.CloseConnection)
objDR = objCMD.ExecuteReader(CommandBehavior.CloseConnection)

'loop through DataReader and create output for Flash
If objDR.Read Then
    strLabels = objDR("Month")
    strData = objDR("Basket Items")
    Do
        strLabels = strLabels & "," & objDR("Month")
        strData = strData & "," & objDR("Basket Items")
    Loop While objDR.Read
End If
objDR.Close()
strOutput = "dummy=1&ChartTitle=Baskets+Items+Per+Month&XAxis=Month&YAxis=↵
Number+of+Baskets&strLabels=" & strLabels & "&strData=" & strData

End Sub
```

Save, compile, and run the page. You should see the data come alive on three different charts for each button clicked (see Figures 8-19 and 8-20).

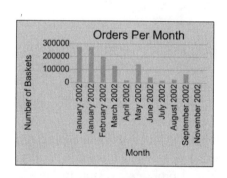

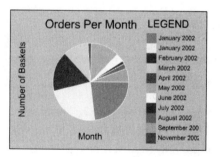

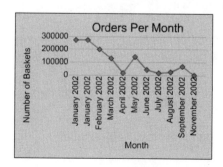

Figure 8-19. Orders Per Month chart output

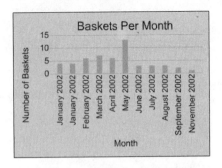
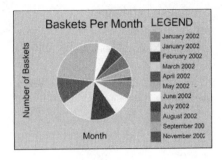

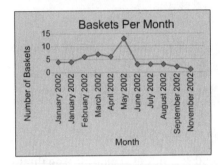

Figure 8-20. Baskets Per Month chart output

Summary

In this chapter, you explored new techniques for utilizing business data in a Flash-based reporting environment. Flash can easily spice up boring business data and is easy to deploy. You also saw how with ASP.NET you can use Microsoft Access as the backend database as easily as SQL Server.

You also learned about the Macromedia Exchange for finding some great components to save time and the Extension Manager to install them into Flash MX. Finally, you utilized the Macromedia Charting Components extension and learned how to create and use a DataSet within Flash MX.

INDEX